INTENTIONALITY,
MINDS,
AND PERCEPTION

INTENTIONALITY,
MINDS,
AND PERCEPTION

Discussions on Contemporary Philosophy

A Symposium

Compiled with an Introduction
by Hector-Neri Castañeda
Wayne State University

WAYNE STATE UNIVERSITY PRESS   DETROIT
1967

CONTENTS

INTRODUCTION

THIS VOLUME contains, with some revisions, the papers, the comments, and the replies presented at the seven colloquia constituting the Wayne State University Symposium in the Philosophy of Mind, which took place in December, 1962.

The authors of the principal papers were asked to write essays that either clarified the bases of, or formulated a new solution or approach to, some problem in the philosophy of mind. The commentators were asked to be merciless in their criticism. The goal was to have, as a result of the collective effort, a network of challenges to prevailing views, as well as an array of suggestions or proposals. The ultimate purpose was to bring the philosophical controversy about some of the problems in the philosophy of mind either to new levels of precision or to other channels of discussion.

The papers follow a natural order from generality to specificity. Chisholm's paper is an appropriate introduction to the whole volume, being an attempt to formulate precise characteristics of intentional or psychological statements: it hurls a challenge to philosophical behaviorism, still a favorite among analytic philosophers, in spite of the increasing attraction of the so-called identity theory, i.e., that states of consciousness are contingently identical with brain states. Ayer's essay deals in a general fashion with the relation of consciousness to bodies, and after a detailed examination of Strawson's views on the definability of persons as bodies having experiences in a certain causal sense, Ayer puts forward a new proposal. Castañeda's essay attempts to clarify the logical bases that give rise to the problem of one's knowledge of other minds, and proposes a recursive analysis of the structure of ordinary, intersubjective mental concepts. Putnam's paper proposes analogies between machines and persons and explores their consequences for the traditional views on the relation of body and mind, thus putting the traditional problems in a larger setting. Sellars' paper contains a thorough examination of epistemological and ontological problems in perceptual knowledge, and defends a semi-Kantian view according to which ordinary physical objects do not really exist, but are only the phenomenal counterparts of the micro-particles of scientific theories, thus vigorously challenging still widespread positivistic doctrines that treat scientific theories as merely computational devices with, at most, heuristic value. Alston's essay develops a devastating critique of current arguments that purport to dissolve the traditional free will problem by claiming that human action cannot be causally determined. Finally, Firth's essay, the most specific of the lot, analyzes the role of causation in seeing and challenges current views on perception that do not provide room for any causal element.

The comments attack fundamental presuppositions, central theses, and crucial arguments of the papers. They, together with the replies, provide starting points for further investigation of the issues involved.

This symposium was one of a continuing series supported by the Wayne State University Alumni Association. This association has been providing the funds for two yearly research awards to assistant professors of Wayne State University, one in the humanities and the other in the sciences. In 1961, H-N. Castañeda received the first Wayne State Fund Recognition Award for Research in the Humanities, which both gave him time for the research that, in part, produced his essay for this symposium, and furnished the funds to meet the expenses of the symposium.

The editor wishes to thank the Wayne State University Alumni Association for having supported his research and the symposium, and for its financial aid for publication of this volume. He also wishes to thank Dr. Randall M. Whaley, former Vice-President for Graduate Studies and Research at Wayne State University, and the members of the philosophy department, especially the chairman, Professor George Nakhnikian, for their unstinting help in handling the arrangements for the symposium. He also thanks the philosophy department of the University of Texas, especially its chairman, Professor John Silber, for duplicating "Consciousness and Behavior" and paying the editor's expenses during the symposium, while he was a visiting lecturer at the University of Texas.

ON SOME PSYCHOLOGICAL
CONCEPTS AND THE "LOGIC"
OF INTENTIONALITY

Roderick M. Chisholm

Brown University

1

IN DEFENSE OF the general thesis that "intentionality" is a
mark of the psychological, it has been held that there is a
"logical," "grammatical," or "linguistic" property which may
be called "intentional" and which characterizes language
about the psychological. But attempts to formulate just
what this "logical," grammatical," or "linguistic" property
might be have been unsuccessful. Every proposed mark of
intentionality has turned out to be a mark, more generally,
of intensionality (or nonextensionality). There are ethical
sentences containing "ought" and modal sentences containing "necessary" which are intentional but presumably not
psychological. Hence it has been suggested—for example, by
Alonzo Church—that intentional language can be characterized only as intensional language having a psychological
subject matter.[1] If this suggestion is true, then we cannot
claim any particular significance for the thesis that intentional
language pertains to the psychological.

I shall set forth a procedure by means of which we can investigate the "logic" or "grammar" of some of our intentional
concepts and which will enable us to contrast them with
other modal concepts. I shall propose certain criteria of intentionality and inquire if these criteria are satisfied by
sentences which do not have a psychological subject matter.
Whether or not these criteria are adequate, I believe they

will throw some light upon the nature of our intentional concepts.

2

Let us speak of ordinary language into which we have introduced the notation of universal and existential quantification with its variables, and let us assume that we know what a modal prefix is. (Perhaps the following is an adequate characterization of a modal prefix in English. A modal prefix is a phrase ending with "that," or at the end of which the word "that" may be inserted; it is not itself a sentence, but if it is inserted at the beginning of a sentence the result will be another sentence. "It is necessary that," "Jones believes that," and "The authorities have taken every step to insure that," are examples of modal prefixes.) I shall discuss what we may call "intentional modal prefixes," or the "intentional modalities."

By appealing to the fact that men need not be rational—that a man may have contradictory beliefs and contradictory desires—we might be able to formulate a fairly simple criterion of an intentional modality. We might say: A modal prefix "it is M that" is intentional if (perhaps among certain other conditions), for any statement p, (i) "it is M that p" implies neither "it is M that not-p" nor "it is false that it is M that not-p" and (ii) "it is false that it is M that not-p" implies neither "it is M that p" nor "it is false that it is M that p." It may seem unfortunate to proceed in this way if intentionality is to be used to establish a distinction between the psychological and the nonpsychological and to show, perhaps, that what it is to be a *person* is something that cannot be described or understood in "physicalistic" terms.[2] For we would be saying, in effect, that the possibility of *irrationality* is what separates the psychological from the physical. It may be, however, that this is the best we can do. And in any case, the other criterion I shall propose will be based upon the possibility of a certain kind of *error*.

Let us restrict ourselves to statements having an initial quantifier, the scope of which extends to the end of the statement, but having no other quantifier. We may say that if the quantifier is universal, the statement is a U-statement; if the quantifier is existential, the statement is an E-statement. Let us assume that our universe of discourse is non-empty ("There exists an x such that x is identical with x" might be thought of as a tacit premise in each of our arguments). And let us restrict ourselves to those U-statements and E-statements which are such that the part following the quantifier is "logically neutral" (i.e., the quantified part is such that no prefixing of quantifiers and negation signs will turn it into a statement which is logically true). We may now single out four ways in which a modal prefix M (e.g., "it is possible that") may occur in such statements:

(1) UC: the result of inserting M at the beginning of a U-statement; e.g., "It is possible that, for every x, x is material."

(2) UD: the result of inserting M immediately after the quantifier of a U-statement; e.g., "For every x, it is possible that x is material."

(3) EC: the result of inserting M at the beginning of an E-statement; e.g., "It is possible that there exists an x such that x is material."

(4) ED: the result of inserting M immediately after the quantifier of an E-statement; e.g., "There exists an x such that it is possible that x is material."

The letters "C" and "D" in the initials used here are taken from the medieval terms *in sensu composito* and *in sensu diviso*.[3] Thus UC may be taken as abreviation for "universal quantification modalized *in sensu composito*," and ED for "existential quantification modalized *in sensu diviso*," and analogously for "UD" and "EC." It may be noted that a modal operator *in sensu diviso* "divides up" the quantified statement and that one *in sensu composito* does not—though this was not the original point of the terms. (We must not be misled by quantifiers that similarly divide up modal prefixes, as in the statement "It is possible, for every *x,* that *x* is material," where the quantifier comes between part of the modal prefix and the "that." A quantifier thus dividing up a modal prefix may be taken out and inserted in front of the prefix; hence the example, easily taken to be *in sensu composito,* is equivalent to our original example of a universal quantification *in sensu diviso.*)

We may now speak of modal prefixes, or modalities, in the forms UC, UD, EC, and ED, where this way of speaking is understood in the manner just described. And we may ask, for any modal prefix and any such form for that prefix, whether statements in that form imply statements in any of the other three forms. (To say that, for a modal prefix M, UC implies UD, is to say: if *p* has M as its only modal prefix and is of the form UC, and *q* is like *p* except that *q* is of the form UD, then *p* implies *q;* and analogously for the other possibilities.) In this way we may distinguish some of the logical properties of the various modalities and possibly find a mark of intentionality.

3

The relevant logical properties of the modal prefix "it is true that" may be represented in the following way:

	UC	UD	EC	ED
UC			—	—
UD			—	—
EC				
ED				

The top line indicates what is taken as implicans, the vertical line what is taken as implicate; the occurrence of a minus sign in any place in a column indicates that the implication which that place represents does *not* hold; an empty place in a column indicates that the implication which that place represents does hold. Thus the first column tells us that "it is true that" in the form UC implies "it is true that" in the forms UD, EC, and ED ("It is true that, for every x, x is material" implies "For every x, it is true that x is material," "It is true that there is an x such that x is material," and "There is an x such that it is true that x is material"). The second column tells us that UD also implies the other three forms; the third column tells us that EC does not imply UC or UD and that it does imply ED; and the fourth column tells us that ED does not imply UC or UD and that it does imply EC.

"It is false that" has the following table:

	UC	UD	EC	ED
UC				
UD	—			—
EC	—			—
ED				

Thus the table for "true" is distinguished by one set of our failures, the table for "false" by another. We will find that most of the other familiar modalities have the following property in common with "true" and "false": the pair consisting of the modal prefix and its negation (i.e., the modal prefix preceded by "it is false that") are such that one of them has at least the four failures of "true" and the other has at least the four failures of "false."

4

The pattern for *believing* ("S believes that," or "It is believed that") may indicate something about the nature of intentional prefixes. Our four forms are exemplified by:

UC: "S believes that, for every x, x is F";
UD: "For every x, S believes that x is F";
EC: "S believes that there exists an x such that x is F";
ED: "There exists an x such that S believes that x is F."

It will be clear that the pattern for *believing* has the four failures we find in the pattern for *truth*: EC does not imply UC or UD, and ED does not imply UC or UD. And if we do not consider "empty universes," it will be clear that, for every modality, UD implies ED. Thus, there remain seven possibilities to consider.

(i) For *believing*, EC does not imply ED. There are many people S of whom we may say, "S believes that there exists an *x* such that *x* will succeed Johnson as President" (EC), but not "There exists an *x* such that S believes that *x* will succeed Johnson as President" (ED).[4]

(ii) UD does not imply UC. "For every *x*, S believes that *x* is material" (UD) does not imply "S believes that, for every *x*, *x* is material" (UC). If somehow, S has come to decide, with respect to each thing, that that thing is material, then UD will be true. But if he believes mistakenly that, in addition to the things he believes to be material, there are still other things and that some of these other things (e.g., God) are not material, then UC will be false.

(iii) UC does not imply UD. The following suppositions are consistent with each other. (1) S has information about each material thing, *a, b, c, . . . n*. (2) S believes, correctly, that each of these things is material. (3) He believes, mistakenly, that *a, b, c, . . . n* comprise all the things there are. Hence, being reasonable, (4) he believes that, for every *x*, *x* is material (UC). But (5) there is, in addition to the material things *a, b, c, . . . n*, still another thing—namely, God—and that thing is not material. These suppositions, which include UC, imply that UD—"For every *x*, S believes that *x* is material"—is false. S has made a mistake, we have supposed, but his mistake does *not* consist in identifying God with *a, b, c, . . .* or *n*, or in supposing God to be a material thing. Believing that there is no God, and believing that God is a material thing, are two quite different heresies; on our suppositions, S is guilty of the former but not of the latter. Hence, for *believing,* UC does not imply UD.

(iv) UD implies EC. I think we may say, of believing generally, that to believe with respect to anything *x* that *x* has a certain property F is, in part at least, to believe that there exists an *x* such that *x* has that property F.[5] If this thesis is true, then, if we can say "For every *x,* S believes that *x* is material" (UD), we can also say "S believes that there exists an *x* such that *x* is material" (EC).

(v) The same thesis about belief, moreover, enables us to say that ED implies EC: if there exists an *x* such that S believes that *x* is material (ED), then S believes that there exists an *x* such that *x* is material (EC).

One may protest: "But suppose that God exists; then, if S is an atheist, we may say 'There exists an *x* such that S believes that *x* does not exist' (ED); but if S is reasonable, we can hardly conclude 'S believes that there exists an *x* such that *x* does not exist' " (EC).[6] We have anticipated the objection by stipulating that the U-statements and E-statements, in terms of which we define our four forms, be statements which are logically neutral. The E-statement "There exists an *x* such that *x* does not exist" is logically false. (We may be tempted also to *deny* that the atheist believes, concerning God, that God does not exist. For there is some plausibility in the thesis that no one can be said to believe, with respect to any particular thing, that that thing does not exist. And this thesis would imply that, instead of believing with respect to God that he does not exist, the atheist believes, with respect to the things that do exist, that none of them is God—or that none of them has the properties which theists believe they attribute to God. But this thesis, attractive as it is, may not be consistent with what I have said above, concerning the failure of the implication from UC to UD for believing.)

(vi) Does UC imply EC, for *believing?* If we are talking about rational beings, then we must say, surely, that if any such being believes that everything is material (UC), he also believes that there is something which is material (EC). The matter would be more difficult if we could contemplate the possibility of a rational man who believes that there isn't anything. I suggest, however, that we need not accommodate our theory to this possibility.

(vii) Finally, does UC imply ED? If (UC) a man S believes that, for every x, x is material, doesn't it follow (ED) that there exists an x such that S believes that x is material? The possibility of UC being true and ED being false, in such a case, would require that S be able to refer to everything without in fact being able to refer to anything. This possibility, too, seems to me to be one that we need not provide for. I shall conclude, therefore, that for believing UC implies ED.

We may summarize these conclusions in the following table and refer to it as Pattern I:

	UC	UD	EC	ED
UC		—	—	—
UD	—		—	—
EC				
ED		—		

5

We may now formulate a possible criterion of intentionality: A modal prefix M is *intentional* provided that: either (1) M conforms to Pattern I, or (2) the result of prefixing M to "it is false that" is intentional. This way of defining intentionality has the consequence that "it is M that" is intentional if and only if "it is M that it is false that" is intentional.

We may also say, if we choose, that a compound of modal prefixes (e.g., "it is M that, or it is N that") is intentional if any of its components is intentional; and if we may speak of modal prefixes as being logically equivalent to other modal prefixes (as "it is necessary that" is usually thought to be logically equivalent to "it is not possible that it is false that"), we may say that a modal prefix is intentional if it is logically equivalent to one that is intentional.

Speaking more informally, we may also say, of those verbs (e.g., "believes") which may be used to construct an intentional prefix, that they, too, are intentional; we may also say of the state, disposition, or event which the verb is used to designate that it is intentional.

In what follows, I shall (i) consider certain other psychological modalities in the light of this definition of intentionality, (ii) discuss the question whether any nonpsychological modalities satisfy the terms of the definition, and (iii) consider the controversial question, with respect to certain other modalities, whether those modalities are psychological.

6

I suggest that *knowing*, like believing, conforms to Pattern I. It is clear that UC implies EC and ED ("He knows that every" implies "He knows that some" and "He knows of some"); and EC implies none of the other three. It is also clear that UD does not imply UC. "For every x, S knows that x is material" (UD) does not imply "S knows that, for every x, x is material" (UC); the first statement, unlike the second, is consistent with supposing S to believe, mistakenly, that there are certain additional things which are *not* material.[7]

We have said that, for believing, UC does not imply UD. What of knowing? Our subject S knows that, for every x, if x is red then x is colored. Does it follow that, for every x, he knows that if x is red then x is colored? Let us consider a certain speck of dust, A, which exists some miles beyond Andromeda. A exists, but S does not know that it does; and therefore S cannot be said to know, with respect to A, that if *it* is red then it is colored. For S to know, with respect to A, that if it is red it is colored, then S must know, *of* some thing, *that* that thing is A.[8] But (we are supposing) there is no thing of which S knows that that thing is the particular piece of dust A; hence even though (UC) S knows that, for every x, if x is red then x is colored, it is not true that (UD) for every x, S knows that if x is red then x is colored. I would conclude, therefore, that for knowing UC does not imply UD, and hence that knowing and believing follow the same intentional pattern.*

Desiring, fearing, approving, and *wondering* all seem to conform to Pattern I. The grounds for asserting this are substantially the same as those considered in the case of *believing*. Perhaps only three cases call for particular attention.

(i) Of a man S, who would like to marry someone or other but who hasn't yet found the right one, we may affirm "S desires that there be (exist) an x such that S marry x" (EC) and yet deny "There exists an x such that S desires that S marry x" (ED); hence, for *desiring*, EC does not imply ED.** The example may be accommodated to *fearing, approving,* and *wondering.*

(ii) If S has been able to find out, with respect to each thing, that that thing is material, and if he desires, with respect to each material thing, that that thing be transformed into something immaterial, then we may affirm "For every x, S desires that x be transformed" (UD). But if he believes that there is another entity, God, and that this other entity is not material, and if he has no desire that this other entity, God, be transformed, then we must deny "S desires that, for every x, x be transformed" (UC). Here, too, the example may be accommodated to *fearing, approving,* and *wondering.*

(iii) Let us revise our assumptions, once again, concerning the truth of materialism and the nature of S's own meta-

* Cornman (footnote 1) seems to argue that since (1) "know" is used as an "achievement-word," therefore (2) knowing cannot be psychological; but he does not defend any premise which would warrant the inference from (1) to (2).

** Quine (*op. cit.*) makes this point saying of the man who wants "mere relief from slooplessness," that although the man desires to own a sloop, there may yet be no particular sloop that he desires to own. Quine does not discuss the forms that I have called "UC" and "UD."

physics. If S is familiar with each of the members of the class of material things, if he desires that whatever is material be transformed, and if he believes that the class of material things includes everything there is, then we may affirm "S desires that, for every x, x be transformed" (UC). But if, unknown to him, there is a God, who has just those characteristics that S wants each thing to have, then we must deny "For every x, S desires that x be transformed" (UD). Analogously for *fearing, approving,* and *wondering.*

The examples of intentional prefixes given so far are of prefixes which have been said to conform to Pattern I. We have also said that a prefix M is intentional if the result of prefixing M to "it is false that" is intentional. Hence *disbelieving* ("S disbelieves that") is intentional, inasmuch as "S disbelieves that it is false that" (= "S believes that") is intentional. Since *desiring* is intentional, "S desires that it be false that" is also intentional; similarly for *fearing, approving,* and *wondering.* ("Believing p" is equivalent to "disbelieving not-p"; but "disapproving p" might be held not to be equivalent to "approving not-p"—the reason being, that although a man disbelieves as many things as he believes, some men may disapprove of more things than they approve of. *Disapproving* is intentional, however, since "S disapproves that it be false that" is intentional.)

Our criteria have been so formulated that the following prefixes cannot be said to be intentional: "It is false that it is believed that," "It is false that it is disbelieved that," and "It is neither believed nor disbelieved that." And similarly for the prefixes that result when the other psychological verbs we have mentioned are substituted for "believed" and "disbelieved" in these prefixes. But this is as it should be, because statements beginning with these prefixes would be true even if there were no persons or no psychological states, dispositions, or processes.

Let us now ask whether our criterion has the defects of

former criteria. Are there nonpsychological modalities which must be called intentional?

7

To show that a certain modal prefix, "it is M that," is not intentional, according to our criterion, it will be sufficient to show that both "it is M that" and "it is M that it is false that" deviate in some respect from Pattern I which we have attributed to *believing* and to other psychological terms. That is to say, it will be sufficient to show that any one of the following is true for "it is M that" and any one of the following is true for "it is M that it is false that":

UC implies UD; UC does not imply EC; UC does not imply ED; UD implies UC; UD does not imply EC; UD does not imply ED; EC implies UC; EC implies UD; EC implies ED; ED implies UC; ED implies UD; ED does not imply EC.

To "show" any of these things we must appeal to the reader's intuition. This is most readily done in those cases where we wish to show that an implication fails, for we can then describe a possible situation in which the antecedent of the implication is true and the consequent false.

Let us consider, in order, the "deontic" modalities, the "alethic" modalities, and the "causal" modalities and see whether we can find any that are intentional.

8

There are a number of different senses of "obligation" and our "deontic logic" will depend in part on which of these senses is the object of our concern. Let us begin with "obligation" in its most imposing sense.

It has been held that there are obligations which are absolute (in that they hold in every possible world), unconditional (in that they hold for each person no matter what he may happen to do), and objective (in that they hold independently of what anyone desires, wishes, feels, approves, commands, or forbids). An example of such an obligation (let us suppose) is that of promise-keeping: every promise must be kept, no matter what, and in every possible world. There is no such obligation (let us suppose) to walk, but if everyone should promise to walk, then (in this world) everyone would have the conditional (but still objective) obligation to walk.

The pattern for "absolute obligation" would seem to be the following:

	UC	UD	EC	ED
UC			—	—
UD			—	—
EC				
ED			—	

The pattern differs from that of *truth* only in that, for absolute obligation, there is no implication from EC to ED. "It is obligatory that there be an *x* such that *x* is a place set aside for worship" (EC) does not imply "There is an *x* such that it is obligatory that *x* be a place set aside for worship" (ED): the people may choose whatever place they would like. The other points on the table need no comment.*

Obligation, in this absolute sense, is not properly indicated by "it is commanded that"—much less by "it is desired that" or any other such intentional expression. "Doing A is *forbidden*," therefore, is not a proper paraphrase of "It is obligatory not to do A"; and "Doing A is *permitted*" is not a proper paraphrase of "It is not obligatory not to do A." We may use

* But compare Jaakko Hintikka, "Quantifiers in Deontic Logic," *Societas Scientiarum Fennica: Commentationes Humanarum Litterarum,* XXIII (1957), 1–23. Hintikka asks whether "There is an action *x* such that *x* ought to be A" implies "There ought to be an action *x* such that *x* is A," which is tantamount to asking whether ED implies EC. Contrary to our table, Hintikka rejects the implication on the ground that "it is conceivable one could have avoided running into the situation where he ought to do A by changing some of his earlier non-obligatory acts" (p. 22). The remark indicates that Hintikka is discussing what I have called "conditional obligation" and not "absolute obligation."

"wrong" and *"not wrong";* as we shall see, the logical properties of these terms differ from those of "forbidden" and "permitted."

Deontic modal prefixes, when taken in this absolute sense, are not intentional. The pattern for *obligatory,* formulated above, may be seen to differ in two respects from the intentional pattern attributed to *believing:* for *obligatory,* unlike *believing,* UC implies UD, and UD implies UC. The pattern for *not wrong* ("it is false that it is obligatory not to do A") differs from that of *believing,* in that, for *not wrong,* UC implies UD. Restricting our variables to persons, we may illustrate the latter point as follows: "It is not wrong that, for every *x, x* walk" (UC) implies "For every *x,* it is not wrong that *x* walk" (UD).

To show that our other deontic terms differ from *believing,* it will be sufficient to make clear that, for them, ED does not imply EC. "There is an *x* such that it is *wrong* that *x* be made a guardian" (ED) does not imply "It is wrong that there is an *x* such that *x* is made a guardian" (EC). Analogously for *non-obligatory* ("it is not obligatory that"), *indifferent* ("it is neither wrong nor obligatory that"), and *nonindifferent* ("it is either wrong or obligatory that"). Possibly *nonindifference* requires illustration. There is a certain person who should *not* be made a gate-keeper; hence (ED) there is an *x* such that it is nonindifferent that *x* be a gate-keeper; but it may yet be indifferent that (whether) there be an *x* such that *x* is made a gate-keeper (not-EC).

It would seem, then, that when we take the deontic modalities in their absolute sense, they are not intentional.

9

Let us now consider the deontic modalities when they are taken in such a way that "obligatory," "wrong," and "not wrong," respectively, may be replaced by "commanded," "forbidden," and "permitted." We are now thinking of those obligations which are "laid down" by God, or by the ruler, or by the state, or by the "mores" of the "culture circle" in which we live. This is the sense in which the terms of "deontic logic" have been interpreted by a number of recent authors.[9]

One may wish to contend that commanding, forbidding, and permitting should be counted as intentional, for they are, without doubt, intimately related to what is intentional. But let us reject this contention, at least provisionally, on the ground that posters and signs ("Do not enter") may command, forbid, and permit.

The pattern for "it is commanded that," I suggest, is the following:

	UC	UD	EC	ED
UC		—	—	—
UD			—	—
EC				
ED			—	

The pattern resembles that for *obligatory*, except that for *commanded*, UD does not imply UC. "For every x, it is commanded that x enlist" (UD) does not imply "It is commanded that, for every x, x enlist" (UC); the latter statement describes a blanket order, but the former does not.*

We do not prove that the commander is inconsistent if we ascribe to him UD and also "It is permitted that there be someone who does not enlist"; he may have told each of his subjects to enlist (UD) while believing, mistakenly, that he has still other subjects. (He may command each of his subjects to enlist without commanding that they all enlist, and he

---

* It is essential to distinguish two different uses of "it is commanded": its use, as above, to *describe* what it is that the commander orders, and its use, by the commander himself, to issue those orders. In its latter use, UD would at least "contextually imply" UC. Similarly, although for the third person "S believes," UD does not imply UC, and UC does not imply UD, for the first person "I believe," these implications may be said to hold "contextually."

may thus command each to enlist without issuing a separate command for each. Suppose that, contrary to his beliefs, his subjects comprise only adult males. In commanding that all adult males enlist, he has, therefore, commanded that each of his subjects enlist without having commanded that they all enlist and without having issued a separate command for each).

The pattern for "commands" differs from that for "believes," in that, for "commands" but not for "believes," UC implies UD. "It is commanded that, for every *x, x* enlist" (UC) is a command which applies to each subject (any subject who refused to enlist would be guilty of insubordination) and thus implies "For every *x*, it is commanded that *x* enlist" (UD).

To show that the other terms of this type of deontic logic are not intentional, it will be sufficient, once again, to show that each term ("it is M that") and its contrary ("it is M that it is false that") differ in some respect from the pattern attributed to *believing. Permission* ("it is not commanded that") differs from believing in that, for permission, UC implies UD: "It is permitted that, for every *x, x* attend the meeting" (UC) implies "For every *x*, it is permitted that *x* attend the meeting" (UD). The other terms differ from believing in various respects; for each of them, unlike believing, ED does not imply EC. "There is an *x* such that it is *forbidden* that *x* attend the meeting" (ED) does not imply "It is forbidden that there is (be) an *x* such that *x* attend the meeting" (EC): analogously for *indifferent, unrequired* ("it is not commanded that"), and *nonindifferent.*

Hence the deontic modalities, when taken in this relative sense, would seem not to be intentional.

10

We have distinguished conditional and unconditional obligation. Given the concept of unconditional obligation, as that which holds for all persons, at all times, and in every possible world, we may describe conditional obligation as follows: A man has the conditional obligation to perform a certain act A if he is in a situation C such that (i) it is unconditionally obligatory that if a man is in situation C then he perform act A and (ii) it is not unconditionally obligatory that he be in this situation C. (A similar distinction could be made for *commands*.) From the fact that a man has the conditional obligation to perform A, we cannot infer that he has an unconditional obligation to perform A (though we can infer, presumably, that he does not have the unconditional obligation not to perform A). How would the "logic" of such obligations differ, so far as our forms UC, UD, EC, and ED are concerned, from the two types of deontic logic just considered?

I feel that the answer to this question is not entirely clear; what does seem clear, however, is that the terms of conditional obligation are not intentional. If the "logic" of these terms does differ from that of absolute obligation and from that of commanding (and I'm not at all sure that it does), it would be in the following respect: for conditional obligation, the forms taken *in sensu diviso* do not imply the corresponding forms *in sensu composito*—i.e., UD implies neither UC nor EC, and ED implies neither UC nor EC. The variants of this modality will differ from *believing* in that, for them, ED does not imply EC, and UC does not imply EC; hence we may conclude that they are not intentional.

11

What of "alethic logic"—the logic of *necessity* and *possibility*? Here the relations among our four propositional forms may vary, depending upon (i) whether we are speaking of logical, physical, or metaphysical necessity, (ii) whether we are speaking of these modalities *de re* or *de dicto,* and (iii) how we deal with certain controversies concerning the relation between these modalities and quantification. But I think it is clear that if we preserve the usual meanings of these terms, none of them will follow the intentional pattern of *believing*. Both *necessity* and *possibility* are such that UC implies UD: "It is necessary that, for every x, x is F" implies "For every x, it is necessary that x is F"; similarly for possibility.* The other alethic modalities—*impossibility, nonnecessity* ("it is not necessary that"), *contingency* ("it is neither necessary nor impossible that"), and *non-contingency* ("it is either necessary or impossible that")—are such that, for them, ED does not imply EC. "There exists an x such that it is impossible that x was the first thing created" (ED) does not imply "It is impossible that there exists an x such that x was the first thing created" (EC); similarly for the other variants of these modalities.[10]

12

Expressions of the following sort may be said to indicate *causal* modalities: "There is (occurs) something sufficient for bringing it about that," "Someone does something sufficient for bringing it about that." We also obtain causal modalities by substituting "necessary" for "sufficient" in these expressions; also by adding "not" at the end, or by saying instead ". . . bringing it about that it is false that," or ". . . preventing it from happening that," *etc.*

It should be clear, I think, that the tables for "sufficient for bringing it about that" and "sufficient to prevent that" are the same, respectively, as those for "it is true that" and "it is false that":

	UC	UD	EC	ED
UC			—	—
UD			—	—
EC				
ED				

	UC	UD	EC	ED
UC				
UD	—			—
EC	—			
ED				—

---

* Strictly speaking, we need not consider logical necessity and logical impossibility in this context, since we have restricted the U-statements and E-statements, in terms of which we have defined the four forms, UC, UD, EC, ED, to statements which are logically contingent.

Indeed, these expressions may be replaced by "makes it true that" and "makes it false that." Hence they do not follow the intentional patterns. Nor do their denials ("does not make it true that" and "does not make it false that") since, for each of these, ED does not imply EC.

"Something occurs which is *necessary* for making it *true* that," "Something occurs which is necessary for making it *false* that," and their denials also appear to be such that, for them, ED does not imply EC.

The causal modalities, then, would seem not to be intentional.

13

We may obtain further light on intentionality by contrasting the following patterns:

	I					II			
	UC	UD	EC	ED		UC	UD	EC	ED
UC		—	—	—	UC		—	—	—
UD	—		—	—	UD			—	—
EC					EC				
ED			—		ED			—	

Pattern I, we have said, is exemplified by "it is believed that" and Pattern II by "it is commanded that." (It will be recalled "it is absolutely obligatory that" differs from "it is commanded that" in that, for absolute obligation, UD implies UC.) Commanding, we have said, is intimately related to what is intentional.

Stating, asserting, and *affirming* are like *commanding* in that they, too, are intimately related to what is intentional and in that they conform to Pattern II. If it were possible for S to state (assert, or affirm) with respect to each *x*, that *x* is material (UD), he could accomplish this act without making the generalization involved in saying that, for every *x, x* is material (UC). (The example is more plausible, of course, if we restrict the values of our variables to some more limited universe of discourse.) Suppose now that S *believes* that, for every *x*, *x* contains an evil principle (UC); this supposition, as we have seen, does not imply that, for every *x*, S believes that *x* contains an evil principle (UD). If he believes, correctly, that all material things contain an evil principle, and if he believes, mistakenly, that there are no things which are not material, then UC may be true and UD false. But if he were to *express* his belief, if he were to *state, assert,* or *affirm* that for every *x*, *x* contains an evil principle (UC), then it will also be true that, for every *x*, S has stated, asserted, or affirmed that *x* contains an evil principle. His statement, but not his belief, is blasphemy.

Again the point will be clearer if we restrict our universe of discourse—say, to the people in the room. Suppose the people in the room comprise *a, b, c,* and *n;* S believes that *a, b,* and *c* are dishonest; he believes, mistakenly, that they are the only people in the room; and he thus concludes that everyone in the room is dishonest (UC). Were these people somehow able to divine his thoughts, then *a, b,* and *c* might have the right to feel offended (if, say, they are not dishonest), but *n* would not. If, however, S were to express his belief and *say* that everyone is dishonest, then, if none of them is dishonest, *n* like the others could charge S with slander. He could accuse S of *saying* that he, *n,* is dishonest, but he could not accuse S of believing that he is dishonest. (Here we have an interesting situation: *n* understood perfectly well what it was that S was saying; S was using his language correctly; S was speaking sincerely and not lying or trying to lie; and yet *n* is justified in attributing to S a statement which S in fact does not believe.)

Although these terms conforming to Pattern II are intimately related to what is intentional, we cannot describe Pattern II itself as an alternative mark of intentionality. For *possibility,* in at least one of its senses, conforms to Pattern II. Restricting our universe of discourse to people who are competing for a prize which one at most can win, we may say: "It is possible that everyone will lose" (UC) implies "Everyone is such that it is possible he will lose" (UD), "It is possible some will lose" (EC), and "There is someone such that it is possible he will lose" (ED). If everyone has an equal chance, we may say "Everyone is such that it is possible he will win" (UD), and this will imply the corresponding EC and ED: but it will not imply "It is possible that everyone will win" (UC). "It is possible that someone will win" (EC) implies neither UC nor UD: similarly "There is someone such that it is possible he will win" (ED) implies neither UC nor UD, but it does imply EC. Does EC imply ED? We may wish to say, of our particular example, that "It is possible that someone will win" implies "There is someone such that it is possible that he will win." But surely we do not want to say that "It is possible that there is an x such that x is God" (EC) implies "There is an x such that it is possible that x is God" (ED). If this interpretation of possibility is correct, we cannot say that Pattern II gives us a mark of intentionality.

What shall we say, then, about the relation of *commanding, stating, asserting, affirming,* and related concepts to what is intentional? We could say of each of these concepts that it implies *believing,* or that it cannot be exemplified unless *believing* is also exemplified.[11] And in such a case we could say that, if these concepts are not strictly intentional, they do at least involve what is strictly intentional. But there are philosophers who appear to be willing to interpret these concepts in such a way that they need not involve what is intentional. They would say, if I interpret them correctly, that any set of objects that happens to be arranged in the pattern or configuration of the printed English sentence "All men are mortal" could be said to *state that* all men are mortal.[12] A configuration of objects having the configuration of *Rauchen Verboten,* wherever and however it may be brought about, might similarly be said to *command that* no smoking occur. If we decide to interpret "state," "assert," "affirm," "command," and related concepts in this way, then, of course, we shall want to deny that they are intentional or that they necessarily involve what is intentional.

Wishing, and perhaps also *willing* and *hoping,* may be interpreted in such a way that, unlike *wanting* and *desiring,* they conform to Pattern II and not to Pattern I. It has been thought by many people that if a man wishes hard enough his wishes will come true. If the man S of our earlier example (who believed that *a, b,* and *c* were all dishonest and comprised everyone in the room) merely *wanted* all the people in the room to be arrested, then, as we have said, his want does not apply to *n* whom he believes, mistakenly, not to be in the room. But if now S acts upon the superstition that sufficient wishing will realize its object and wishes that, for every *x, x* be arrested (UC), and if *n* knows of the wish and shares the superstition, then *n* may reasonably fear for his own freedom, on the ground that UC implies UD. *Willing* and *hoping* may be less clear; on some interpretations, they resemble *desiring* and *wanting* and thus conform to Pattern I, but on others they resemble *praying* and *requesting* and thus conform to Pattern II.

14

What of *thought, love,* and *action?* The grammatical object of the verb "think" may be either propositional or nonpropositional. The former possibility is realized in such sentences as "He is thinking about Alaska having been admitted into the Union" and "He is thinking about what would have happened had the matter been handled differently"; the latter is exemplified by "He is thinking about Alaska" and "He is thinking about the largest state." (Every sentence in which "think" has a propositional object implies one in which "think" has a nonpropositional object; "He is thinking about *a*'s being F" implies "He is thinking about *a*." This point is sometimes put by saying that judgments and assumptions presuppose ideas. An interesting philosophical question is whether ideas presuppose judgments or assumptions. Can a man think of an object *a* without thinking of *a* as having certain properties or as being in a certain state?) When we wish to use "think" with a propositional object, we may introduce grammatical auxiliaries to construct a modal prefix; e.g., "He is thinking about the possibility that." And this modal prefix follows the intentional pattern of *believing*.

We may construe the objects of desiring and wanting, and possibly the objects of liking, as being propositional. But this is less plausible in the case of *loving*. In one common use of the verb "love," it would make no sense to use the term with a quantified statement as its grammatical object. Using "love" in this way, perhaps we can say that people love only those things which they believe to exist. In this case, love is like knowledge in that its existence presupposes that which is intentional. In other uses, "love" may imply "want" or "desire" and not "believe"; here, too, it may be said to presuppose what is intentional. Such terms as "worship," "respect," and "adore" are similar to "love" in these respects.

Is *acting* intentional? "S *does* so-and-so" may often be interpreted as saying that S produces a condition sufficient for the existence of so-and-so. *Doing,* taken in this way, is one of the causal modalities, and we have said that the causal modalities are not intentional. But *trying, attempting, intending,* and *purposing* ("S does something in order to bring it about that . . .") are easily seen to be intentional. And *doing,* surely, implies or involves some one or another of these intentional concepts. We may not wish to say that acting always involves *trying* or *attempting,* if these latter concepts are taken, as they usually are, to imply *exertion* or *effort.* But it is plausible to say that acting always involves purposing ("doing something in order to bring it about that . . ."), and since purposing is intentional, acting involves what is intentional.[13]

Let us abbreviate "Mr. Jones is dead" by "*p*"; "S brings it about that" by "A"; and "it is false that" by the hyphen. Then we may distinguish Ap, A-p, -A-p, and -Ap, and construct a square of opposition, as illustrated here.[14] Ap tells us that S brings about or causes the death of Mr. Jones, but leaves open the question whether the death is accidental or intentional;

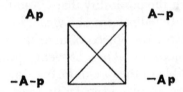

A-p tells us that S prevents the death (perhaps, without realizing it, he causes Mr. Jones to miss the boat, which is destined to sink); -A-p tells us that S does nothing which prevents Mr. Jones from dying (but it does not tell us whether or not Mr. Jones is dead); and -Ap tells us that S does nothing which causes Mr. Jones to die. If we wish to say that S does something *in order* to bring about the death, that he "purposed" it, we might say "S purposes that S brings it about that Mr. Jones is dead"—PAp—and make similar distinctions. And if we wish to say that he is successful, i.e., that he brings it about intentionally that Mr. Jones is dead, in short, that he murders him, we might say: "PAp and Ap." The expression "P" in "PAp" is intentional.*

* Using "W" for "it is wrong that," and "B" for "it is believed that," we could formulate some of the problems which give rise to "moralities of intention" by considering the logical relations holding among such formulae as the following:

$$p$$
$$Wp$$
$$Ap$$
$$PAp$$
$$BWp$$
$$BWAp$$
$$BWPAp$$

along with the formulae obtained from these by putting the negation sign in admissible places.

15

The epistemic modalities, e.g., "it is evident that," "there is no ground for believing that," "it is probable that" also ought to be considered. But the properties of most of these remain problematic, possibly because they combine logical, ethical, and intentional elements. Thus "*h* is probable in relation to *e*," in one familiar use, might be interpreted as saying, among other things, that the logical relations between *h* and *e* are such that, if *e* were *known* to be true (or, possibly, if nothing other than *e* and what it entails were known to be true), then there would be a certain amount of justification, for *believing*, or for *acting upon* the proposition that *h* is also true. These modalities, so far as I have been able to see up to now, do not provide counterexamples to what I have said about intentionality.

COMMENTS

Robert C. Sleigh, Jr.

Wayne State University

1

I shall make few references to the notion of "intentionality." I take the main burden of the paper to be the discovery of some pattern to which all the members of a certain set of basic psychological prefixes conform but to which no nonpsychological prefix conforms. Further, I take it that Chisholm either explicitly asserts each of the following theses in his paper or he explicitly asserts something that entails it.

> Thesis I: Pattern I is such that the prefixes "S believed that," "S knows that," "S desires that," "S fears that," "S wonders whether it is the case that," "S is thinking about the possibility that," conform to it.

> Thesis II: Pattern I is such that no non-psychological prefix conforms to it.

> Thesis III: There is some Pattern P_1 such that the prefixes "S believes that," "S knows that," "S desires that," "S fears that," "S wonders whether it is the case that," "S is thinking about the possibility that," conform to it.

> Thesis IV: Whatever pattern it is to which the above mentioned prefixes conform, there is no nonpsychological prefix which conforms to it.

First, a note concerning an apparent presupposition in Chisholm's method of distinguishing psychological prefixes from nonpsychological prefixes: it is evident from the remarks in the initial section of Chisholm's paper that his primary interest is in distinguishing psychological prefixes from other nonextensional prefixes. And, it is also evident that the method which Chisholm proposes for marking this distinction involves the logical behavior of quantified statements containing nonextensional prefixes. In cases of quantification modalized *in sensu diviso* with a nonextensional modal prefix, the resulting statement apparently involves a quantification into what Quine has called an "opaque context." Apparently, Chisholm is presupposing in certain cases the legitimacy of quantifying into opaque contexts. I shall discuss this assumption with respect to the prefix "S believes that."

Sentences like the following are ambiguous:

(i) Dorothy believes the chairman is in his office.
(ii) Dorothy believes everyone in 106 Lincoln Hall is a philosopher.

Consider (i). This sentence usually asserts that Dorothy accepts the proposition that the chairman is in his office. But (i) may also be used to assert that a certain relation obtains between Dorothy and a certain person, i.e., the chairman. Thus (i) may be used to assert that the chairman is such that Dorothy believes of him that he is in his office and this assertion may well be true even though Dorothy does not accept the proposition that the chairman is in his office. Suppose that you are concerned to know what belief Dorothy holds with respect to a certain man whom you know to be the chairman and who, in fact, is George Nakhnikian, though you do not know this. Suppose I discover that Dorothy accepts the proposition that George is in his office. I note that Dorothy does not know or even believe that George is the chairman. In this situation I might well tell you what you want to know by employing (i) without thereby in any way committing myself to the claim that Dorothy accepts the proposition that the chairman is in his office. Following Quine, let's say that the first use of (i) outlined above involves "believe" in its notional sense; the second, "believe" in its relational sense.[1]

Consider (ii). Its notional use is obvious. And, again, a relational use comes to mind although it is not common. Suppose you know that Tom, Dick and Harry and no one else occupies 106 Lincoln Hall. Suppose you are concerned to know what belief Dorothy holds about the vocations of these men. In this situation I might employ (ii) to tell you what you want to know even though I know that Dorothy (mistakenly) thinks that Jones is in 106 Lincoln Hall and that Jones is not a philosopher.

This distinction may be stated somewhat more exactly for very simple cases in the following schemata:

$$a \; : \; \text{S believes Fx}$$
$$b \; : \; \text{S believes (Qx) (Fx)}$$

Let us say that a sentence, c, is an instance of the schema a just in case c results from a by substituting a name or description of a person for "S"; a one place predicate for "F"; and, a name or description for "x."

Let us say that a sentence, d, is an instance of the schema b just in case d results from b by substituting a name or description of a person for "S"; a quantifier, universal or existential, for "(Qx)"; a propositional function in which a one place predicate replaces "F" and an individual variable bound to whatever replaces "Qx," replaces "x."

Df. I: If a sentence, c, is an instance of the schema a, then c contains "believe" in its relational sense, if and only if, whatever name or description replaces "x" in a to obtain c occurs transparently in c.*

---

* A name or description e occurs transparently in a sentence S just in case the proposition expressed by S, or its negation, entails that there is such an object as e purports to denote and the principle of substitution holds for e in S.

Where that which replaces "x" in a to obtain c is a description, then Df. I is tantamount to saying that c contains "believe" in its relational sense just in case the description replacing "x" has a primary occurrence in c. The distinction between primary and secondary occurrences of a description in a sentence may be extended to names in a perfectly natural way. Hence, Df. I is tantamount to saying that c contains "believe" in its relational sense just in case the name or description replacing "x" has a primary occurrence in c.

Let us carry over the idea of transparency to instances of b. Consider a list of names or descriptions L_1: a_1, a_2, . . . a_n. Consider a sentence d which is an instance of b. Consider the result of dropping the quantifier in d to obtain an instance of "S believes Fx" and replacing "x" (or whatever replaces "x" in b to obtain d) by the elements of L_1 alternatively. This gives us a new list, L_2: S believes Fa_1, S believes Fa_2, . . . S believes Fa_n. We may then employ Df. I to insure that each item in L_2 contains "believe" in its relational sense.

Let E be the disjunction of the items in L_2.

Df. 2.1: If a sentence d is an instance of the schema b and the quantifier replacing "(Qx)" in b to obtain d is existential, then d contains "believe" in its relational sense, if and only if, d is equivalent to E in the presence of the assumption that L_1 contains at least one name (or description) of each existing thing.

Let U be the conjunction of the items in L_2.

Df. 2.2: If a sentence d is an instance of the schema b and the quantifier replacing "(Qx)" in b to obtain d is universal, then d contains "believe" in its relational sense, if and only if, d is equivalent to U in the presence of the assumption that L_1 contains at least one name (or description) of each existing thing.

Although nothing has been said explicitly about sentences of the form "(∃x) [S believes (relationally) that Fx]" or "(x) [S believes (relationally) that Fx]," something about them follows from what has been said. Clearly, since names occur transparently in instantiations of "(∃x) [S believes (relationally) that Fx]" a sentence of this form will be true just in case E is true on the usual assumption. But Df. 2.1 has as a consequence that "S believes (relationally) that (∃x) (Fx)" is true under exactly the same circumstances. Analogous remarks apply to universal quantification. These results may be summarized by saying that, for the relational sense of "believe," the quantifier, existential or universal, is commutable with the prefix "believes that," hence the pattern to which the relational sense conforms appears to be:

| | Believing (relationally) | | | |
	UC	UD	EC	ED
UC			—	—
UD			—	—
EC				
ED				

Since, obviously, this is not Pattern I, we may skip Theses I and II and turn to III and IV. Note that, for the relational sense of "believe," IV is clearly false, because "it is true that" conforms to the above pattern and is not psychological.

I assume that sentences which are instances of the schemata *a* or *b* contain "believe" in either its notional or relational sense; hence, if not in the relational sense, then in the notional sense.

I assume that the distinction between relational and notional senses formulated for "believe" may be extended in an analogous fashion to the other members of the set of basic psychological prefixes. The results of the discussion of "believe" in its relational sense suggest that Theses I through IV had best be limited to the notional senses of the basic psychological prefixes. Obviously, when Theses I through IV are so construed they involve the assumption that it is legitimate to quantify into contexts which are prefaced by "believe" (and the other members of the basic set) in its notional sense. If this assumption is mistaken, then Chisholm's procedure is misguided. Moreover, Quine's arguments that this assumption is mistaken are well-known and it seems to me that Chisholm's program cannot be regarded as complete until Quine's arguments are countered and an acceptable system for mixing quantification and opacity is at hand.[2] In any case, there are questions concerning Chisholm's theses that may be discussed profitably prior to the development of such a system and to these I now turn.

2

Consider the following patterns:

PATTERN I

	UC	UD	EC	ED
UC		—	—	—
UD	—		—	—
EC				
ED		—		

THE MINIMUM PATTERN

	UC	UD	EC	ED
UC		—	—	—
UD	—		—	—
EC	—	—		—
ED	—		—	

According to Chisholm (and this is Thesis I) the members of the basic set of psychological prefixes conform to Pattern I. In the light of the preceding discussion, we may take this to mean that the members of the basic set of psychological prefixes in their notional senses conform to Pattern I. My view is that this claim is mistaken, and, that the members of the basic set conform to the Minimum Pattern. Apparently, in claiming that *believing* conforms to Pattern I, Chisholm is employing some principle of rationality. He says:

> By appealing to the fact that men need not be rational —that a man may have contradictory beliefs and desires —we might be able to formulate a fairly simple criterion of an intentional modality. . . . It may seem unfortunate to proceed in this way if intentionality is to be used to establish a distinction between the psychological and the nonpsychological and to show, perhaps, that what it is to be a *person* is something that cannot be described or understood in "physicalistic" terms. For we would be saying, in effect, that the possibility of irrationality is what separates the psychological from the physical.

Chisholm has not defined "rationality" and after considering various alternatives, I would suggest a definition that seems to have the results Chisholm desires. With respect to believing it is this: "S is rational with respect to his beliefs" means that: for any propositions p and q, if S were to believe p and if p entailed q, then S would believe q. Unhappily, it is unclear in Chisholm's paper just how this definition could be employed. Clearly, the prefix "S is rational with respect to his beliefs and S believes that" *does* conform to Pattern I. But it is not at all clear what the relevance of this fact is to the claim that "S believes that" conforms to Pattern I. Indeed, the difference in meaning between "S believes that" and "S is rational with respect to his beliefs and S believes that" seems to confirm the view that "S believes that" *does not* conform to Pattern I. We can, of course, simply *make* the fact that "S is rational with respect to his beliefs and S believes that" conform to Pattern I relevant to Chisholm's claim by adopting some such condition as the following: A prefix—M—is intentional if, when conjoined with a suitable instance of the schema "—is rational with respect to his—," the resulting prefix conforms to Pattern I. But this procedure, as Chisholm would surely agree, is utterly ad hoc and, perhaps, circular. In addition, to preserve Thesis I, it would be necessary to accept such definitions as the following:

> "S is rational with respect to his wonderings" means that: for any propositions p and q, if S were to wonder whether it is the case that p, and if p entailed q, then S would wonder whether it is the case that q.

I conclude that it is best to consider Thesis I without employing any assumptions about rationality.

To what pattern the prefix "S believes that" conforms is a matter not easily settled. There appear to be conflicting intuitions on crucial cases, e.g., whether UC implies EC. Nonetheless, we may settle the question whether Thesis I is true. It is not; it is false. Surely "S wonders whether it is the case that" does not conform to Pattern I, but rather to the Minimum Pattern. Hence, if my view is correct, Thesis I is false, but Thesis III is true. But if Chisholm is right about *believing* then both Theses I and III are false.

Let us now consider Theses II and IV. In the light of my partiality for the Minimum Pattern, let us construe Thesis IV as saying that no nonpsychological prefix conforms to the Minimum Pattern.

I suggest the following counterexamples:

> *a*) To Thesis II: "With respect to the propositions expressed by the sentences on page 31 of *Perceiving,* it is more probable than not that"
>
> *b*) To Thesis IV: "There is a sentence derivable in the system explained on page 32 of *Perceiving* which expresses the proposition that"

In claiming that these prefixes constitute counterexamples to Theses II and IV, it is claimed that i) prefix *a* conforms to

Pattern I, and ii) the prefix *a* is nonpsychological; iii) prefix *b* conforms to the Minimum Pattern, and iv) prefix *b* is nonpsychological. In prefix *a,* it is intended that "is more probable than not" be taken in the logical sense; that is, any substitution instance of "h is more probable than not with respect to e" is either logically true or logically false provided that: a) the substitution instance is well-formed, and b) "h" and "e" are schematic letters to be replaced by sentences expressing propositions and not propositional variables to be replaced by names of propositions. Note that with "is more probable than not" so understood, a sentence employing this predicate in the logical sense is contingent ("With respect to the propositions expressed by the sentences on page 31 of *Perceiving,* it is more probable than not that Urbana is in Illinois"). This is crucial; otherwise, the proposed counterexample would violate Chisholm's requirement of logical neutrality. Now note that the analysis of "*h* is probable in relation to *e*" proposed by Chisholm in order to reduce the notion of probability to one that is partly psychological is not at all plausible for the concept of probability employed in the proposed counterexample.

Chisholm may claim that "there is a sentence derivable in the system explained on page 32 of *Perceiving* which expresses the proposition that" is psychological or involves what is psychological, in virtue of its entailing, when appended to a sentence p, that there is some person who interprets some sentence to mean that p. If this entailment (or some similar entailment) does not hold, then we have our counterexample. Indeed, in one passage he seems to provide all that is necessary to sustain our counterexample. He acknowledges that there are philosophers who would say:

> That any set of objects that happens to be arranged in the pattern or configuration of the printed English sentence "All men are mortal" could be said to *state that* all men are mortal. If we decide to interpret "state," "as-

sert," "affirm," "command," and related concepts in this way, then, of course, we shall want to deny that they are intentional or that they necessarily involve what is intentional.

This passage suggests that we can *decide* to interpret these concepts in this way. If so, then I so choose. In any case, if Chisholm claims that the prefix "there is a sentence derivable in the system explained on page 32 of *Perceiving* which expresses the proposition that" is psychological, then we surely require a detailed account of what is involved in the pre-analytic concept of a "psychological" prefix. Suppose that Chisholm is right in counting this prefix as psychological. Is there a way of marking off the class of psychological prefixes so construed, other than in terms of the logical behavior of quantified statements containing nonextensional prefixes? It seems to me the following shows promise:

Df. 3: A modal prefix, M, is intentional (psychological), if and only if, $(\exists p) (\exists q) \sim \{[M(p) \cdot (p \longleftrightarrow q)] \rightarrow M(q)\}$.
(Read "$[p \longleftrightarrow q]$" as: p is logically equivalent to q.)

I realize that this is inadequate as it stands. It shares a difficulty with Chisholm's definition. Consider these prefixes: "Jones believes that," "God believes that," "It is believed that." I assume that Chisholm wishes to regard all of these as intentional prefixes. Yet, obviously they do not conform to the same pattern and only the first and third are intentional by Df. 3. What seems to be required is a suitable definition of a "prefix" family so that these prefixes are all members of one and the same family. With such a definition, we could say that a prefix is intentional in the event it is a member of a prefix family at least one member of which satisfies the definiens of Df. 3.

REJOINDER
Roderick M. Chisholm

Mr. Sleigh's discussion contains many useful and penetrating observations. Some of his criticisms are sound and point to the need of modifying what I have said. But some of his criticisms and some of his more positive remarks do not seem sound. I shall begin with his comments on the "legitimacy" of quantifying into intentional contexts.

The general phenomenon of intentionality has two sides. One is that our beliefs, desires, and other intentional attitudes may be "directed upon" objects which do not exist (Diogenes looked for an honest man). The other is that, among the objects that do exist, there are some upon which our beliefs, desires, and other intentional attitudes may be directed (there is a dishonest man whom the police are looking for). Some philosophers are puzzled about one side and ask "How can our beliefs and desires refer to objects that do not exist?" Other philosophers are puzzled about the other side and ask "How can our beliefs and desires refer to objects that do exist?" Those who question the "legitimacy" of quantifying into intentional contexts would seem to belong with the second group.

Unless we are prepared to say that "the mind cannot get beyond the circle of its own ideas," we must recognize that some of the things in the world may in fact become objects of our intentional attitudes. One of the facts about Oliver B. Garrett is that he once lived in Massachusetts; another is that the police have been seeking him for many years; another is that I first learned of his existence in my youth; and another is the fact that I believe him still to be in hiding. If we wish to use "exists" tenselessly, we may infer from the latter fact that there exists something such that I believe it to be in hiding, or, if there is need to be more precise, we may say "($\exists$x) (I believe that x is hiding)." Analogously for the second and third of these facts. I would say, therefore, that unless we are prepared to accept the subjectivist view, we can hardly question the "legitimacy" of quantifying into intentional contexts. What we should do, of course, is to note the logical behavior of sentences in which quantifiers range over intentional contexts, and of sentences in which intentional operators range over quantified contexts. Then, if possible, we might formulate rules to tell us, with respect to such sentences, what legitimate inferences may be made among the types. This is what I have tried to do. In this connection, Sleigh says that the sentence "Dorothy believes that the chairman is in his office" is *ambiguous* and that it might be re-expressed either by saying "The chairman is such that Dorothy believes of him that he is in his office" or by saying "Dorothy believes the proposition—the chairman is in his office." This interpretation suggests that the original belief sentence may be telling us that Dorothy is related to one or the other of two quite different objects—either to the chairman or to something called a "proposition."* But this is misleading. I would prefer to say, first, that the original

---

* Sleigh describes a "relational" use of "believe," which, apparently, he proposes we use in connection with the first type of case and which is such that "S believes that," has the same pattern as "It is true that" with respect to UC, UD, EC, and ED. But if what I have said about believing is correct, this use of "believe" would be inadequate for the description of what we ordinarily call "believing." Unless we were to use "S believes that," in this "relational" sense, as a synonym for "it is true that," or "S brings it about that," it will be problematic whether this "relational" sense of "believe" has any significant use at all.

belief-sentence is *indeterminate* in that it presents us with two different possibilities and the realization of either is sufficient to make the sentence true. (The context of utterance, however, will often indicate which possibility is intended.) And, secondly, I would relate these two possibilities in the following way: If we are justified in saying, with Quine, that any noun or substantival expression used to designate an object may be readily transformed into verbs or adjectives which are true of that object, then we may set forth the two possibilities presented by the belief sentence without appealing to any such locution as "Dorothy believes the proposition —the chairman is in his office." Let us replace "chairman" by "chairs," and "in his office" by "officially located." Then the unambiguous but indeterminate "Dorothy believes that the chairman is in his office" becomes: "Either (i) there is just one thing *x* such that *x* chairs, and Dorothy believes that *x* is officially located; or (ii) Dorothy believes that there is just one thing *x* such that *x* chairs and *x* is officially located."*

* (The "just one thing," of course, may be eliminated.) One of the advantages of this type of formulation is that it enables us to deal with Russell's puzzle about the author of *Waverley* and hence with the principal reason for supposing that quantification into belief contexts is "illegitimate." The sentence "Although it is true that George believes that the author of *Marmion* is Scottish, it is false that George believes that the author of *Waverley* is Scottish," would be paraphrased as follows (for simplicity we retain the substantives *"Waverley"* and *"Marmion"*): "It is false that: there exists just one thing *x* such that *x* wrote *Waverley*, and George believes that *x* is Scottish. It is false that: George believes that there exists just one thing *x* such that *x* wrote *Waverley* and that *x* is Scottish. Either: (i) there exists just one thing *x* such that *x* wrote *Marmion*, and George believes that *x* is Scottish; or (ii) George believes that there exists just one thing *x* such that *x* wrote *Marmion* and that *x* is Scottish." This sentence is consistent with saying: (1) "For every *x* and every *y*, if *x* is identical with *y*, then whatever is true of *x* is true of *y*"; (2) "The author of *Waverley* is identical with the author of *Marmion*"; and (3) "For every *x*, if anyone believes that *x* has a certain property F, then his believing that *x* is F is something that is true of *x*; and if he does not believe that *x* is F, then his not believing that *x* is F, is also something that is true of *x*." Paraphrasing the original belief

Sleigh's remarks about "rationality" convince me that it was a mistake to try to bring this concept into the discussion of the logic of other intentional concepts. But if we eliminate our requirements about rationality, thus providing for the fact that people do contradict themselves and have contradictory beliefs, there is no longer any justification for saying that, for believing or for knowing, UC implies EC, or that UC implies ED. Thus there is no contradiction in saying "There is a person who believes that everything is material, but who does not believe that there is anything material"; and there is no contradiction in saying "There is a person who believes that everything is material, and yet there is nothing that he believes to be material." In this case, the pattern for *believing,* and also the pattern for *knowing,* is:

	UC	UD	EC	ED
UC		—	—	—
UD	—		—	—
EC	—			
ED	—		—	

This pattern, as far as I know, is not satisfied by any modality which is nonpsychological. If all of this is true, then this pattern yields one criterion for saying that a prefix is intentional. We should note, however, that what the pattern yields is at best a *criterion,* and not the means for a definition, for there are many psychological or intentional prefixes which do *not* conform to this pattern.

I now believe that Sleigh is also right in saying that "S wonders whether it is the case that," "S is thinking about

---

sentences in the way proposed enables us to conjoin it with these three sentences without becoming committed to the contradictory conclusion, "There exists an x such that George believes that x is Scottish, and such that it is false that George believes that x is Scottish," and also without becoming committed to the Protagorean conclusion (evidently acceptable to many contemporary philosophers), "There exists an x such that, under one description of x, George believes that x is Scottish, and such that, under another description of x, George does not believe that x is Scottish."

the possibility that," and "S fears that" conform to what he calls the "minimum pattern." They do not conform to the pattern just assigned to knowing and believing since they are such that neither ED nor UD imply EC. ("There is someone such that I wonder whether he will be the next President" does not imply "I wonder whether there is someone such that he will be the next President"; *etc.*) "S desires that," however, would seem to be more problematic. Consider a man who (i) desires not to marry, but (ii) desires that if he is going to marry he marry Jane and (iii) knows that he is going to marry. Does it follow that he desires to marry Jane —or only that he desires that, since he must marry, he marry Jane? In the former case, but not in the latter, we must say that, for desiring ED does not imply EC. Analogously for UD, EC, and desiring.

In eliminating our requirements about "rationality," we also make available the following criterion which I proposed in Section 2 of my paper and which Sleigh does not discuss:

> By appealing to the fact that men need not be rational— that a man may have contradictory beliefs and contra- dictory desires—we might be able to formulate a fairly simple criterion of an intentional modality. We might say something like: A modal prefix "it is M that" is intentional if (perhaps among certain other conditions), for any statement p, (i) "it is M that p" implies neither "it is M that not-p" nor "it is false that it is M that not-p" and (ii) "it is false that it is M that not-p" implies neither "it is M that p" nor "it is false that it is M that p."

The qualifying phrase, "perhaps among certain other con- ditions," is needed because the criterion as it stands is satis- fied by certain causal prefixes ("Jones being in Boston would require it to be true that Jones is in Massachusetts") and also by certain ethical prefixes ("Jones' commitments require him to make it true that Jones is in Massachusetts"—where "require" is so interpreted that we can say of a man that he is subject to conflicting requirements). But if we amend the passage quoted by adding that an intentional prefix is one having forms UC, UD, and EC such that, for that prefix (iii) UC does not imply UD, and (iv) EC does not imply UD, then the resulting criterion will not be satisfied by such causal or ethical prefixes.* Of both senses of "require" we may say: the prefixes "X requires it to be true that" and "X does not require it to be false that" violate (iii); the negations of these prefixes violate (iv); and "either X requires it to be true that, or X requires it to be false that," as well as its negation, violates (i).

We would seem to have, then, at least two separate criteria for intentionality—i.e., two sets of conditions either one of which would be sufficient for saying that a modal prefix is intentional. These are (1) the new pattern for believing and knowing and (2) the pattern just described. These criteria may be strengthened by adding the stipulation proposed in Section 5 of the original paper—*viz.*, that a prefix may also be said to be intentional if the result of prefixing it to "it is false that" is intentional.

Let us now consider the four theses which Sleigh attributes to me.

Thesis I: "Pattern I is such that the prefixes 'S believed that,' 'S knows that,' 'S desires that,' 'S fears that,' 'S wonders whether it is the case that,' 'S is thinking about the possibility that' conform to it." Sleigh is right in saying that this thesis is false, since, as we have just seen, some of these concepts do not conform to Pattern I.

Thesis II: "Pattern I is such that no nonpsychological prefix conforms to it." Sleigh proposes the following prefix as a

---

* Because of some of the examples that may suggest themselves in this context, we should remind ourselves that "UD" and "ED" are to be so interpreted that the scope of the quantifier in UD and in ED extends to the end of the statement.

counterexample to Thesis II: "With respect to the propositions expressed by the sentences on page 31 of *Perceiving* it is more probable than not that . . ." But is this prefix nonpsychological? What does it mean to say, of a sentence appearing in some book, that the sentence "expresses" a proposition? Surely this—that certain people use the sentence, or may use the sentence, in order to assert, express, or otherwise convey the proposition. And to say of a man that he *does* something *in order to assert, express,* or otherwise *convey* a proposition is to make a statement that is obviously intentional and therefore psychological.*

I would say, more generally, that semantic sentences, as such, are intentional.** (On Sleigh's own definition of "inten-

---

* Anticipating this objection, Sleigh appeals to the following passage in my paper: There are philosophers who would say . . . that any set of objects that happens to be arranged in the pattern or configuration of the printed English sentence "All men are mortal" could be said to *state that* all men are mortal. If we decide to interpret "state," "assert," "affirm," "command," and related concepts in this way, then, of course, we shall want to deny that they are intentional or that they necessarily involve what is intentional. (The point of these remarks might be put more clearly by saying, for example, that if we redefine "state that" in such a way that a sufficient condition for the truth of "X states that all men are mortal" will be the truth of "X is the string of English words 'All men are mortal'," then there will be no ground for saying that "state that," as so redefined, is intentional.) Sleigh comments: "This passage suggests that we *can decide* to interpret these concepts in this way. If so, then I so choose." I find the latter sentence difficult to understand, for the passage quoted gives us no directions at all for interpreting, or for reinterpreting, Sleigh's prefix, "With respect to the propositions expressed by the sentences on page 31 of *Perceiving,* it is more probable than not that. . . ." Sleigh may mean to be saying that, according to the passage quoted, he has the right to give his prefix any meaning he chooses and hence one that is nonintentional, and also that if he has this right he is prepared to exercise it. But if he does reinterpret the prefix in any nonintentional way, then he must tell us what this reinterpretation is before he can claim to have shown that the prefix conforms to Pattern I.

** I have defended this general point of view in the papers cited in my essay, footnote 1.

tional," as indicated below, such prefixes as " 'This triangle is equiangular' means that . . ." become intentional.) And I would add that there is good reason for saying that sentences in which such words as "implies" take propositional clauses as their grammatical objects (e.g., "There is something which implies that all Greeks are men") are semantic and therefore, if my more general thesis is correct, intentional. But this point, it is only fair to add, is controversial.

Thesis III: "There is some Pattern P_1 such that the prefixes 'S believes that,' 'S knows that,' 'S desires that,' 'S wonders whether it is the case that,' 'S is thinking about the possibility that,' conform to it."

Thesis IV: "Whatever pattern it is to which the above mentioned prefixes conform, there is no nonpsychological prefix which conforms to it." I interpret this to mean that the Pattern P_1, referred to in the statement of Thesis III, is one to which no nonpsychological prefix conforms.

If what I have just said is correct, then the criterion quoted in Section 4 from Section 2 of the original paper, with the qualifications noted, satisfies Thesis III and Thesis IV, and both theses, therefore, are true.

Sleigh proposes the following *definition*—as distinguished from a *criterion*—of "intentional prefix":

A modal prefix M is intentional (psychological), if and only if $(\exists\ p)\ (\exists\ q) \sim \{[M(p) \cdot (p \longleftrightarrow q)] \rightarrow M(q)\}$.

"Jones believes that" is intentional by this definition, since there are statements p and q which are such that the conjunction of "Jones believes p" and "p is logically equivalent to q" does not imply "Jones believes q."* If this definition were

---

* Compare Carnap's *Meaning and Necessity,* p. 53: "We study sentences of the form 'John believes that. . . .' If here the subsentence '. . .' is replaced by another sentence L-equivalent to it, then it may be that the whole sentence changes its truth-value. Therefore, the whole belief sentence is neither extensional or intensional with respect to the subsentence."

adequate, it could be used to reinforce the general point, above, according to which semantic sentences are intentional.* But does it give us a *necessary* condition for saying that a prefix is intentional? Consider the prefix "Jones has a belief the truth-value of which is logically independent of that of the proposition that. . . ." Does the definition give us a *sufficient* condition for saying that a prefix is intentional? Consider: "The proposition that no Romans are Greeks is the converse of the proposition that . . ." (M), "No Greeks are Romans" (p), and "No Romans are Greeks" (q). Or: "If it is neither true nor false that I will be in Warsaw tomorrow, then . . ." (M), "It is not true that I will be in Warsaw tomorrow (p), and "It is false that I will be in Warsaw tomorrow" (q).

A more promising formula would be this: a sentence prefix M is intentional if, for every sentence q, the result of modifying q by M is logically contingent; and a sentence is intentional if it is the result of modifying a sentence by an intentional prefix or if it implies a sentence that is intentional.**

---

* Consider: *"Dieses Dreieck ist gleichwinklig* means that . . ." (M), "This triangle is equiangular" (p), and "This triangle is equilateral" (q); "Application of *modus ponens* to 'If John is here then two and two are four, and John is here' is sufficient to yield the proposition that . . ." (M), "Two and two are four' (p), and "Two and three are five" (q).

** "Sentence prefix," in all of this, might be thought of as designating a phrase which ends with a right-hand and a left-hand parenthesis, in that order, and which is such that the result of inserting a well-formed sentence between the parentheses will be another well-formed sentence. For a continuation of these discussions see: Roderick M. Chisholm, "Notes on the Logic of Believing," *Philosophy and Phenomenological Research,* XXIV (1963), 151–201; David R. Luce, "On the Logic of Belief," *Philosophy and Phenomenological Research,* XXV (1964), 259–260; Robert C. Sleigh, Jr., "Notes on Chisholm on the Logic of Believing," *ibid.,* pp. 261–265; and Roderick M. Chisholm, "Believing and Intentionality: A Reply to Mr. Luce and Mr. Sleigh," *ibid.,* pp. 266–269.

NOTES FOR CHISHOLM ESSAY

1. Alonzo Church, "Logic and Analysis," *Proceedings of the XIIth International Congress of Philosophy* (Florence: Sansoni, 1958–1961), IV, 77–81: "And it would seem that intentionality is merely that special case of obliqueness in which the oblique context is introduced by a word (such as believe) that has a psychological reference"—an oblique context being characterized in terms of the failure of substitutivity for identity or for material equivalence. Compare James Cornman, "Intentionality and Intensionality," *Philosophical Quarterly*, XII (1962), 44–52. Both papers refer to criteria of intentionality proposed by myself in *Perceiving: A Philosophical Study* (Ithaca, N.Y.: Cornell Univ. Press, 1957) Chapter XI, and in "Sentences about Believing," *Proceedings of the Aristotelian Society*, LVI (1955–56), 125–147, and reprinted in Herbert Feigl, Michael Scriven, and Grover Maxwell (eds.), *Minnesota Studies in the Philosophy of Science,* Vol. II (Minneapolis: Univ. of Minnesota Press, 1958), pp. 521–539.
2. Compare Herbert Spiegelberg's remark about the appearance of intentionality in the world: *Hier beginnt der Einbruch eines ganz Neuen in die Welt. Totes Sein erhebt sich aus der Befangenheit in sich selbst und greift über sich hinaus. Das bedeutet einen Wendepunkt im kosmischen Geschehen.* In "Der Begriff der Intentionalität in der Scholastik, bei Brentano und bei Husserl," *Philosophische Hefte,* V (Prague: 1936), pp. 75–91.
3. See Duns Scotus, *Quaestiones: in Librum Primum Priorum Analyticorum,* in Volume II of *Opera Omnia* (Vivès edition, Paris, 1891), especially Question 36 (p. 173 ff.). This work is now attributed to "Pseudo-Scotus."
4. This point was made by W. V. Quine, in "Quantifiers and Propositional Attitudes," *Journal of Philosophy,* LIII (1956), 177–187.
5. The most plausible case for the denial of this thesis was made by Alexius Meinong. See his distinction between *Seinsmeinen* and *Soseinsmeinen* in Sec. 45 of *Über Annahmen* (2nd. ed.; Leipzig: J. A. Barth, 1910) and the distinction between "thetic" and "athetic" predication in *Zur Grundlegung der allgemeinen Werttheorie* (Graz: Leuschner and Lubensky, 1923), pp. 126–129. I have criticized Meinong's theory in "Jenseits von Sein und Nichtsein," in Karl S. Guthke (ed.), *Dichtung und Deutung: Gedächtnisschrift für Hans M. Wolf* (Bern: Francke Verlag, 1961), pp. 23–31. Compare James Mish'alani, "Thought and Object," *Philosophical Review,* LXXI (1962), 185–201. Brentano and Russell, of course, also criticized Meinong's theory of judgment or belief.

6. This type of objection was brought to my attention by John R. Wallace of Stanford University.

7. The failure of UD to UC, for knowing, was noted by G. H. von Wright, *An Essay in Modal Logic* (Amsterdam: North-Holland Publishing Co., 1951), p. 49.

8. This point is made in Jaakko Hintikka's *Knowledge and Belief* (Ithaca: Cornell Univ. Press, 1962), Chapter VI. Hintikka's discussion is excellent, but made somewhat difficult by the fact that he uses the formula, "For every x, S knows that x is F," *not* to express what we would ordinarily take the formula to express (and thus not to express what we have been taking it here to express), but rather to express what we might express by saying, "For every x, if there exists a y such that S knows that x is identical with y, then S knows that y is F." Hintikka also notes the failure, for knowing, of UD to UC and of EC to ED.

9. For example by Alan Anderson in *The Formal Analysis of Normative Systems* (New Haven: Yale University. Sociology Dept., Interaction Laboratory. Pub. as U.S. Office of Naval Research, Group Psychology Branch Technical Report No. 2, 1956), see pp. 63–64.

10. In *Symbolic Logic* (New York: Ronald Press, 1952), F. B. Fitch makes substantially the following points on p. 165: for *necessity*, (i) UC implies UD, (ii) UD implies UC, (iii) ED implies EC, but (iv) EC does not imply ED. On the first two counts, then, *necessity* would differ from *believing*. He also notes that, for *possibility*, (i) ED implies EC, and he is inclined to say (ii) EC does not imply ED; in these respects *possibility* would resemble believing. According to Miss Barcan, however, for possibility, EC *does* imply ED. See Ruth C. Barcan, "A Functional Calculus of First Order Based on Strict Implication," *Journal of Symbolic Logic*, XI (1946), 1–16; "Interpreting Quantification," *Inquiry*, III (1962), 252–269. In *Meaning and Necessity* (Chicago: Univ. of Chicago Press, 1947), Rudolph Carnap states that for *logical necessity*, UC implies UD, and UD implies UC. Arthur Burks, in "The Logic of Propositions," *Mind*, LX (1951), 363–382, states that for *causal necessity*, UC implies UD, and UD implies UC.

11. I have defended such a view in "Statements about Believing"; see footnote 1.

12. Such a view is suggested in the writings of Wilfrid Sellars and of Israel Scheffler. See, for example, Sellars' correspondence with the present writer in Herbert Feigl, Michael Scriven and Grover Maxwell, eds., *Minnesota Studies in the Philosophy of Science*, Vol. II (Minneapolis: Univ. of Minnesota Press, 1958), pp. 521–539, and Scheffler's "An Inscriptional Approach to Indirect Quotation," *Analysis*, XIV (1954), 83–90.

13. *Acting on* the proposition that . . . ," I suggest, *is* intentional. I have

discussed this concept and its relation to purposing in "What Is It To Act Upon A Proposition?" *Analysis,* XXII (1961), 1–6. In "Freedom and Action" included in *Freedom and Determinism,* ed. Keith Lehrer (New York: Random House, 1966), I have discussed in considerable detail *purposing* and the related concept of *undertaking.*

14. St. Anselm made a similar distinction, using the terms *facere esse, facere non esse, non facere non esse,* and *non facere esse.* See D. P. Henry, "Saint Anselm's *De 'Grammatico',*" *Philosophical Quarterly,* X (1960), 115–126.

NOTES FOR SLEIGH COMMENT

1. W. V. Quine, "Quantifiers and Propositional Attitudes," *Journal of Philosophy,* LIII (1956), 177–187.
2. *Op. cit.*

THE CONCEPT OF A PERSON*

A. J. Ayer

Oxford University

1

THE PROBLEMS which I intend to discuss are excessively familiar to students of philosophy. They are concerned with persons in the broad sense in which every individual human being can be counted as a person. It is characteristic of persons in this sense that besides having various physical properties, including that of occupying a continuous series of spatial positions throughout a given period of time, they are also credited with various forms of consciousness. I shall not here try to offer any definition of consciousness. All I can say is that I am speaking of it in the ordinary sense in which, to be thinking about a problem, or remembering some event, or seeing or hearing something, or deciding to do something, or feeling some emotion, such as jealousy or fear, entails being conscious. I am not at this stage committting myself to any view about the way in which this notion of consciousness should be analyzed.

The first question which arises is how these manifestations of consciousness are related to the physical attributes which also belong to persons. The answer which I think would still be most acceptable to common sense, at least when it is made to consider the question in these terms, is that the relation is contingent, not logical, but only factual. In philosophy this

* This essay appeared in A. J. Ayer's *Concept of a Person* (London: Macmillan; New York: St. Martin's Press, 1963).

view is mainly associated with Descartes; if he did not originate it, he put it forward in the clearest and most uncompromising way. The view is that a person is a combination of two separate entities, a body and a mind or soul. Only the mind is conscious; the physical properties which a person has are properties of his body. The two entities are separate in the sense that there is no logical connection between them. It is conceivable that either should exist without the other; that is, there is no contradiction in supposing that a person's mind exists in some other body, or apart from any body at all, and equally none in supposing that a person's body is animated by some other mind, or not by any mind at all. This does not, however, exclude the possibility of there being causal connections between them; so that even if they are separable in principle, there may still be grounds for holding that they are inseparable in fact. Descartes himself prejudged this question by defining the mind as a substance, which implied, in his usage, that its existence was causally as well as logically independent of the existence of the body. But this view that the mind is a substance is not entailed by the view that mind and body are logically distinct. It would be compatible with this sort of dualism to reject the notion of mental substance altogether and conceive of the mind, in Humean fashion, as a series of experiences.

Whatever may be the attractions of this dualistic view for common sense, the tendency of philosophers has been to try to replace it by some form of monism. Thus Berkeley, who held that physical objects were collections of sensible qualities which were dependent for their existence upon being perceived, and Hume, who saw no grounds for holding that anything existed but sensory impressions and the ideas which copied them, may both be regarded, in their different ways, as having tried to effect the reduction of body to mind. In more recent versions of this type of theory, such as those developed by William James and Bertrand Russell, the sense-data and images, which are taken as fundamental, are held to constitute a kind of neutral stuff, itself neither mental nor physical, out of which both mind and matter are to be constructed. Conversely, it was held by Hobbes, in opposition to Descartes, that there was no need to postulate the existence of minds in addition to bodies; conscious states and activities could be attributed to the body itself. And modern philosophers, like Ryle and Carnap, have argued that it is a mistake to think of conscious states and processes as ghostly inhabitants of a private mental stage; statements about people's mental life are reducible to statements about their physical constitution, or their actual and potential behaviour.

With all of these theories, except perhaps the last, there is a corresponding problem of personal identity. On any dualistic view an account is required of the way in which the mind is lodged in the body. Could there be more than one mind in a single body? Could the same mind dwell in more than one body, at the same or at different times? If the relation is one to one, how are its terms paired off? How is it decided which mind goes with which body? The most plausible answer is that they are causally connected in some special way, but it is not easy to see how this connection is to be defined. If the mind is regarded as a substance, the question arises how such a substance could ever be identified. If it is regarded as a collection of experiences, there is the problem, to which Hume himself confessed that he could see no answer, of showing how the collection is united. What is it that makes a given experience a member of one such collection rather than another? With any view of this type, there is also the problem of identifying the experiences themselves. In the ordinary way, we identify experiences in terms of the persons whose experiences they are: but clearly this will lead to a vicious circle if persons themselves are to be analyzed in terms of their experiences.

An argument in favor of the physicalistic type of monism is

that these difficulties are avoided. At least there is then no special problem of personal identity. The criteria for the identity of persons will be the same as those that determine the identity of their bodies; and these will conform to the general conditions which govern the identity of all physical objects of a solid macroscopic kind. It is primarily a matter of spatio-temporal continuity. Moreover, if persons can be equated with their bodies, there will no longer be any need to specify how minds and bodies are correlated. Once it is shown how states of consciousness can be ascribed to bodies, this problem will have been solved. But whether this can be shown is itself very much an open question. It is obvious that any view of this type encounters very serious difficulties; and it is not at all so clear that they can be satisfactorily met.

What is common to all these theories is the view that the concept of a person is derivative, in the sense that it is capable of being analyzed into simpler elements; they differ only about the character of these elements and the way in which they are combined. But this premise itself has recently been challenged. In his book *Individuals,* Mr. P. F. Strawson has attempted to prove that the concept of a person is a primitive concept; and what he means by this is just that it is not analyzable in any of the ways that we have outlined.[1] Not everything that we want to say about persons can be construed as a statement about the physical objects which are their bodies; still less when we refer to persons are we referring to mental substances, or to collections of experiences. Neither, in Mr. Strawson's view, can it be maintained that persons are compound; that they are the product of two separate entities, or sets of entities, one the subject of physical characteristics and the other the subject of consciousness. He holds, on the contrary, that the subject to which we attribute the properties which imply the presence of consciousness is literally identical with that to which we also attribute physical properties. And if we ask what this subject is, the only correct answer is just that it is a person.

Mr. Strawson's main reason for rejecting dualism is, in his own words, that "the concept of the pure individual consciousness—the pure ego—is a concept that cannot exist; or, at least, cannot exist as a primary concept in terms of which the concept of a person can be explained or analyzed. It can exist only, if at all, as a secondary, non-primitive concept, which itself is to be explained, analyzed in terms of the concept of a person."[2] It might be thought that this would not affect the dualist who rejects the notion of the pure ego, and thinks of the conscious subject as a collection of experiences, but in fact the reasons which Mr. Strawson has for denying that there can be a primary concept of the pure ego apply equally to any idea of a non-physical subject of consciousness, whatever its composition may be thought to be.

His argument runs as follows: The first premise is "That it is a necessary condition of one's ascribing states of consciousness, experiences, to oneself, in the way that one does, that one should also ascribe them, or be prepared to ascribe them, to others who are not oneself."[3] Now this is understood to imply that one ascribes experiences to others in exactly the same sense as one ascribes them to oneself. It excludes the view, which has been held by some philosophers, that the statements which a person makes about the experiences of others are to be analyzed quite differently from the corresponding statements that he makes about his own, that whereas in his own case he is to be understood as speaking literally, what he says about the experiences of others can only be construed as a reference to their behavior. But when one talks about the experiences of another person one cannot be attributing them to a pure consciousness; neither is it possible to regard the subject of one's statement simply as a collection of experiences. The reason for this is that in the case of another person neither the pure consciousness nor the collection of experiences would be things that one could have any means of identifying. But if our attributions of experiences to others cannot be understood in this way, neither can our attributions of experiences to ourselves: this follows from the principle that the same analysis must be applied to both.

An important consequence of this argument, if it is sound, is that we must give up the argument from analogy on which many philosophers have relied as a justification for believing in the existence of other minds. It is tempting to think that one can come by the idea of one's own experiences through introspection, observe that in one's own case experiences of certain kinds are characteristically associated with certain forms of behavior, and so, when one observes other people behaving in similar ways, infer that they are having similar experiences. Even if one does not acquire the belief that there are other minds in this fashion, it may still be the ground for holding that the belief is rational. This reasoning has, indeed, met with various objections. Assuming that it is logically impossible for anyone directly to observe what goes on in another person's mind, some philosophers have maintained that this is not a valid argument from analogy; for they hold that no inductive argument can give us any reason to believe in the existence of something which could not even in principle be observed. Others who think that this difficulty can be overcome find fault with the argument because its basis is so weak. As Wittgenstein put it, "How can I generalize from the *one* case so irresponsibly?" The novelty of Mr. Strawson's attack lies in his refusal even to allow the argument to start. If my knowing how to ascribe experiences to others is a necessary condition of my being able to ascribe them to myself, then, Mr. Strawson suggests, the argument begins by presupposing what it is intended to justify.[4]

Moreover, even if, without consideration of others, I could initially distinguish what are in fact my experiences from the body with which they are associated, and this body from other bodies, this still would not give me any ground, in Mr. Strawson's view, for supposing that any of these other bodies were "owned" by subjects who also had experiences. I should discover empirically that certain feelings occurred when this body was acted on by certain stimuli, and that they did not occur when other bodies were so treated. But all that could ever be in question would be the presence or absence of experiences of my own. And even this goes too far, if it only makes sense for me to talk of my experiences in contradistinction to those of other people. To some extent this argument was anticipated by G. E. Moore, who maintained in his essay on "The Nature and Reality of Objects of Perception" that if one assumes with Berkeley that the objects of perception exist only so long as one is perceiving them, then no reasoning by analogy could give one any ground at all for ascribing experiences to other people; the most that it could possibly authorize would be a belief in the existence of unconscious experiences of one's own. But for Moore this was just an argument against idealism; he thought that if the objects of perception were allowed to be physical bodies which existed independently of our perceiving them, then we could rely upon analogy as a ground for believing that some of these bodies were inhabited by minds like our own.[5] Mr. Strawson, on the other hand, holds that even if we grant this premise about the objects of perception, there is still no basis for the argument from analogy.

It might be thought that this line of reasoning would result in the elimination of anything but the body as a possible subject of consciousness, but Mr. Strawson does not take this view. He does not in fact discuss the thesis of physicalism, according to which statements about experiences are transformable into statements about physical occurrences, but instead goes on to examine a hybrid theory which he calls the "no-ownership" doctrine of the self. This is the theory that the only sense in which experiences can significantly be said to have an owner is that they are causally dependent upon the state of some particular body. It is perhaps misleading to call this a "no-ownership" theory, since in the sense which it allows to ownership, it does not imply that any experiences are unowned. Mr. Strawson's reason for so calling it is not so much that this sense of ownership is Pickwickian as that it does not yield a guarantee that experiences are private property. For he holds that it must on this theory be regarded as a contingent fact that the experiences which a person owns are causally linked to his body and not to some other body instead.

Mr. Strawson's objection to this theory is that it is incoherent. The proposition which it tries to state is that, with respect to any given person, all his experiences are dependent upon the state of his body; and this proposition is supposed to be contingent. But how are his experiences to be identified? In accordance with what principle are my experiences classified as mine? If the answer is that they are just those experiences which are causally dependent, in the requisite way, upon the state of this body, then the proposition that all my experiences are causally dependent upon the state of this body becomes analytic; it is just a way of saying that all the experiences which are causally dependent upon the state of this body are causally dependent upon the state of this body. But what the theory requires is that this proposition be contingent. And since it admits no other way of identifying a person's experiences, the consequence is that it defeats itself.

It is also true of physicalist theories that they admit no other way of identifying a person's experiences than by identifying his body. It might, therefore, be thought that they too were exposed to Mr. Strawson's argument, especially as it seems to be a contingent proposition that some particular body is the body of such and such a person. But here the physicalist has an effective answer. He can argue that the reason why this proposition is contingent is just that it pre-supposes that the body in question has been independently identified, either ostensively or by some other form of description. If we have identified a person, it follows on his view, that we have identified that person's body; but the converse need not hold. Neither is there any further problem for the physicalist about the identification of experiences, since he maintains that statements about a person's experiences are logically equivalent to statements about the condition or movements of his body. As we shall see, there are serious objections to any view of this kind; but on this score at least, it is not incoherent. We may, therefore, conclude that Mr. Strawson's argument is not fatal to theories of this type. Whether it is fatal even to the "no-ownership" theory is one of the questions that we shall have to consider later on.

Physicalist theories are based on a consideration of the way in which we ascribe experiences to other people. Since our only ground for this proceeding is our observation of their physical condition and behavior, it is assumed that this is all that we can be referring to. Then, on the assumption that we must mean the same by the ascription of experiences to ourselves as we do by ascribing them to others, it is inferred that even when we speak about our own experiences we are referring to our physical condition or behavior. To dualists, on the other hand, it is evident that when we speak about our own experiences we are not referring to the physical manifestations by which other people may be made aware of them. Our knowledge of our own experiences is of an entirely different character. So again assuming that when we speak about the experiences of others we must mean the same as we do when speaking about our own, they infer that the physical events on which we base our attributions of experiences to others are signs of these experiences and not to be identified with them. They hold that we have direct knowledge of our own experiences; but that such knowledge as we can have of the experiences of others is only inferred from their physical manifestations. And then they are faced with the problem how these inferences can be justified.

In maintaining that the concept of a person is logically primitive, Mr. Strawson hopes to secure the advantages and at the same time avoid the difficulties of both these lines of approach. He admits that the basis on which we ascribe experiences to others is different from that on which we ascribe them to ourselves, but he denies that, in the case of other people, we are reduced to making an inductive inference. There is not merely a factual connection between certain physical events and the experiences which they are understood to manifest. It is true that when we ascribe experiences to others we do not simply mean that they are in such and such a physical condition or that they are behaving, or disposed to behave, in such and such ways. These are just the criteria by which we determine that they are having the experience in question. But the point is that these criteria are "logically adequate." In our own case, we do not rely on these criteria. Our knowledge of our own experiences is not obtained by observation. But this does not mean that the sense in which we ascribe experiences to ourselves is in any way different from that in which we ascribe them to others. On the contrary, it is a necessary feature of predicates which imply that the subject to which they are attributed is conscious, "it is essential to the character of these predicates, that they have both first and third person ascriptive uses, that they are both self-ascribable otherwise than on the basis of observation of the behavior of the subject of them, and other ascribable on the basis of behavior-criteria."[6] If we did not understand the use of predicates of this kind, we should not possess the concept of a person. For persons are essentially the subjects to which such predicates are attributed.

But how, to echo Kant, are such predicates possible? Or, as Mr. Strawson puts it, "What is it in the natural facts that makes it intelligible that we should have this concept (of a person)?"[7] He does not attempt to answer this question in any detail, but he does suggest that if we are looking for an answer we should begin by directing our attention to predicates which are concerned with human action. He thinks that it is easier to understand how we can see each other, and ourselves, as persons, "if we think first of the fact that we act, and act on each other, and act in accordance with a common human nature." His reason for thinking this is that a study of the ways in which we do things should rid us of the belief "that the only things we can know about without observation and inference, or both, are private experiences." In cases of intentional action, we also have knowledge, not based on observation and inference, about the present and future movements of our bodies. Not only that but predicates which refer to forms of action do so as a rule "while not indicating at all precisely any very definite sensation or experience." The result of this is that although we ascribe such predicates to others on the basis of observation and do not in general ascribe them on this basis to ourselves, we find it much easier in their case than in the cases where there is a reference to some distinctive experience to recognize that what is attributed on these different bases is nevertheless the same.

The suggestion that persons are to be distinguished in the first instance by their capacity for action has also been put forward by Professor Hampshire in his recent book on *Thought and Action.*

> The deepest mistake in empiricist theories of perception, descending from Berkeley and Hume, has been the representation of human beings as passive observers receiving impressions from "outside" of the mind where the "outside" includes their own bodies. In fact, I find myself from the beginning able to act upon objects around me . . . I not only perceive my body, I also control it; I not only perceive external objects, I also

manipulate them. To doubt the existence of my body would necessarily be to doubt my ability to move . . . I find my power of movement limited by the resistance of objects around me. This felt resistance to my will defines for me, in conjunction with my perceptions, my own situation as an object among other objects.[8]

And not only is this in fact so: according to Professor Hampshire, it could not conceivably be otherwise. It is only because persons are themselves physical objects with a situation in space and time and with a power of movement which brings them into contact with other physical objects, including other persons with whom they can communicate, that they can even form the idea of an objective world.

Professor Hampshire also thinks that the concept of human action provides the key to the problem of personal identity.

We have no reason to seek for some criterion of personal identity that is distinct from the identity of our bodies as persisting physical objects. We find our intelligence and our will working, and expressing themselves in action, at a particular place and a particular time, and just these movements, or this voluntary stillness, are unmistakably mine, if they are my actions, animated by my intentions . . . I can only be said to have lost a sense of my own identity if I have lost all sense of where I am and what I am doing.[9]

It appears that the action here envisaged is always at least partly physical; so that it follows, in Professor Hampshire's view, that the notion of a disembodied person, and, therefore, the notion of personal survival in a disembodied state, is self-contradictory or meaningless. Mr. Strawson does not go quite so far. As we have seen, he thinks that there could not be an underived concept of a pure individual consciousness, but he sees no reason why such a concept should not have what he calls "a logically secondary existence." One can, therefore, intelligibly think of oneself as surviving one's bodily death. For one can imagine oneself continuing to have experiences of various kinds, without having any power to make physical changes in the world, and without having any perception of a body which is related to these experiences in the way that one's living body is related to one's present experiences. I suppose it might be necessary to add the further condition that one's experiences should not in any way suggest that other people perceived such a body either. If these conditions were fulfilled, then one could legitimately think of oneself as surviving in a disembodied state. It is not suggested that this could actually happen, in the sense that it is causally possible for there to be experiences which are independent of a body, but only that the idea is intelligible. Having made this concession, Mr. Strawson goes on to remark that there are two essential features of this form of existence which may somewhat diminish its appeal. The first is that one would be entirely solitary; if there were other creatures in the same condition one would have no means of knowing it. The second is that one could retain one's sense of one's own identity only insofar as one preserved the memory of one's embodied existence; this might be eked out by taking a vicarious interest in the state of the world which one had left. In short one would exist, as it were on sufferance, as a former person. From this point of view the idea of there being persons, even of such an attenuated sort, who were not at any time embodied, is not intelligible.

2

I have made a detailed summary of Mr. Strawson's theory because it gives an account of persons which, if it were acceptable, would remove many of the difficulties of the mind-body problem. It seems to me, however, that the theory has serious difficulties of its own. The cardinal point is the attempt to stop short of physicalism on the one hand, and dispense with the argument from analogy on the other, by maintaining that our observations of the physical condition and behavior of other persons, on the basis of which we attribute experiences to them, are logically adequate for this purpose. But what exactly is meant here by saying that a criterion is logically adequate? Not that the evidence entails the conclusion, for in that case we should not stop short of physicalism: if a statement about a person's experiences is to follow logically from a statement about physical events, it also must be construed as a statement about physical events. Not that the evidence provides sufficient empirical support for the conclusion, for then the reasoning is inductive: we are back with the argument from analogy. What is envisaged is something between the two, but what can this be? What other possibility remains?

That there can be a relation between statements which is not deductive and yet is in some sense logical is a view which Mr. Strawson is not alone in holding. It is maintained also by the followers of Wittgenstein, especially in connection with this problem, but they too fail to make it sufficiently clear what the relation is supposed to be. What Wittgenstein himself appears to have held is that it is only insofar as our so-called inner experiences have characteristic outward expressions that the statements which we make about them can have any meaning for us; and that so far as this goes it makes no difference whether one is referring to one's own experiences or to those of other people; it is in this sense that he denied the possibility of a private language. I do not think that he was right on this point, as I have argued elsewhere, but even if he were right, even if it is only through their having physical manifestations that our experiences are communicable, even to ourselves, the relation between the statements which refer to these experiences and those which refer to their outward expressions remains obscure. We are not allowed to say that the experiences are identical with their outward expressions; and yet we are not allowed to say that they are logically distinct. This would seem to indicate that there is a relation of one-way entailment; but the entailment cannot run from the manifestations of the experiences to the experiences themselves, for the manifestations may be deceptive; and if it goes in the reverse direction, then in talking about our experiences we must be talking about their outward expressions and something else besides. But then the question arises what is this something else besides; and to this we are not given any answer.

But may not the reason why we get no answer be that the question itself is wrongly framed? If we begin by assuming a dichotomy between experiences on the one side and physical states or processes on the other, we shall surely end in the unhappy position of having to find some inductive ground for bridging the gap between them. But is this not just the assumption that Wittgenstein was trying to discredit? His followers will claim that our notion of a "pure experience" is utterly obscure to them. We talk of the experience of feeling pain, but do we really understand what it would mean to be in pain without having at least the tendency to display some physical reaction? Can we significantly divorce our thoughts and our emotions from their characteristic expressions in action or in speech? And when it comes to the way in which one observes the behavior of another person, it is surely quite wrong to treat this as an ordinary instance of the observation of physical events. Human behavior does not present itself to us as a physical process from which we have to make a dubious inference to the thoughts and feelings and purposes which lie "behind" it. It is itself expressive of these thoughts and feelings and purposes; and this is how we actually see it. From the outset we observe it *as* human behavior with all that this implies.

I do not question the facts on which this argument is based. No doubt we attach a significance to human behavior which we do not attach to the movements of inanimate things; there is, indeed, a sense in which one can simply observe what another person is thinking or feeling. But however natural this process may be, it is still a process of interpretation; there is a distinction to be drawn between the sign and what it signifies. However intimate the relation between our "inner" states and their "outward" expressions, it is surely a relation between distinguishable terms. Indeed this is already implied by saying that the outward experience is a criterion for the existence of the inner state. But then we are entitled to ask what sort of criterion it is and what can be meant by the claim that it is logically adequate.

Mr. Strawson himself has tried to illustrate what he means by logical adequacy by appealing to another example.

> If one is playing a game of cards, the distinctive markings of a certain card constitute a logically adequate criterion for calling it, say, the Queen of Hearts; but in calling it this, in the context of the game, one is ascribing to it properties over and above the possession of these markings. The predicate gets its meaning from the whole structure of the game.[10]

In the same way, he suggests, the physical criteria which are held to be logically adequate for the ascription to persons other than oneself of predicates which imply the presence of consciousness do not exhaust the meaning of these predicates. The predicates get their full meaning from the structure of the language.

But what does this analogy come to? It is quite true that we recognize a card, such as the Queen of Hearts, by its markings; and it is also true that, in most contexts, when we identify a card as the Queen of Hearts we are saying not merely that it has a certain characteristic appearance, but also that it stands in certain relations to other cards, that it occupies a certain position in one of the series that makes up a suit. Even to say of it that it is a card implies that it is meant to figure in a game. This is one of the numerous cases in which the applicability of a term to a given object depends, in part at least, upon the object's function. All the same it is always a contingent fact that a thing with such and such a characteristic appearance fulfills the function that it does. If the observation that it has certain markings is an adequate criterion for a particular card's being the Queen of Hearts, the reason is that the role which is played by the Queen of Hearts in various card games is commonly bestowed on cards of that design. But this is an inductive generalization; there is no logical connection between the fact that a card looks as it does and the fact that if it is used in a game it is allotted certain powers, for example that of outranking other cards whose markings are in some respects like and in other respects unlike its own. That a card has the look of the Queen of Hearts does not itself guarantee that it would be suitable to play the role of the Queen of Hearts in any particular sort of game, or indeed that it is fitted for a part in any game at all. The correlation of its appearance with its function is a matter of convention; but it is an empirical fact that this convention holds.

This may, however, be mistaking the point. Perhaps the point is that, given the appropriate conventions, it is not a matter for empirical discovery that a card with such and such markings plays such and such a role. In the context of a game of bridge, to identify a card as the Queen of Hearts is to identify it as a card which outranks the Knave of Hearts and is outranked by the King. The reason why the appearance of the card is a logically adequate criterion for its function is that the connection between them is established by the conventions which allot to cards of various designs their respective powers in the game.

But if this is the point of the analogy, it does not achieve its end. For the connection between a mental occurrence and its bodily expression is just not on a par with that which is conventionally established between the appearance and function of a token in a game. To identify a piece in a game of chess as a bishop and to count anything other than a diagonal move with it as a move in the game would be a contradiction; the rules of chess being what they are, the identification of a piece can be construed as carrying with it the delimitation of its powers. On the other hand, there would be no contradiction in identifying a man's grimace as one which was characteristic of a man in pain, and yet denying that he felt any pain at all. The grimace and the feeling are logically separable in a way that, given the appropriate conventions, the appearance and function of a token in a game are not.

It has been suggested to me by Professor Alston that the analogy may hold in a weaker form. So long as we confine our attention to particular instances, we shall not find anything more than an empirical connection between a mental occurrence and its bodily manifestation. It will always be logically possible in any given case that either should exist without the other. And if this is possible in any given case, it is natural to infer that it must be possible in all cases. The view suggested to me by Professor Alston, which he thinks may also have been held by Wittgenstein, is that this inference is incorrect. Though the liaison between the characteristic outward expression of an inner state and the inner state in question may fail in any particular instance, it is not logically possible that it should fail in all instances, or even in any high proportion of them. So the reason why behavioral criteria can be said to be logically adequate is that even though they are not infallible, their overall success is logically guaranteed.

The source of this guarantee is supposed to lie in the fact that it is only through their being associated with certain outward expressions that we are able to talk significantly about our inner experiences. As has already been noted, this is Wittgenstein's ground for denying the possibility of a private language. We are taught the use of a word like "pain" in contexts in which the feeling for which it stands is outwardly manifested in some characteristic way; and the result is that this association is retained as part of the meaning which the word has for us. The association is not so close as to exclude the possibility of anyone's ever feeling pain without displaying it, or of anyone's ever displaying signs of pain, without actually feeling it, but it is close enough to make it a logical certainty that such cases are the exception and not the rule.

One of the attractions of this theory is that it bars the skeptical approach to the problem of one's knowledge of other minds. For if we have the a priori assurance that the passage from outward manifestation to inner state is generally secure, we need no further justification for trusting it in any given instance; the onus then falls upon the skeptic to show that in these special circumstances it is not to be relied on. The question is, however, whether we are entitled to this assurance; and here I am still disposed to think that the skeptic can maintain his ground. For even if one grants the premise that we should not in practice be able to acquire an understanding of words which refer to inner states or processes, unless these inner states were outwardly detectable, it does not seem to follow that once our understanding of these words has been acquired, we cannot divorce them from their original associations. Indeed it is admitted that we can do so in particular instances; and it is not clear what should prevent us from doing so in all. If the suggestion is that we should then be landed in a contradiction, I can only remark that I do not yet see where the contradiction lies.

Whatever difficulties there may be in supposing that our mental states could in general be dissociated from their characteristic physical manifestations, the admission they can be so dissociated even in a few particular instances is fatal to the strict theory of physicalism. For if to speak about a so-called mental event were always logically equivalent to speaking about its physical manifestations, it would not be possible even in a single instance that one should exist without the other. Physicalism of this type again has the merit of removing any difficulty about one's knowledge of other minds; but it achieves this by too desperate a measure. The decisive objection to it was put most succinctly by Ogden and Richards in their *Meaning of Meaning:* one cannot apply it to oneself except at the cost of feigning anesthesia.[11] Not only do we not have to observe our own behavior, or take account of our physical condition, in order to know what experiences we are having, but in many cases at least the occurrence of the experience appears to be logically consistent with the absence of its customary outward expression, or indeed of any outward expression at all. The exceptions are those cases where the words which we use to refer to the experience already associate it with some pattern of behavior: this applies especially to words which stand for emotions, perhaps also to statements of intention. But even here it would seem that if we thought it useful, we could cut away the references to behavior, and thereby obtain statements which were understood to refer to the experience alone. Even if it were true, as Wittgenstein seems to have thought, that our ability to talk significantly about our "inner" experiences depends upon their having characteristic outward expressions, it still would not follow that these outward expressions could not be deceptive; not just in the sense that they failed to cohere with other physical manifestations, but in the sense that the person in question simply did not have the experience which they led us to attribute to him.

It has been suggested that even if statements about experiences are not logically equivalent to statements of a purely physicalistic character, it may still be the case that experiences are identical with physical events. To speak of the brightness of the Morning Star is not logically equivalent to speaking of the brightness of the Evening Star; the sense of these two expressions is not the same; nevertheless the fact is that the

Evening Star and the Morning Star are identical. So also lightning is in fact a discharge of electricity, though the terms are not logically equivalent. In the same way, it is argued that even though the reports which we make of our experiences do not entail any descriptions of the condition of our brains, it does not follow that the two are not to be identified. It may be that all that actually takes place in this connection is a physical process in the brain; and that when it is one's own body which is in question one is able to apprehend this physical process in the form of an experience.

The difficulty here is to see what can be meant by saying that our experiences are not merely caused by physical occurrences which take place in our brains, but are literally identical with them. How could this claim be tested? What kind of experiment would establish that they were or were not identical? In the case of the Morning and the Evening Star we have a criterion of identity; there is empirical evidence that a star which is observed to shine at one period of the day is spatio-temporally continuous with one which is observed to shine at a different period; but this criterion is not applicable here. The case of lightning is more promising; for part of our reason for identifying the flash of lightning with an electrical discharge is that the electrical discharge produces it; even so what is more important is that they occur at the same time and place. But although there are philosophers who have taken this view, it does seem rather strange to hold that our experiences are literally located in our brains. This is not, as in the other case, a spatial coincidence which can be empirically discovered; it is rather that if one makes the assumption that experiences must be somewhere in physical space, the brain seems the obvious place in which to put them. But of course the dualist's answer to this would be that they are not in physical space at all.

The most that can be empirically established is that our experiences are causally dependent upon the condition of our brains. To go beyond this and maintain that what appears to us as a correlation of the mental with the physical is really an identity, is simply to take a decision not to regard the mental correlates as entities in their own right. But even if this decision were accepted, it would not dispose of all our problems; for the identification of experiences with events in the brain is based on the acceptance of psychological laws. And how do we know that these laws themselves are valid? A possible answer is that I can find out the connection in my own case, whether or not I choose to regard myself as "owning" the experiences with which my body is associated; and that I can then infer that what has been found to hold for this body holds for other bodies also. But this brings us back once more to the argument from analogy.

3

An essential feature of the argument from analogy is that the justification, as distinct from the cause, of my ascribing experiences to others must issue from the premise that I have experiences myself. The assumption is that I can come to think of myself as having both a body and a mind without having to raise the question whether or not I am unique in this respect; then, knowing myself to be a person in this sense, I can go on to consider what grounds I have for believing that others are so too. But this is just the assumption that Mr. Strawson wishes to deny. He maintains, as we have seen, that it is a necessary condition of one's ascribing states of consciousness to oneself that one should also ascribe them, or be prepared to ascribe them, to others who are not oneself; and from this he infers that any attempt to justify the belief that there are other persons by relying on the premise that one knows oneself to be a person would be circular; the premise would already assume what the argument is supposed to prove.

I shall now try to show that this inference is not correct. It is, indeed, a mark of a general concept, such as the concept of being a person, that no limitation is placed upon the number of individuals to which it can apply. It is, therefore, true that I could not think of myself as satisfying the conditions of being a person unless I admitted the possibility that others satisfied them too. But all that this excludes is the view, which has indeed been held by some philosophers, that it is meaningless to ascribe states of consciousness to anything but oneself; it is perfectly compatible with the view that one does not know, or even with the view that one can not know that such an ascription is ever true in fact. But if I can know that I am a conscious subject without knowing that there are any others, there need be no circularity in an argument which proceeds from the premise that I have experiences and arrives at the conclusion that others have them also.

To this it may be objected that when it is said that I must be prepared to ascribe states of consciousness to others in order to be able to ascribe them to myself, what is meant is not just that I must be willing to regard the existence of other conscious beings as something which is abstractly possible, but rather that I must be disposed to treat it as established by certain observations which I actually make. In other words, I must already believe that I can be justified in ascribing experiences to others before I can significantly ascribe them to myself, and in that case an attempt to base this justification on my knowledge of my own experiences will be circular.

But the answer to this is that there is a difference between my believing that I am justified in accepting a given proposition and my really being so; and not only that, but a belief in a proposition may be justified without the proposition's being true. So even if I could not think of myself as a person unless I also thought that I had reasons to think the same of others, I could still consistently raise the question whether these reasons really did the work that was required of them; and even if I were able to decide that they were good reasons, I still should not be bound to hold that they were conclusive. It seems to me, therefore, that Mr. Strawson's argument needs a stronger premise than the one that he states. It must hold it to be a necessary condition of one's ascribing states of consciousness to oneself not merely that one should ascribe them, or be prepared to ascribe them, to others, but that one should be sure of doing so successfully. It must, in other words, exclude the possibility of one's being invariably mistaken.

This premise would establish Mr. Strawson's case if it were true. My objection to it is that it is false. I do not mean by this that one is invariably mistaken in ascribing states of consciousness to others: if this were put forward as a general proposition implying that everyone was so mistaken, it would be self-contradictory; and I certainly do not in fact believe that I am the only conscious subject in the world. What I mean is that if there were someone who was invariably mistaken in ascribing states of consciousness to others, whether because there were no other persons in the world or merely because he never encountered any, this would not necessarily prevent him from being able to ascribe them to himself. Since this degree of solitude has never been attained by anyone who has acquired the use of language, I cannot prove my point by citing any actual case. The only way I can substantiate it is by constructing a rather artificial example.

Imagine a child who, for reasons which need not trouble us, is kept from having any contact, at least throughout his formative years, with any other human being. He is fed by mechanical means, and confined to a nursery which contains, in addition to the usual furniture, a number of automata. These automata, some of which roughly imitate the appearance of human bodies, are so constructed that they respond to his actions in certain limited ways; cry out, for example, when he hits them, or retaliate by striking out at him; they can be made to nod or shake their heads in answer to his questions, and also to utter certain simple sentences; these utterances may be triggered off by visual or auditory signals. For his instruction in the use of language, and in other forms of behavior, the child depends upon a voice which addresses him through a loudspeaker. If it be objected that even though the child never sees the owner of the voice, it still introduces a human element, we can suppose that the sounds which the child hears are not spoken by any person, but transmitted, perhaps from written messages, by a machine. The voice teaches the child the names of the various types of objects in the room; it formulates sentences for him to imitate, which are sometimes also responded to by the automata. It teaches him his own name, the use of pronouns and demonstratives, and the use of words which describe his "inner" states. In very much the same way as children normally do learn these things, he learns to say when he is hungry or satisfied, happy or in pain; he is coached, as other children are, to distinguish what he sees from what he imagines, or from what he remembers; and among his memories to distinguish those that are memories of dreams. Part of the method by which this is achieved is a stressing of the similarity between himself and the automata; the voice always speaks of them as though they too were conscious, and he finds that the attribution of consciousness to them, but not to the "inanimate" objects in the room, corresponds to differences in their behavior. In this way he learns how to apply the concept of a person: and he satisfies the condition of being ready to apply it to other things beside himself.

I said that this was an artificial example, but it is not excessively fanciful. The idea of such an experiment may be morally repugnant, but it would not be very hard to stage, and I see no reason to suppose that it could not lead to the result which I have described. But if this is so, the consequences are important. The example shows not only that one might be able to ascribe experiences to oneself, while being invariably mistaken in ascribing them to others, but also that the criteria which are taken to be logically adequate for ascribing experiences to others may determine no more than that some locution is correct, that in such and such conditions this is the proper thing to say; it does not necessarily follow that what is said is true. Nor can this conclusion be escaped by saying that the child in my example would not possess our concept of a person, that the automata which he had been taught to regard as conscious subjects really would be persons in his sense of the term. There is no warrant for assuming that his concept of a person could not be the same as ours. He applies it to himself on the basis of his experiences and he applies it to the automata on the basis of their behavior, which if they were very skillfully constructed, might not appear very different, within their limited field of operation, from that of human beings. It is not that he has a different concept of what it is to be conscious, or that he applies the concept incorrectly, but that he just happens to be in a situation where the things which he has every reason for thinking to be conscious are really not so. If he were an infant philosopher, he might begin to wonder whether his companions really did have experiences in the way that he did and infer that they did from their resemblance to himself. Or perhaps if he were struck by some stereotyped quality in their behavior he would rightly conclude that they did not. Whichever conclusion he came to, his skepticism would not be senseless. How could it be if it were actually justified?

The reason for saying that a doubt of this kind would be senseless, even in this artificial instance, is that it could never be laid to rest. There is nothing in this child's world, as we have described it, which would allow him to find out that his companions were, or were not, automata. If he were released from his nursery and allowed to mix with other human beings, he would have a standard of comparison. He would be able to observe how differently these human beings spoke and acted from the things which he had been brought up to regard as persons; if he discovered how the automata were constructed, he would have a further reason for placing them in a different category from himself. But would this mean more than that he was requiring a stronger basis for his argument from analogy? And might he not still doubt whether it was strong enough? But then what would make it strong enough? If no behavioral criteria are logically sufficient, there must always be room for doubt. But what is the significance of a doubt which could never be allayed?

I do not know the answer to this question. The difficulty is not just that the argument from analogy, at least in the form in which it is usually presented, does not seem very powerful; it is rather that any inductive argument allows for its conclusion to be false. So if my belief that other beings are conscious can be defended only as an inference from their behavior, it is at least possible that I am the only person in the world. The short answer to this is that I know that I am not; but this still leaves the problem how I can have the right to be so sure. If physicalism were true, this problem would give no trouble, but I do not see how the obvious objections to physicalism are to be overcome. I am, therefore, inclined to agree with Mr. Strawson that we ought to try to find a middle way. For the reasons which I have given, I do not think that he has yet succeeded: among other things, his notion of logical adequacy is rather too nebulous to bear the weight which he puts upon it. Nevertheless, I think that the development of this notion, along the lines suggested by Professor Alston, may at least be along the road in which the solution of this problem lies.

Though I am by no means fully satisfied with the argument from analogy, I think it can be defended against the objection that the only experiences which it can give us any reason to believe in are experiences of one's own. This objection rests on the premise that if the behavior of others did not provide me with a logically adequate criterion for ascribing experiences to them, the very idea of their having experiences could have no meaning for me. The only facts in my possession would be that when my body was stimulated in certain ways, certain experiences occurred, and that when bodies similar to mine were stimulated in similar ways no such experiences occurred. But if this were all I had to go on, then, it is suggested, I could not even form the hypothesis of there being experiences which were enjoyed by persons other than myself.

This objection has force when it is backed by the assumption that my successfully ascribing experiences to others is a precondition of my being able to ascribe them to myself; but when this assumption is discarded, all that remains for the objection to rely on is a strict interpretation of the verification principle. Its conclusion will follow from the ruling that I cannot attach sense to any statement which I could never be in a position to verify directly. But this in itself appears to me now to be an objection against maintaining the verification principle in such a stringent form. If no more is required than that the statement be indirectly testable, then the argument from analogy will at least not be excluded at the outset. Whether its conclusion satisfies this condition of significance will in fact depend upon the question whether it is a legitimate form of inductive argument. There is indeed a special difficulty for those who think that one can not conceive of physical objects except as logical constructions out of one's own private sense-data; for it may well be asked how I could possibly suppose that a logical construction out of my sense-data was endowed with a private world of its own. On the other hand, if I am entitled to assume that what I perceive, in some cases at least, are public objects which exist independently of myself, there seems to be no good reason why I should not be able to form the hypothesis that certain of these physical bodies have experiences connected with them in the way that experiences have been found by me to be connected with particular states of my own body. The objec·

tion that I must in that case already be conceiving of the physical bodies as the bodies of other persons does not seem to hold; the identification of such a body as a particular physical object will, as I hope to show, itself be sufficient for the numerical identification of the experiences which are causally dependent on it; further than that, the experiences themselves need be identified only in a qualitative fashion, as experiences of a certain kind.

If we are able to dispense with the notion of a subject, other than the body, to which both states of consciousness and physical properties are attributed, there will be no reason why we should especially direct our attention to predicates which are concerned with human action. The importance which was attached to these predicates was that they were supposed to provide us with an instance in which we had knowledge not based on observation and inference of something other than our own experiences. Thus our immediate knowledge of our own bodily movements would supply a precedent for taking our knowledge of the experiences of other persons to be noninferential. But, if, as I have tried to show, our knowledge of the experiences of others is inferential, the need for this precedent will not arise. In any case, it seems to me very doubtful whether the precedent itself is valid. It is indeed true that we are made aware of our bodily movements by kinesthetic sensation, and it is also true that we usually do what we intend to do, especially when the intention is one that can be immediately carried out. Nevertheless our kinesthetic sensations can be delusive; they are not sufficient conditions of the physical movements with which we associate them; neither is one's consciousness of an intention a guarantee that it will be fulfilled. In both instances the exceptions are rare enough for us to overlook the distinction between the sign and what it signifies; we speak of feeling a movement or of doing things intentionally, as though the sensation were inseparable from the movement, and the intention from the action which fulfills it; but the distinction is there none the less.

Neither does it seem that the analysis of predicates, which are concerned with human action, will provide us with the answer to the problem of self-identity. Professor Hampshire may well be right in claiming that even in our infancy we are not simply the passive recipients of sensory impressions; it may be true that one comes to think of oneself as an object among other objects through feeling the resistance which these other objects oppose to one's will. But this fact, if it be a fact, about the way in which a person acquires the idea of his own identity does not tell us in what this identity consists.

4

If the thesis of physicalism is to be rejected, it does not follow that we are forced back into the position of Descartes. It is possible to hold that states of consciousness are distinct both from their physical causes and from their physical manifestations, without being obliged to hold that there is a mental substance to which they are ascribable. Indeed, if this is what Hume was seeking when he tried to distinguish himself from his perceptions, it is not merely a contingent fact that he was unable to find it; there is no possible way in which such a substance could be identified.

It might seem, however, that we were then committed to Hume's own position. If experiences can be logically distinguished from physical events, then it might appear to follow that one can at least conceive of their existing on their own. Having rejected the notion of a mental substance, we shall have to look upon the self as "a bundle of perceptions," in Hume's terminology; and it will be a contingent fact that separate bundles are associated with particular bodies. If we take the short step from Hume to John Stuart Mill and regard these bodies themselves as "permanent possibilities of sensation," it will be a contingent fact that some particular

"perception" is both an element of a collection which constitutes a certain body and an element of a collection which
constitutes an individual self.

But the answer to this is that all that we have so far allowed
is that a statement which ascribes an experience to some person need not be equivalent to any statement which refers to
that person's physical condition or behavior. And from this it
does not follow that it is even logically possible for states of
consciousness to exist independently of any physical body.
The reason why it does not follow is that it may not make
sense to talk of states of consciousness except as the experiences of some conscious subject; and that it may well be that
this conscious subject cannot be identified except by reference
to his body.

In favor of this view, it may be argued that the alternative
of equating the conscious subject with the series of his experiences leaves us without any explanation of the nature of
personal identity. Not only is it not clear how the individual
experiences are to be identified, but there appears to be no
principle according to which they can be grouped together;
there is no answer to the question what makes two experiences, which are separated in time, the experiences of the
same self. The most promising suggestion is that the bundles
are tied together by means of memory; but this meets with
serious difficulties. In the first place, it is exposed to the
charge of circularity; for it is plausible to argue that remembering an experience already implies thinking of it as an
experience of one's own: and even if this charge can be met,
it is clear on other grounds that memory alone will not suffice.
For not every experience can be remembered; otherwise each
piece of remembering, which is itself an experience, would
have to be remembered, and each remembering of a remembering and so *ad infinitum:* how then is it to be determined
that two memory experiences which occur at different times

are members of the same bundle? The only answer which suggests itself is that one of them accompanies an experience of which the other is directly or indirectly a memory: the relation may be said to be indirect when the second memory is a memory of some experience accompanying a memory which is either directly, or at one or more such removes, a memory of the experience in question. But what is this relation of accompanying? When dealing with the question in my *Problem of Knowledge* I said that it might be taken to be "the relation that holds between two items of experience if and only if they are parts of the same total experience at any given moment."[12] But this does involve us in a circle, for

> what is meant here by a total experience is just the experience of one and the same person. We can hold that the relation between its parts is *sui generis,* but then we can also hold that the relation between the successive experiences of the same person is *sui generis;* and in that case we do not need to bring in memory at all.[13]

In the *Problem of Knowledge* I did indeed fall back upon a solution of this kind: I spoke of a "relation of which, perhaps, nothing more illuminating can be said than that it is the relation that holds between experiences when they are constituents of the same consciousness."[14] But to be driven to postulating an unanalyzable relation is, in this as in other instances, simply to abandon the problem, not to solve it.

One objection to making personal identity depend upon the identity of the body is that it rules out even the logical possibility of a person's existing in a disembodied state. On any view, the evidence that states of consciousness are causally dependent upon physical processes is strong enough to make it extremely improbable that any person ever does succeed in doing this; but the idea of its happening might at least appear to be intelligible. Surely one can imagine oneself continuing to have experiences which are very like the ex-

periences which one has at present, except that they include
none of the perceptions which establish the existence of one's
own body; and if one can imagine that this could happen to
oneself, one should also be able to imagine that it could
happen to others. This is a legitimate form of argument, but
in the present instance it may be deceptive. For if this picture
of oneself in a future disembodied state is intelligible in its
own right, why should it have to contain any link with one's
present form of existence? Is it not also imaginable that one
should lose all memory of one's embodied self? And could
we not go even further? If it is conceivable that one should
exist at some time without having any experiences which
were indicative of one's having a body, why should it not be
conceivable that this should be so at all times? Could it not
be imagined that the whole of one's existence was passed in
a disembodied state? The objection to these flights of fancy
is that there would then be no means by which one could be
identified. But does this not equally apply to the idea of a
person's surviving the destruction of his body? The experiences which might then ensue may themselves be imaginable;
but it would seem that in crediting them with an owner we
are making a tacit reference to the body which is supposed
to have been forsaken. Mr. Strawson's idea appears to be that
one could retain one's identity through having memories of
one's former life. But here he seems to have forgotten that
something is needed to secure one's continued existence as a
person; and for this we have seen that memory will not
suffice.

I do not present these arguments as being in any way conclusive; I am, however, inclined to think that personal
identity depends upon the identity of the body, and that a
person's ownership of states of consciousness consists in their
standing in a special causal relation to the body by which he
is identified. I am not maintaining of course that this is how
one actually becomes aware of one's own experiences, but

only that the fact that they are one's own, or rather the fact that they are the experiences of the person that one is, depends upon their being connected with this particular body. This amounts in effect to adopting what Mr. Strawson calls "the no-ownership doctrine of the self." We must, therefore, try to rebut his charge that this theory is internally incoherent.

His argument, as we have seen, is that the theory requires it to be a contingent proposition that all my experiences are causally dependent upon the state of my body; but if my experiences are identified as mine only in virtue of their dependence on this body, then the proposition that all my experiences are causally dependent on the state of my body must be analytic; and so the theory is committed to a contradiction. I think, however, that these propositions can be reformulated in a way which shows that the contradiction does not really arise. The contingent proposition is that if my body is in such and such a state then an experience of such and such a kind results; the analytic proposition is that if an experience is causally dependent in this way on the state of my body, then the experience is mine. But now it is obvious that these propositions are distinct; so that there is no inconsistency in holding that one is contingent and the other not. There would indeed be a vicious circle if the experiences had first to be identified as mine before it was discovered that they were dependent on my body, but this is not the case. The position is that a person can be identified by his body; this body can be identified by its physical properties and spatio-temporal location; as a contingent fact there are certain experiences which are causally connected with it; and these particular experiences can then be identified as the experiences of the person whose body it is. There is nothing inconsistent in this.

What may have misled Mr. Strawson is the picture of a heap of experiences which have to be assigned to their respective owners. For this makes it natural to ask which of these experiences are dependent upon a given body, and to believe that one is raising a question of fact; it will then seem to be an objection to our theory that it only allows the trivial answer that the experiences which are dependent on this body are those which are dependent on this body. But it is the picture that is at fault; and the question to which it leads is illegitimate. We cannot ask *which* experiences are dependent upon a particular body, and are, therefore, to be assigned to such and such a person, because this is to assume improperly that the experiences have been independently identified. The question which we can ask is *what* experiences are dependent upon a particular body, if this is just a way of asking what experiences the person who is identified by the body is having at the relevant time. It is analytic that if the experiences are connected with his body, they are his experiences; but of course it is not analytic that experiences of one sort rather than another are at any given time connected with his body. Neither does our theory require that it should be.

Our difficulties, however, are not yet at an end. Merely to say that a person's experiences are causally dependent on the state of his body is to speak too vaguely. The nature of the causal relation which is to do the work of assigning experiences to persons needs to be precisely specified. If we are to do justice to the assumptions that are ordinarily made about the way in which experiences are distributed, this relation must operate in such a way that any individual experience is linked to one and only one human body. The problem is to find a causal relation which not only fulfills this task but is also such that its existence can plausibly be taken to follow from every statement in which a person is credited with some experience.

A simple answer would be to regard the relation as being that of causal sufficiency. An experience would then be said to be mine if and only if some state of my body were causally sufficient for its occurrence independently of the state of any other body; this would exclude the experiences of other people on the assumption that I cannot act upon another person except by producing some physical change in him which is then itself sufficient for the occurrence of his experience. But apart from its needing this questionable assumption, the objection to this answer is that it relies on a causal relation, the existence of which we are hardly entitled just to take for granted. It is by no means universally agreed that all our experiences are physically determined, in so strong a sense as this would imply; it has even been maintained, in the interests of free will, that there are experiences which have no sufficient conditions at all. Now this may very well be wrong; there is certainly no means of showing that any experience lacks a sufficient condition, and it may in fact be true of every experience that its sufficient condition consists in some state of its owner's body. But the point is that even if this hypothesis is true, it can significantly be questioned. It is not at all plausible to hold that its truth is logically implied by every statement in which a person is credited with some experience. To say that the experience is not physically determined may be false, but it does not appear to be self-contradictory.

I think, therefore, that the most that we can hope to maintain is that an experience belongs to a given person in virtue of the fact that some state of that person's body is a necessary condition of its occurrence. The justification for this would be first that experiences are individuated only by reference to the persons who have them, and secondly that persons are identified only by reference to their bodies. If these premises are admitted, it follows that no experience of mine would have occurred unless my body had existed; more particularly, it follows that the existence of my body will be implied by any statement in which an experience is attributed to me. But this does not settle the argument. For even if it were granted that an experience could not be mine unless it stood in this relation of causal dependence to my body, one might still maintain that something more than this was required to identify the experience as mine.

A strong argument in favor of this view is that if the relation of dependence is to be merely one of causal necessity, then every one of my experiences is dependent upon the existence of bodies other than my own. This follows simply from the fact that I must have had ancestors: since the existence of their bodies is a necessary causal condition of the existence of my body it is also a necessary causal condition of the existence of my experience. Moreover, apart from this general condition which applies indifferently to all my experiences, a great many of my experiences owe their special character in part to the behavior of other persons. It is very often the case that I should not be having the particular experience that I am having unless some other persons had spoken or acted in some particular way, or been in some particular state; and in all such instances the existence of these person's bodies will also be a necessary condition for the occurrence of my experience. It would appear, therefore, that while the relation of causal sufficiency is too strong for our purposes, the relation of causal necessity is too weak. It does not fulfill the task of assigning each experience to one and only one body.

The only way that I can see of overcoming this difficulty is to make a distinction between mediate and immediate necessity. Let us say that the existence of an event x is mediately necessary for the existence of another event y if and only if there is some event z such that x is a necessary condition for the existence of z and z is a necessary condition for the existence of y; and let us say that the existence of x is immediately necessary for the existence of y if and only if it is necessary for the existence of y, but not mediately so. Then we may claim that the causal relation which links a person's experience to his and only his body is that of immediate necessity. What makes a given experience mine is the fact that the existence of some state of my body is an immediately necessary condition of the occurrence of the experience and that no state of any other body is so.

Let us now see whether this criterion gives an adequate result. If our reasoning has been correct, the first of its requirements presents no difficulty. Not only is the existence of my body a necessary condition for the existence of any of my experiences, but it also seems clear that it is immediately necessary. There is no other factor that intervenes between my body and this set of experiences which are dependent on it: indeed it is hard even to imagine in this case what such an intervening factor could be. The question is whether there is any difficulty about the second requirement. Does it safeguard us from having to assign experiences to what would ordinarily be regarded as the wrong owners?

With some misgiving, for reasons which we shall come to, I am prepared to maintain that it does. The fact that the physical existence of my ancestors is also a necessary condition of my having any experiences now presents no problem. For clearly this is a case of mediate necessity. The existence of my own body is an intervening factor. It is also an intervening factor in at least the overwhelming majority of cases in which the character of my experiences depends upon the state or behavior of another person. For in the normal course of things the only way in which another person can act upon me is by affecting my perceptions. If I am to be in any way influenced by him I must observe him, or observe some effect of what he has done. But in that case the existence or state of his body can at best be a mediately necessary condition of my having the experience which depends upon it. It is mediated by the occurrence of my perception, and so by a bodily state of my own.

We could leave the matter there were it not that we must

allow at least for the possibility of para-normal experiences. Thus, there are alleged to be cases in which one person acquires information about the mental or physical condition of another without having to rely upon any form of sense perception. Now one may be skeptical about the authenticity of these reported cases of telepathy, though some of them at least appear to be very well-attested; one may accept them as authentic, but still believe that they can somehow be explained in physical terms. This would be in line with the assumption that it is impossible to act upon another person except by causing him to undergo some physical change. Nevertheless, however little we may like the idea of accepting telepathy at its face value, that is, as a form of communication between persons which does not operate by physical means, I do not think that we are entitled to exclude it a priori. It may be a far-fetched notion, but it does not appear to self-contradictory. But if we allow this, then the adequacy of our criterion for assigning experiences to persons is put in question. For suppose that someone communicates a thought to me in this telepathic fashion. In that case, his bodily state will be a necessary condition for his having the thought which he communicates; it will, therefore, also be a necessary condition of my having the experience which results. But *ex hypothesi,* the state of my own body is not in this instance an intervening factor. It is of course itself a necessary condition of my having the experience, but an independent one. It might, therefore, be thought that according to our criterion we should be obliged in a case of this kind to deny me the ownership of the experience.

This would, however, be a mistake. For what is required of our criterion is that no experience of mine shall have for an immediately necessary condition the state of any other body but my own. And this requirement is satisfied even in the case which we have just been envisaging. If we allow telepathy of this kind to be possible, then we are indeed allowing that the state of another person's mind may be an immediately necessary condition of my having some experience; but the state of his body will still be only mediately necessary. It will give rise to my thought only through the medium of his. There is, therefore, still an intervening factor: not, as in this normal case, some state of my own body, but the other person's experience.

The only type of para-normal case which we could not so easily accommodate would be that in which my experience was dependent on the action of another person, without my being in telepathic communication with him and without my perceiving his action or any of its physical effects. Thus in an experiment on extra-sensory perception, in which one of the experimenters selects a card and the subject, sitting in another room, is required to guess what it is, it may be discovered that the subject scores significantly better when the experimenter touches the back of the card with his finger, even though the subject does not know what the experimenter is doing, and the experimenter himself does not know what the card is. If this were to happen, there would be a ground for saying that the experimenter's bodily movement was an immediately necessary condition of the subject's thinking as he did. But then we should be faced with the impossible consequence that, according to our criterion, the subject's thought was not ascribable to any single owner.

This example is troublesome, but not, I think, necessarily fatal to our theory. One way of meeting it would be to construe our criterion in such a way that the only type of bodily state which came within its scope would be an internal state. Such overt performances as the movement of a finger would not qualify. So certain experiences would be mine in virtue of the fact that such things as the condition of my brain and nerves were immediately necessary for their occurrence, and that they did not stand in precisely this relation to any other body but my own. Another defense would be simply to refuse to admit our para-normal case as a counterexample. It is not possible, one might argue, that the experimenter should affect the subject's thought under these conditions simply by moving his hand. This type of action at a distance is unintelligible. There must be some intervening mechanism, even though we do not know what it is. But the trouble with this defense is that it already assumes that the subject's thought has been assigned to him. Without this assumption the complaint about action at a distance would have no basis as it stands. We could, however, attempt to modify it in such a way as to avoid this objection. We should have to maintain, as a general principle, that in a case where an experience would be manifested in a given body, if it were manifested at all, it was impossible that it should be causally dependent upon a different body, without the operation of some intervening factor. But how are we to decide which is the body in which the experience would be manifested? If we are reduced to identifying it as the body of the person who has the experience, then clearly we are back in our circle; and it does not seem certain that it could always be identified by other means. In view of these difficulties it seems preferable to adopt the course that I first suggested: that is, to try to deal with the awkward para-normal example by narrowing our interpretation of what is to count for our purposes as a bodily state. *163492*

A more far-reaching objection to this whole procedure is that we are introducing a recondite, if not dubious, theory into the analysis of statements which function at a much simpler level. The use of statements which ascribe experiences to persons is an everyday occurrence: one of the first things that a child learns is to employ and understand them. Can we seriously maintain that these statements incorporate such a sophisticated and unfamiliar notion as that of an immediately necessary condition?

The answer to this objection is that it is beside the point.

In attempting to analyze statements about persons, we are not proposing to discover what those who make such statements commonly have in mind. Our aim is rather to redescribe the facts to which the statements refer in such a way that their nature becomes clarified; and for this purpose there is no reason why we should not resort to technical terms. In the same way, it is not a fatal objection to a causal theory of perception that a child may learn to talk of the physical objects which he perceives before he has acquired the notion of cause, neither is it fatal to a phenomenalist theory that comparatively few people understand what is meant by a sense-datum. The only relevant question is whether these theories are adequate to the facts: that is, whether they correctly represent the truth-conditions of the statements which they serve to analyze. In the present instance, the way to refute our theory would be to find an example in which it clearly made sense to speak of a person's having some experience, even though the experience was not uniquely dependent on his body in the way that the theory requires. So long as no counterexample is forthcoming which the theory cannot be adapted to meet, we may regard it as provisionally acceptable. In a field in which so many theories have had to be discarded, I should not wish to claim more for it than that.

In claiming even so much, I am assuming that it has at least been shown that the theory is free of any vicious circularity. But this may still be questioned. The reason why it may be questioned is that the theory presupposes the existence of psycho-physical laws. Admittedly they are fairly modest laws: we are not assuming that every experience is physically determined; the physical factor is taken only to be necessary, not sufficient. Even so, it may be argued, these laws have had to be empirically discovered. And how could we ever have set about discovering them unless the experiences, which were found to be correlated with certain physical states, had themselves been independently identified? But this means that the charge of circularity returns in full force. How is it finally to be met?

The only way that I can see of meeting it is to draw a distinction between the general proposition that every experience is causally dependent, in the required sense, upon a body and the more specific propositions which describe the different forms that this dependence takes. The general proposition must be held to be necessary, on the ground that causal dependence upon a body is an essential part of what we mean by an experience. On the other hand, the more specific propositions are contingent. The precise nature of the psychophysical laws which correlate experiences of various types with certain sorts of physical conditions remains a matter for empirical discovery.

In taking the more general proposition to be necessary, I am not implying that in order to know that I am having some experience, I have first to find out that it is dependent on my body. I do not need to find this out, any more than I need to find out that this body is my own. The identification of the body, which carries with it the numerical identification of the experience, is a problem for other people not for oneself. The reason for this is that in referring to myself at all I am presupposing my ownership of this body; in claiming an experience as mine, I imply that it is dependent on this body and not on any other. This does not mean of course that my body could not have been qualitatively different; we are concerned here only with numerical identity. It is not a necessary fact that my body has the physical attributes that it does, but given that this is the body by which I am identified, it is a necessary fact that *this* body is *mine*.

But now a further question arises. If my argument is correct, it is essential that a person be identified at any given time by reference to some body. But is it essential that he be identified at all times by reference to the same body? It would seem natural and convenient to hold that it is, but the consequence of this would be that certain hypotheses which have been thought to be significant, even if highly improbable, would be ruled out a priori. We should, for example, be making it logically impossible that a person should be reincarnated, or that two persons should exchange bodies with one another. Yet however fanciful a story like Anstey's *Vice Versa* may be, it is not ordinarily thought to be self-contradictory.

What makes such fantasies appear legitimate is that there are subsidiary criteria of personal identity which may at least be conceived as running counter to the main criterion of physical continuity. These are the criteria of memory and continuity of character. Thus, in Anstey's story, the ground for saying that Mr. Bultitude has been translated into the body of his schoolboy son is that from a certain moment onwards the person who is identified by the schoolboy's body displays the mental characteristics which previously belonged not to the son but to the father, and that it is the father's and not the son's experiences that he ostensibly remembers. In such a case, we could insist on saying that the persons who were respectively identified by the two bodies remained the same as before but that they had mysteriously acquired each other's character and memories; it does, however, seem a more natural way of telling the story to say that the two persons have exchanged bodies. On the other hand, even if some one could convince us that he ostensibly remembered the experiences of a person who is long since dead, and even if this were backed by an apparent continuity of character, I think that we should prefer to say that he had somehow picked up the dead man's memories and dispositions rather than that he was the same person in another body; the idea of a person's leading a discontinuous existence in time as well as in space is just that much more fantastic. Nevertheless, I think that it would be open to us to admit the logical possibility of reincarnation merely by laying down the rule that if a person who is physically identified as living at a later time does have the ostensible memories and character of a person who is physically identified as living at an earlier time, they are to be counted as one person and not two. For given that this condition is satisfied, the question of their numerical identity is a matter for decision and not a question of fact.

But even if the subsidiary criteria of personal identity could in these strange cases be allowed to override the primary physical criterion, they are still parasitical upon it. It is only because the different bodies provide us with subjects of reference that we can entertain these queer hypotheses at all. What we should in fact be doing in these cases would be to revert to a Humean theory in which a person's identity is made to depend upon relations between experiences, irrespective of the body with which they are associated. But we have seen that a theory of this kind is not tenable unless the experiences themselves can be identified; and I have argued that the only way in which they can be identified is through their association with a body, the body being that which supplies an immediately necessary condition of their occurrence. It may well be thought a defect in my position that it requires the existence of these psycho-physical relations to be assumed a priori. But if this is a defect it is one that I see no way to remedy.

COMMENTS

Edmund L. Gettier III

Wayne State University

1

I CANNOT in this comment discuss all that Professor Ayer has to say in his paper. I shall restrict my comments to section 4 of the paper, where he states views of his own. In order to make discussion easier, I should like to begin by listing five propositions. Throughout these comments assume that the variable "S" ranges over persons, "B" over bodies, "E" over experiences, and "x" and "y" over the class of contingently existing objects.

a) If S identifies S′, then S identifies S′ by reference to the body of S′.

b) If S identifies an experience E, then S identifies E by reference to the person who has *E*.

c) E is an experience of S if and only if there exists some internal state of S's body that is an immediate necessary causal condition of the existence of E.

d) Then S asserts or judges that Fx S has identified x.

e) Then S identifies S′ by reference to B (there is a relation R such that

    i) S knows that there is one and only one that has R to B, and

    ii) S refers to S′ as the one and only one person that has R to B.)

I believe that it is clear from Ayer's paper that he holds propositions (a) through (c) to be true. I think that he would want to hold (d) or something like (d), for one of the points of the paper seems to be that for any group of particulars, if we cannot identify particular members of that group, then we cannot make assertions or have beliefs about particular members of the group. Thus, if we cannot identify disembodied persons, then we cannot make assertions about particular disembodied persons. I do not know whether Ayer would accept proposition (e) or not. I shall not at this moment anyway attribute proposition (e) to him.

It is obvious that the expressions "identified" and "by reference to" are key expressions in the sentences used to state propositions (a) through (d). Clearly, also, if one does not understand these key expressions, then one would not know what propositions are being expressed by (a) through (d), and hence, what propositions Ayer is here holding to be true. Certainly these expressions need some explanation, possibly even definition, since they seem to occur as technical terms in the sentences used to express propositions (a) through (d). However, in his paper Ayer does not give any explanation of them at all! And in the absence of such explanations, it seems fair to say that Ayer has not presented us with one clear view to be discussed.

In order to make it quite clear that the terms "identified" and "by reference to" need explanation, I shall present *prima facie* counterexamples to proposition (a) and (b), and maintain that in the absence of some elucidation of these two terms it is impossible to tell whether these apparent counterexamples are or are not really counterexamples.

First consider proposition (a). According to it, if I identify Albert Einstein then I must have made some reference to the body of Albert Einstein. But suppose on some given occasion I refer to Einstein as the person who first thought of the theory of relativity. Clearly I can so refer to Einstein. And just as clearly, the definite description that I used contained within it no expression that refers to Einstein's body. Now, have I, by so referring to Einstein, identified him? It is impossible to tell from what Ayer says in his paper. Perhaps I can successfully refer to a man without identifying him. Perhaps all successful references to a person are identifications. Perhaps a successful reference to a person is an identification only if there is another person who witnesses the reference and knows to whom the reference is made. Suppose that by referring to Einstein by means of this definite description I *did,* according to Ayer, identify Einstein. Have I done so by reference to Einstein's body? Clearly, my description contains no expressions referring to the body of Einstein. But does it or does it not follow from this that I have identified him without referring to his body? Again it is impossible to tell.

Now, consider proposition (b). According to it I can identify a particular experience E only by making some reference to the person who has experience E. But suppose I have a pain in my shoulder, and, referring to the pain in my shoulder, I say to myself, not to someone else, "That pain is getting worse." It seems that I can refer to my own pains in this way, provided I am talking to myself. But again, the expression "that pain" by which I referred to the pain in my shoulder, does not contain any expressions referring to myself, or for that matter to any person. Have I by referring to my pain with the expression "that pain" identified the pain? Might this not be a case of what Ayer calls "ostensive identification"? Or, again, is it required for a successful reference to a pain to be a case of identification, that there be a hearer who, upon hearing the reference, knows to what object the reference is made? Whether these two cases of a reference are or ar not counterexamples to propositions (a) and (b) cannot be determined by anything that I can find in Ayer's paper. I feel, therefore, that I don't know exactly what view he is asking us to consider.

2

In spite of the obscurity surrounding the expressions "identified" and "by reference to," it seems possible to argue that if (a), (b), and (c) are true, then (a) and (b) are both false. I shall first argue that if (a), (b), and (c) are all true, then (b) by itself is false. I shall then argue that from what was established in deducing the falsity of (b) it follows also that (a) is false.

Let us assume that B_1 is a particular body that has been identified without any reference to a person or to any experiences. Let us say, as Ayer asserts is possible, that body B_1 has been identified by its place at a certain time. Let us assume also that a certain person S_1 has been identified by reference to B_1, and that B_1 is the body of S_1. All of this is said to be possible in (a) and (b). Now consider the following list of definite descriptions:

    f) The experience E such that:
       i) E is P, and
       ii) E belongs to S_1
    g) The experience E such that:
       i) E is P, and
       ii) There exists some internal state of the body of S_1 that is an ICNC (immediate causal necessary condition) of the existence of E.
    h) The experience E such that:
       i) E is P, and
       ii) There exists some internal state of the body B_1 that is an ICNC of the existence of E, and
       iii) B_1 is the body of S_1
    i) The experience E such that:
       i) E is P, and
       ii) There is an internal state of B_1 that is an ICNC of the existence of E.

It follows from (b), no matter what the words "identified by reference to" mean, that it is possible to identify an experience by reference to the person who has E. If Ayer holds that (b) is true, then it would seem that he would hold that an experience can be identified by means of description (f). The first constituent of (f), that E is P, is inserted because for most people if they are having one experience, they are having many. Hence, it would be impossible to refer uniquely to one particular experience of a given person by saying merely that it is the experience had by that person. Some other properties of the experience must be mentioned. In this case, let us imagine that the property of being P is the property of being a thought about the number eight.

The second constituent of description (f), *i.e.*, that E belongs to S_1, is analyzed by Ayer in proposition (c) above. If we substitute the analysis of "E belongs to S_1" for this expression in description (f), the result is description (g). If Ayer holds that an experience can be identified by description (f), then it would seem that he must hold that the very same experience can be identified by description (g), since he holds that (c) states a logical equivalence.

Description (g) contains the expression "the body of S_1." We are assuming that a body B_1 has been identified, and that B_1 is the body of S_1. Hence, if we substitute the name "B_1" for the expression "the body of S_1" and then add a condition to the effect that B_1 is the body of S_1, we should get a description that uniquely refers to the same experience that is referred to by description (g). By making this substitution and addition we get description (h). It seems, then, that if Ayer holds (b) true, he would hold that it is possible to identify an experience by means of description (h).

But I think that it can be shown that if (h) uniquely refers to some experience, then (i) uniquely refers to an experience. We can see this by considering the transposition, i.e., if (i) does *not* uniquely refer to an experience, then (h) does *not* uniquely refer to an experience. Let us suppose that (i) fails to refer uniquely to an experience because there is more than one experience that satisfies this description. If description (i) fails in this way then there are at least two experiences such that for each there is an internal state of body B_1 causally related to it in the proper way. If description (i) fails to refer in this way, then clearly adding to (i) the condition that B_1 is the body of S_1 will do nothing to choose between the experiences satisfying (i). But description (g) is just description (i) with this extra condition added. Hence, if (i) fails by virtue of there being more than one experience satisfying it, then (g) will fail for the same reason.

On the other hand imagine that (i) fails because there is no experience satisfying it. It follows logically from the fact that no experience satisfies (i) that no experience will satisfy (h), for both of the conditions mentioned in (i) are mentioned also in (h). For any two conditions, what does not satisfy those two conditions will not satisfy those two conditions in conjunction with a third. My conclusion then: description (i) can fail in only two ways; and for each of these ways in which (i) can fail, (g) fails also. It follows from this that if (g) succeeds in referring to an experience, then (i) succeeds in referring to an experience also.

Therefore, if (b) is true, (i) can be used to refer to an experience. But description (i) makes no reference to a person. In fact, it is just description (g) with the reference to a person dropped out. Hence, if (a), (b), and (c) are true, it is possible for (g) to identify an experience, and it is possible for (i) to identify an experience. But this is to identify an experience without reference to a person. Hence, (b) is false. Therefore, if (a), (b), and (c) are true then (b) is false.

I turn now to showing that if (a), (b), and (c) are true, then (a) is false. We have established that it is possible to identify an experience by means of description (i). In so identifying, no reference would be made to a person. Suppose that the experience so identified is a particular experience E_1. As Ayer says, it is necessarily true that for each experience it belongs to one and only one person. Given the necessity of this proposition, and the fact that we have identified an experience E_1, and that by hypothesis S_1 is the person to whom E_1 belongs, we can identify S_1 by the following description: (j) the person to whom E_1 belongs. Given that we can identify person S_1 by description (j), we have identified a person without reference to his body, solely by reference to an experience of his. Therefore, if (a), (b), and (c) are true it is possible to identify a person by description (j). And if it is possible to identify a person by description (j), then (a) is false.

Ayer could answer my contention that the falsity of (a) follows from (a), (b), and (c) by saying that he meant to use the expression "identified by means of" in such a way that it is transitive. Therefore, he could claim, experience E_1 was identified by means of a body, and S_1 by E_1. Therefore, the identification of S_1 by description (j) was an identification of a person by means of a body. If Ayer were to maintain that the expression "identified by means of" is transitive, then I must give up my contention that if (a), (b), and (c) are true then (a) is false. This reply would not affect my contention that if (a), (b), and (c) are true then (b) is false. I would still have one conclusion left, at least temporarily. If Ayer makes this reply, then we once again see trouble arising because he has made no attempt to elucidate these key concepts in his position, and we do not know, therefore, whether the relation *identifies by reference to* is transitive.

3

In this section I should like to raise a question that Ayer must be able to answer if his view is to be considered tenable. In raising it, I shall be making the assumption that he accepts proposition (e). I do not know that he does but he does hold that a person can be identified by reference to his body. And it does seem reasonable to assume that what this means is that there is some relation R such that it can be known that one and only one person has R to some given body, and that the identification occurs by means of a definite description of the form "the one and only one person who has R to such and such a body." I might identify a person by means of his automobile. And to do this I might identify him as the one and only one person who has the relation of owning to that automobile.

Assuming, then, that Ayer accepts proposition (e), let us imagine (e) instantiated for particular persons S_1 and S_2, and some particular body B_1. Then let us assume that the antecedent of the instantiated form of (e) is true. We will be assuming that a particular person S_1 does identify some particular person S_2 by reference to some particular body B_1. From this assumption together with proposition (e), it follows that S_1, the person doing the identifying, knows that there is one and only one person who has the relation R in question to B_1. The question I wish to raise is this: from what kind of evidence could S_1 infer that there is one and only one person who has R to B_1?

One thing seems clear. It could not be that S_1 infers that there is one and only one person having R to B_1 from the proposition that S_2 and only S_2 has R to B_1. That is, S_1 could not infer that there is one and only one person having R to B_1 from a proposition that asserts of a particular person that he has R to B_1. For, according to proposition (d), to know that such a proposition is true of a particular person, S_1 must be able to identify that particular person. But for S_1 to identify that particular person there would have to be another relation R' such that S_1 knows that one and only one person has R' to *some body*. Thus, an infinite regress seems to follow, given (d) and (e), from the contention that S_1 knows that there is one and only one person who has R to B_1 from evidence consisting of statements about particular persons.

We might imagine that his evidence has the following form: B_1 has P, and for every B: (If B has P *then* there is one and only one person having R to B). These two premises will entail that one and only one person has R to B_1, and hence could serve as the evidence of S_1, provided it is possible for S_1 to get evidence for them. But what kind of evidence can he have for the generalization, other than instances of particular bodies and particular persons related by relation R? The problem comes to this. In order for S_1 to identify S_2, by reference to B_1, he must know of some relation R that one and only one person has R to B_1. The question that is puzzling is how S_1 could have evidence for such a proposition without ever using a proposition about a particular person.

4

In this last section, I should like to make a claim for which I can give no argument. Possibly, the main contention of Ayer's paper is proposition (c). Though I know of no argument to show it, proposition (c) appears to be simply false. Ayer agrees that what internal states of my body are causally necessary for my experiences is a contingent matter to be investigated by scientists. It seems equally true that whether any internal states of my body at all are causally necessary for my experiences, is a contingent matter to be investigated by scientists. For example, it seems logically possible that scientists might have discovered that in the air immediately adjacent to my body, little atomic events occur which are the immediate causally necessary conditions of my experiences; and that all of the internal states of my body are causally irrelevant to the existence of my experiences. For example, there appears to be no contradiction in the supposition that when light waves hit my eyeballs, certain events are brought about just outside of my eyeballs, which are themselves immediate causally necessary conditions of my having the experience of seeing. However, I have no argument to present. I can only put my intuition up against that of Prof. Ayer's.

Ayer does admit that an overt bodily movement of someone other than myself, e.g., the waggling of a finger by the man standing next to me, might be an immediate causally necessary condition of some thought of my own. For this reason, he puts the word "internal" into proposition (c). It seems absolutely astonishing that a philosopher would think it logically possible for someone's waggling of his finger to be an immediate causally necessary condition of my having some thought, but at the same time think it logically impossible for some internal state, e.g., his flexing certain muscles or his heart skipping a beat, to be so related to a thought of mine. It seems clear that whatever is true in the one case is true, also, in the other; and that in both cases it is a contingent fact that such bodily states of other persons are or are not immediate causally necessary conditions of my thoughts and experiences.

I suppose that a philosopher can be justified on holding certain propositions true even though they seem paradoxical or even false, provided no argument is known against their truth. But when confronted with propositions that seem so plainly false, it would be comforting to have at least *some* arguments in their favor.

REJOINDER

A. J. Ayer

I SHALL BEGIN by trying to meet Mr. Gettier's request for a clearer explanation of what I mean by saying that one type of thing is identified by reference to another. In the case of anything of which it can significantly be said that it comes into existence at a particular time and remains in existence for a time, however short, I assume that there must be some way in which its presence can be detected. This is not to say, of course, that the presence of any individual object is detectable by any observer at any time. Clearly I cannot now detect the presence of objects which have ceased to exist or not yet come into existence; and among the objects which do now exist there are many whose presence I have no means of detecting because they are too remote in space for me to have access to them. But if the reference that I make to any such object is to be intelligible there must at least be a standard method of detecting the presence of objects of that kind. There are also, I think two other conditions that have to be satisfied. There must be some criterion by which one member of a given class of objects is differentiated from another; and in the case of things which have more than a momentary duration there must be some criterion of self-identity. There must be some way of determining whether two episodes which are separated in time do or do not belong to the history of the same object.

Now though everything which exists in time must be accessible to observation in some sense or other, the mode of access need not always be straightforward. There are types of objects, or occurrences, the presence of which is detectable only through detecting the presence of objects or occurrences of different types. Thus, one of the standard means of detecting the presence of electrons is to observe characteristic marks on photographic plates; unconscious states of mind are typically manifested by certain forms of behavior; the actions of corporate bodies, like parliaments or armies, are revealed only in the actions of the men and women who compose them. Of course I am not suggesting that the relation between the different types of entities is the same in each of these examples: obviously the relation of a particular soldier to the army of which he is a member is not of the same order as the relation between a particular set of marks on a photographic plate and the electrons of which they are the traces. But what these examples do have in common is that in all of them there is a distinction between something which is manifested and something of a different type through which this manifestation is effected. And this is what I had in mind when I spoke of one thing's being identified by reference to another.

In the case of persons, their bodies, and their experiences, there is, however, a complication which I hoped I had brought out in my essay. Gettier attributes to me the view that experiences can be identified only through the identification of the persons whose experiences they are, and that persons can be identified only by reference to their bodies. Though I believe this to be true of the experiences which one ascribes to other persons, I do not believe this to be true of one's own experiences, as I hoped that my essay had made clear. Consequently, while I hold that the identification of the person whose experience it is can in the appropriate circumstances be a sufficient condition for identifying an experience, I do not hold that it is necessary. This does not mean that I think there could be experiences which were not the experiences of any person. It is just that in one's own case I admit the possibility of one's having what might be called direct access to them.

On the other hand, I do hold that a person can be identified only by reference to his body, even in the special case in which the person is oneself. My reason for this is that even in referring to oneself as a person one has to rely upon some criterion of self-identity; and I do not see how personal identity is to be analyzed except in terms of the identity of a body. I admit that we do make use of other criteria but argue that they are parasitical upon the criterion of bodily identity; I do not think that they could sustain a concept of personal identity on their own. Thus I reject the idea of there being disembodied persons, even as a logical possibility, because I do not see how the experiences of such a person could be held together; that is, I do not see what relation there could be between them in virtue of which they would be the experiences of one and the same person.

In the light of these explanations, I will make some brief comments on the several points which Gettier raises. Of the five propositions which he begins by listing, I accept (a) (b) and (e) and a weaker version of (d), in the sense that I hold that if S is intelligently to assert or judge that fx, x must at least be the sort of thing that he knows how to identify. I do not, however, accept (b) if this is taken to imply that experiences are necessarily identified by reference to the persons who have them.

It should be clear from what I have already said that the first of Gettier's apparent counterexamples is not in fact a counterexample to proposition (a) as I interpret it. There is, indeed, a sense of the word "identify" in which I can properly be said to have identified something if I have given a description which applies to it and to nothing else: and in this sense I might be said to have identified A by reference to B if the description which I had given of A was one in which B was mentioned as standing to A in some unique relation. Thus, in Gettier's example, Einstein is identified by reference to the theory of relativity, as being the person who first thought of it. Hence, if this had been the sort of identification that I had in mind, Gettier would have found a counterexample to my thesis and could easily have produced many others. But I hope that I have now made it clear that the sort of identification which I did have in mind was not one to which such examples would be relevant.

The second of Gettier's counterexamples is a counterexample to proposition (b). But since I do not hold proposition (b) this does not affect me.

In the second part of his paper Gettier develops an elaborate argument to show that, if my theory is correct, an experience E can be uniquely characterized as an experience of a given type which has an internal state of a body B_1 for its immediate necessary condition, and he infers from this, first that on my own principles experiences need not be identified by reference to persons since they can be identified by reference to bodies, and secondly, that persons need not be identified by reference to their bodies since they can be identified by reference to their experiences. I have no fault to find with the argument except that to make it entirely rigorous he should have included a reference to the time at which E occurs, but the inferences which he draws from it do not disturb me. I do not claim immunity on the ground that I reject proposition (b) since I should wish to maintain it with respect to the experiences of persons other than oneself, which, if Gettier were right, I could not consistently do. The point is rather that for me the distinction which he has to make between identifying an experience by reference to a person and identifying it by reference to that person's body presents a false antithesis. In my view, as I thought my essay would have shown, to identify an experience as the experience of a particular person is equivalent to identifying it by reference

to the body by which the person in question is himself identified. If I speak of identifying experiences by reference to persons rather than by reference to bodies, it is only because we
commonly talk of persons rather than of bodies as having
experiences. But I never suggested that to identify an experience by reference to a person was a distinct process from
identifying it by reference to a body. And for the same reason
I do not count the fact that a person may be uniquely characterized as the owner of an experience which is itself identified
by reference to a body as at all an objection to my thesis that
persons are identifiable only by reference to their bodies. In
this case, therefore, the question whether my relation of
"identifies by reference to" is transitive does not arise, but in
fact I do hold it to be transitive.

The same mistake seems to me to vitiate the argument
which Gettier seeks to develop in the third part of his paper.
He maintains that I am committed to holding that if a person
S_1 identifies some other person S_2 by reference to a particular
body B_1, S_1 must know that there is one and only one person
who stands to B_1 in the relation R on which the identification
is based; and he then argues that "it could not be that S_1
infers that there is one and only one person having R to B_1
from the proposition that S_2 and only S_2 has R to B_1." If I
follow him correctly, his ground for this is that S_1 could not
attach sense to the proposition that S_2 has R to B unless he
had independently identified S_2, and that, on my principles,
the only way in which S_1 could identify S_2 independently of
knowing that S_2 bore the relation R to a particular body B,
would be by knowing that S_2 bore the relation R to some body
or other; and he understandably fails to see how one could
come to know that a person bore the relation R to some body
or other except through coming to know that he bore this
relation to a particular body. But the sufficient answer to all
this is that, given that the body in question has the characteristics of a person, as opposed, say to an animal or an inanimate

thing, the identification of the person just consists in the identification of the body. There is no question of the person's having to be independently identified. Of course if the statement that the body is the body of the person whose body it is, is not to be merely trivial, the person will have to be described in some other way than merely as the owner of that body. But, as I have already explained, the fact that a person may be uniquely described in ways that make no explicit mention of his body is not incompatible with the thesis that it is only by reference to their bodies that persons are, in my sense, identifiable.

I may remark in passing that while I do make it necessary that one and only one person "inhabits" a given body at a given time, this rule could easily be relaxed if it were found advisable. At present I do not allow for any other means of describing cases of alleged co-consciousness than by saying that they are cases of one person with a split personality. But it would not be hard to introduce subsidiary criteria of personal identity which would make it significant to talk of there being two or more persons simultaneously inhabiting a single body. However, as in the other para-normal cases with which I dealt, these criteria would still be parasitical upon the primary criterion of physical identity.

Finally, Gettier states that he just does not find it credible that the relation in virtue of which a person's experiences are ascribable to him should consist in their dependence upon some internal state of his body as their immediately necessary causal condition; and he complains that if I was going to advance a proposition which seems so plainly false, I ought at least to have produced some arguments in its favor. My answer to this second charge is that I did produce a number of arguments which seemed to me to leave no alternative to the view that a person's ownership of his experiences consists in their standing in some causal relation to his body; and the theory that this relation was that of their having some internal state of his body as their immediately necessary causal condition seemed to me to fit the facts better than any other that I could think of. I do not deny, however, either that it seems excessively artificial or that it forces me to attribute necessity to propositions which I might otherwise have been more inclined to regard as contingent. It may well be then that on this point Gettier's intuition is to be trusted. My own intuition goes no further than the belief that even if this theory is not the answer, some theory of a similar type is most likely to be true.

NOTES ON AYER ESSAY

1. P. F. Strawson, *Individuals: An Essay in Descriptive Metaphysics* (London: Methuen & Co. Ltd., 1959).
2. *Ibid.*, p. 102
3. *Ibid.*, p. 99.
4. Ludwig Wittgenstein, *Philosophical Investigations* (Oxford: Basil Blackwell, 1953), p. 293.
5. G. E. Moore, *Philosophical Studies* (London: Kegan Paul, Trench, Trubner and Co., Ltd., 1922), pp. 31–96.
6. *Op. cit.*, p. 108.
7. *Ibid.*, p. 111.
8. Stuart Hampshire, *Thought and Action* (London: Chatto and Windus, 1959), pp. 47–8.
9. *Ibid.*, p. 75.
10. *Op. cit.*, p. 110.
11. C. K. Ogden and I. A. Richards, *The Meaning of Meaning* (London: Kegan Paul, Trench, Trubner & Co., Ltd.; New York: Harcourt, Brace and Co., Inc., 1938).
12. A. J. Ayer, *The Problem of Knowledge* (London: Macmillan and Co. Ltd.; New York: St. Martin's Press, 1958), p. 222.
13. *Loc. cit.*
14. *Ibid.*, p. 226.

CONSCIOUSNESS AND BEHAVIOR: THEIR BASIC CONNECTIONS[1]

Hector-Neri Castañeda

Wayne State University

THE RELATIONSHIPS between consciousness and behavior are purely contingent; yet there is an a priori connection between the consciousness of other selves and the consciousness of bodily behavior. How is this possible?

My answer is that the relationship between consciousness of self and consciousness of other selves resembles the connection between observational knowledge and the knowledge of theoretical entities built upon it. These relationships are truly synthetic *a priori,* in a sense I want to specify. I claim there is a sense in which one cannot think of oneself as a self without believing that in certain circumstances and conditions there is probably a self different from oneself. But I insist that even though a fully-rounded idea of a self involves criteria for identifying possible other selves, these criteria are logically inadequate.

In these assertions, I make some assumptions which are not customary. The most important are: (A) that a private language is possible, or better, that it is possible to have thoughts which are not fully communicable; (B) that theoretical entities are real; (C) that it is possible to have thoughts and make judgments without possessing a language; and (D) that it is not necessary to learn one's concepts from others or from experience (whatever this may mean), i.e., that it is possible to be born with all of one's concepts or to acquire them by a causal event in one's history that has nothing logically to do with the concepts in question. I will try both to make clear the role of these assumptions and to defend them.

1. The Problem and Its Data

Section 1. A PRIORI AND CONCEPTUALLY NECESSARY CONNECTIONS. Since every philosophical claim is to the effect that something or other is necessary or impossible, or *a priori* or empirical, and often the necessity in question is not formal logical necessity, we must give some idea of the necessity involved. The following definitions are not precise, but they will be helpful.

A proposition is *conceptually analytic or necessary* if and only if: (a) it is a truth of logic (including modal and deontic logic); or (b) it is an instance of a truth of logic; or (c) it is derivable from definitional rules of inference (not necessarily substitutions by explicit or recursive definition); or (d) it is a proposition which expresses a connection constitutive of the connected concepts; it is a kind of meaning postulate; or (e) it is entailed by a set of propositions all of which are conceptually analytic.

The most obscure category is (d). But the following ten examples may help: "Everything red is colored"; "Everything which is all over a clear-cut instance of red is not all over a clear-cut instance of green"; "Everything colored is extended"; "If X is larger than Y, Y is not larger than X"; "If X is heavier than Y and Y heavier than Z, X is heavier than Z"; "If X judges at time t, while attending to his experiences, that he is in pain, then he is in pain at t"; "If X is a pain, X occupies at least a two-dimensional space"; "If X judges at t that he judges that p, then at t X judges that p"; "If X thinks at t that p and q, then at t X thinks that p and thinks that q"; "If X dreams at t that p, then at t X has a thought that p."

A proposition is *conceptually inconsistent or impossible* if and only if its denial is conceptually analytic.

A proposition is *conceptually synthetic or contingent* if and only if it is neither conceptually analytic nor conceptually inconsistent.

P *conceptually implies* Q if and only if "If P, then Q" is conceptually analytic.

P is an *a priori* proposition if and only if, P is conceptually analytic or inconsistent, or it is conceptually inconsistent that someone knows by experience at some time *t* that P and it is also conceptually inconsistent that someone knows by experience at some time *t* that not-P.

P is *empirical* if and only if it is not *a priori*.

X *knows by experience* at *t* that P if and only if: (a) X perceives at *t* that P; or (b) at *t* X both judges that P and attends to his experiences, and P is such that X's believing that P while attending to his experiences conceptually implies that P; or (c) there is a proposition Q such that at *t* X knows by experience that Q, Q conceptually implies P, and at *t* X infers P from Q; or (d) there is a time *t'* prior to *t* at which X knows by experience that P and at *t* X remembers how he knew by experience that P; or (e) there is a time *t'* prior to *t* at which X knew by experience that P, X has believed that P from *t'* to *t*, and at *t* X knows a way of finding out by experience that P.[2]

Section 2. KNOWLEDGE OF OTHER MINDS IS INFERENTIAL. To think that an entity X is, or has, a mind or a self is to think that X is or was or will be conscious. To think that X is conscious is to think that X is having a thought or an experience. I want to concentrate on the consciousness involved in the awareness of an experience of a given sort. By "experience" I mean here things like bodily sensations, sense data, and mental images. It should be noted that I distinguish experiences sharply from the awareness of them. But an episode of awareness *can* itself be the object of another episode of awareness. We can concentrate our discussion on such experiences without any important loss of generality because, on the one hand, the states of consciousness consisting in the awareness of them must have an experience as an "object" in order to exist and, on the other hand, experiences as illustrated can only exist while sustained by a supporting, even though perhaps merely diffused, consciousness. Thus, the question whether or not one knows that a different self has an experiential state of consciousness reduces to the question whether or not one knows that such a self has an experience of a certain type.

Now, certain propositions which are conceptually analytic entail that if one knows something about another mind or self one knows it by inference. These propositions are not universally accepted as necessary, so that restating them should help to formulate the issue between myself and other philosophers more clearly.

To avoid unnecessary repetitions, let "A" be interpreted alternatively, in each occurrence, as:

A = There is an experience which is not mine.
A = There is no experience of sort S which is not mine.
A = There is a self different from me.
A = There is no self of sort S different from me.

Let us abbreviate "X conceptually implies Y" by "X ⊃* Y."

Let us start by supposing that (1) I know that A. Clearly, in the customary sense of "know that," (2) (X knows that p) ⊃* (p (is true) and X believes that p and X has conclusive reasons for p.) [The reverse entailment does not seem to hold.] Hence, from (1) and (2), (3) I have reasons for A. This can be understood as (4) (X has at time t reasons for p) ⊃* (i) at t X perceives that p; or (ii) at t X believes that p while attending to his own mental goings-on, and believing that p while attending to one's own mental goings-on ⊃* p; or (iii) at t X has some concepts such that having them ⊃* believing that p; or (iv) there is a proposition q such that q implies p [not necessarily conceptually], and at t X has conclusive reasons for q and infers p from q; or (v) at a previous time, X had conclusive reasons for p, and at t X remembers what conclusive reasons he had for p, or (vi) at a previous time, X had conclusive reasons for p, X has believed that P since then, and has conclusive reasons for believing that he can at t verify that p. Since having conclusive reasons of types (v) or (vi) logically entails having had conclusive reasons of one of the types (i) through (iv), we may disregard (v) and (vi) without loss of generality. Thus, we derive; (5) I have conclusive reasons for A of type (i), (ii), (iii), or (iv).

My *first assumption* is: (6) Every proposition that can be known by perception fails to entail conceptually any of the alternative interpretations of A. Since each interpretation of A is incapable of being known by perception, it follows that (7) I cannot have reasons of type (i) for A.

My *second assumption* is: (8) My belief that A while I attend to my mental goings-on does not conceptually entail that A (is true); i.e., I cannot have conclusive reasons of type (ii) for A.

My *third assumption* is: (9) There are no concepts my full possession of which conceptually entails that I believe that A; i.e., I cannot have conclusive reasons of type (iii) for A. Hence, from (5) through (9), and (1): (10) I know that A $\supset$* I know some proposition q implying A from which I infer A. But, by (6), I cannot derive my knowledge that A from a purely perceptual proposition. It is obvious that (11) I cannot infer correctly by induction that A from a proposition q which I know solely by perception. (I cannot perceive the other selves, or experiences not mine, required for the induction.) Hence, (12) I know that A $\supset$* either I inductively inferred A from a set of propositions some of which I know by perception and some by introspection [i.e., by reasons of type (ii)], or I deductively inferred A from a set of premises of type (iii) and by perception, introspection, or both.

My *fourth assumption* is: (13) No inductive argument is capable of yielding knowledge that A. Thus, I conclude that (14) If I know that A, I know this by deduction from premises which I must believe in order to have the concepts of self, and experience, as well as from premises which I know by perception, introspection, or both.

My *last assumption* here is: (15) The deduction as envisaged in 14 is impossible. Therefore, I conclude that in the strong, but conventional sense of "know that" characterized by propositions (2) and (3), I do not really know that there is an experience which is not mine, nor do I really know that there isn't an experience of a sort S which is not mine, nor that there is a self different from me, nor that there isn't a self of sort S different from me. But I want to emphasize that I do have some less certain knowledge, namely, that *very probably* there are selves different from me as well as experiences which are not mine, and, alternately, that *very probably* there are neither selves of certain sorts different from me nor experiences of certain kinds which are not mine.

Section 3. A CONTRARY VIEW: BEHAVIORISM. I pass now to note some of the opposition to my controversial assumptions. Some versions of philosophical behaviorism would object to my assumption that no perceptual proposition conceptually entails that there are experiences which are not mine. Other versions would simply analyze statements about X's experiences of a given sort as conjunctions of statements about X's bodily movements or conditions of X's body, thus making the having of an experience directly perceptible. A more sophisticated version would quarrel only with premise (6). By identifying the having of an experience with a set of dispositions exercised in bodily movement, the sophisticated behaviorist may agree that the having of an experience is not itself perceptible, but can be inferred deductively from perceptible states of affairs.

I am convinced that all versions of philosophical behaviorism are mistaken even if they are dispositional and include other sophistications. (A fashionable sophistication is the view that "He is in pain," and *a fortiori* the concept of pain, is not analyzable in purely behavioral terms because utterances of the sentence play a role in "a way of life" and in expressing an inclination to furnish some aid to the person spoken of.) Their chief difficulty lies in the fact that one has direct, noninferential and incorrigible knowledge of one's own experiences. As far as I can see, the following propositions are conceptually analytic in that they express constitutive connections among the concepts involved:

Postulates of Direct Access:

(1) At *t* X has [does not have] an experience Y, is capable of judging that he has Y, and is attending to his own mental goings-on ⊃* X knows that he has [does not have] Y.

(2) At *t* X has some [no] experience of a phenomenal type ø, is capable of judging that he has an experience of type ø, and is attending to his mental goings-on ⊃* X knows at *t* that he has some [no] experience ø.

Postulates of Incorrigibility:

(1) X believes that he has [does not have] Y, which is an experience of phenomenal type ø, while attending to his mental goings-on ⊃* X has [does not have] Y.

(2) X believes that he has some [no] experience of phenomenal type ø, while attending to his mental goings-on ⊃* X has some [no] experience of phenomenal type ø.

These postulates make it possible to know (by introspection, as I will say) that one has a pain, a sensation of warmth, etc. without having to take note of one's behavior at all. Furthermore, the postulates allow one's claim of being in pain to be correct regardless of one's bodily behavior and circumstances. According to the postulates, Smith will be mistaken in claiming that I am in pain, regardless of how correct his perceptions are, if I believe while attending to my own feelings that I am not in pain. Behaviorism, on the contrary, asserts that there are circumstances in which Smith may be correct in claiming that I am in pain, in spite of my sincere and self-searching denial. Here the fact that we have to accept a person's *statement* that he is in pain speaks against behaviorism.

In general, it is conceptually possible that a person may feign pain by behaving like a person in pain. He has no pain but his behavior is typical of pain. Hence, behavior typical of pain does not conceptually entail that one is in pain. Moreover it is conceptually possible to suppress the expression of pain. Behaviorists sometimes reply that feigning presupposes a connection between behavior and experiential states. This is true. But the presupposed connection is not one of entailment. What is presupposed is a customary association between certain behavior and certain experiences. Such an association is enough for the possibility of deception.

The more sophisticated contemporary behaviorists would attack our postulates on the grounds that the utterance "I know that I am in pain" is senseless, that it does not really express a state of affairs. If this were so, these postulates, instead of furnishing the central part of the "logic" of introspective knowledge, would be sequences of senseless words. On this contention there would be nothing direct about knowledge of one's own experiences; presumably one would know them by observing one's own behavior. If this were so, it would certainly meet the crucial objection to behaviorism. But none of the arguments are convincing. They are all either incoherent or based on a false premise, which I will demonstrate here to defend my postulates.

(a) *The first argument:* If a proposition is contingent, it is logically possible to believe falsely that it is true. If "I am in pain" expresses the contingent proposition we normally understand, one could believe one is in pain without being so.

This is impossible, hence there is no such proposition one can believe or know.

This argument is faulty. From "It is impossible to believe falsely that one is in pain" it follows that it is *necessary* that if one believes himself to be in pain, the belief is true. Furthermore, since "I am in pain" can be only contingent, the proper conclusion is that the first premise of the argument is false. This would be a strong version of postulate E(2). (Actually, we do not have to reject the first premise. Postulate E conforms to it by allowing that an inattentive judgment that I am in pain be false.)

(b) *The second argument:* A contingent proposition can be falsely believed to be true; if "I am in pain" expresses a contingent proposition, sentences of the form "I believed falsely at t that I was in pain at t" would be meaningful. But they are not meaningful, hence there is no such proposition expressed by "I am in pain" and none expressed, *a fortiori,* by "I know that I am in pain."

I do not see how a philosopher is going to prove that "I believed falsely at 9 A.M. that I was in pain at that time" is meaningless. One may even grant that it expresses a false proposition. For instance, I may distract my attention from a mild pain by reading, and suddenly realize that I was reading and felt no pain and judge that I had no pain, but the very act of so judging makes me attend to my mental goings-on and realize almost simultaneously that I was wrong, that the pain was still there. These are facts which may be described somewhat differently, but our postulates provide room for a consistent description, without doing violence to our central conception of pain.

Besides, there is such a proposition expressed by the sentence "I am in pain." As those who propound this argument accept, the sentence "He is in pain" often expresses a proposition. Suppose then that x asserts of me "He is in pain." I can express what he believes by saying "x believes that I am in pain," where "I am in pain" expresses a proposition.[3,4] Furthermore, "I am in pain" expresses something that is true or false, can be contradicted, has entailments, and appears as premise in arguments. These five features together are certainly sufficient to make the utterance the formulation of a proposition. Hence "I know that I am in pain" is just as meaningful.

(c) *The third argument:* In ordinary language it is odd to say that one believes that one is in pain. "I believe that" is used to suggest the possibility of a mistaken belief or doubt. There is no room for doubt about one's own pains. Hence, "I believe that I am in pain" is senseless and so is "I know that I am in pain."

This argument is invalid. Once again, from "There is no room for a mistaken belief" it follows that if one believes he is in pain his belief is true. And this is why it is strange to say "I believe I am in pain," since this assertion suggests the possibility of a mistake.

(d) *The fourth argument:* In ordinary language it is odd to ask a person who has said he is in pain "How do you know?" Hence, it is senseless to say "I know that I am in pain," unless this just means "I am in pain."

This is an inconclusive argument. Since one cannot be mistaken about one's pains, the senselessness of the question lies in asking for an answer the respondent knows is already known. The only answer to, "How do you know?" is, "By having the pain" or "By attending to my feelings." Nothing in the argument shows that it is even pointless to speak of knowing one's own pains. In making an inventory of the ways of knowing, one lists physical objects known by perception, pains known by feeling, or introspection, mathematical theorems known by deduction, etc.

(e) *The fifth argument:* It is correct to speak of knowledge only when there is a procedure for testing it. But it is absurd to suppose there can be tests for whether one is in pain or not.

Since it is correct to speak of knowing one's own pains, the major premise is false.

In sum, it is pointless to inform another person that one believes, thinks or knows one is in pain. But this fact about ordinary *reporting* in no way shows that pointless assertions do not report facts. Indeed, the pointlessness of the assertions presupposes their intelligibility. The crucial thing is, however, to note that these arguments which are meant to be attacks on our postulates of incorrigibility and private access involve premises which entail these very same postulates.

Section 4. THE ANALOGICAL VIEW. The assumption, formulated in premise 8 in Section 2, is questioned by those who explain our knowledge of other minds by sympathy, empathy or telepathy. But here I will ignore these views.

Rush Rhees' paper on private language[5] can be interpreted as denying this assumption. He seems to claim that the very fact I have a language conceptually implies that I am or have been part of a community of speakers in which I learned my language. On the commonly-held assumption that thinking is impossible without experiences and without language, Rhees seems to be committed to the view that my having thoughts conceptually implies that there are or were other persons, different from me with experiences which are or were not mine. Now, direct awareness of one's own thoughts is awareness of a second-order experience. Furthermore "I think that I think that p" conceptually entails "I think that p." Hence, on the view extracted from Rhees, my thinking that I am thinking that p while attending to my thoughts conceptually entails that there have been other selves and experiences which are not mine. Therefore, in contradiction to my assumption there would be an experience, namely, the experience of having a certain thought, whatever this may be, such that my believing that I am thinking, conceptually implies that there has been some other self and some experience not mine.

This argument depends on two important premises: (1) that having thoughts ⊃* having a language, and (2) that having a language ⊃* participation in a community. If both were conceptually analytic, the above argument would be a transcendental deduction of the falsity of solipsism. I suspect the fear of solipsism is precisely the reason why both premises are widely accepted. But I see very little reason for accepting (1), and no reason at all for accepting (2). Premise (2) is a strong version of the view that one has to learn one's concepts from experience. But I see no reason at all to suppose that there is some sort of logical connection between the process of learning and what is learned. I see no reason why a person cannot be born in full possession of all his concepts, or why a person, born with no concepts at all, cannot get all of them by means which have nothing logically to do with the concepts, e.g., by being hit exactly on the top of his head by a bunch of seedless grapes. If this is so, it cannot be a necessary *a priori* truth that one has to get his concepts by a specific series of events, namely communal activities. I have elsewhere[6] discussed both premises (1) and (2), and below I will say something more about the learning of concepts. Clearly, premise (2) is false.

My third assumption that there are no concepts the full possession of which conceptually entails that there are selves different from me, that there are experiences which are not mine, etc., seems, however, to be generally accepted.

My fourth assumption has two parts: (a) "No inductive argument can yield the knowledge that there is a self different from me, or that there is an experience which is not mine," and (b) "No inductive argument can yield the knowledge that there is no self different from me, or that there is no experience of sort ∅ which is not mine." I am more confident of the truth of (b). The premises for the inductive argument mentioned in (b) must be obtained by introspection and perception, and neither can furnish a premise to the effect that awareness is unrelated to a physical object, or that there is no experience of a certain phenomenal sort related to my body when I am not aware of the experience in question and my body fails to exhibit the appropriate behavior. For instance, I cannot claim to know by experience that when my body does not exhibit pain behavior there is no pain in it, say, inside its skull. All I can claim is that *I* feel no pain when my body doesn't exhibit it. Neither through introspection nor through perception can I know that somebody else is not feeling pain in, say, my skull, when I feel none there and my body evinces none. Thus, the impossibility of obtaining inductive arguments for the absence of other selves or of experiences other than ours does show that our ordinary negative knowledge of other minds is not based on induction. Hence, to account for the ordinary certainty of our beliefs about other minds we have to resort to a view allowing noninductive beliefs.

I also think that (a) is true, but I do not have proof. In this case I do not need premises resulting from either introspection or from perceiving somebody else's absence of experience or awareness. I can proceed from my experimental knowledge of the associations between awareness or experiences and behavior, and this knowledge is illustrated fully in my own case. Nevertheless, I will assume that this inductive procedure breaks down somewhere. My justification for this assumption is that I want to develop a plausible alternative to the traditional analogical view of our knowledge of other minds. According to the latter, everything we know about other minds is only probable and inductive.[7] However, if no alternative proves better at this point, to contemplate both can only provide a greater insight into the nature of our concepts or experiences.

It is now customary to hold that the analogical view is

either false or incoherent. But none of the arguments given in support of this claim stands criticism, aside from the criticism that negative knowledge of other minds cannot be inductive.[8]

Section 5. THE CRITERIOLOGICAL VIEW. My last assumption is that my knowledge that there is an experience of sort ∅, which is not mine is a deduction from (1) principles which I must believe inasmuch as I have the concepts of experience, ∅, and self, and (2) premises which I know either (a) by introspection, or (b) by perception, or (c) some by perception and some by introspection. In view of my assumption that nothing perceptible conceptually implies that there is [no] experience, *the principles (1) are not conceptually analytic.* Clearly we may distinguish three types of view: (1a), (1b), and (1c).

Malcolm has advocated a view that Plantinga[9] has called "criteriological." It *looks* very much like (1a). According to Malcolm,[10] sets of behavior together with sets of circumstances are criteria for saying that somebody has a pain, an itch, a sensation of discomfort, a thought, an auditory sensation, etc. He has been emphatic in his contention that these sets of behavior-cum-circumstances are not related by entailment to what they are criteria for. I take it that his denial of entailment goes as far as what I have called conceptual entailment. If it does not, his view is simply a behaviorism distinguished by its awareness of its own difficulties. But Malcolm also insists that the connection between the criteria for an experience and the experience is not empirical. It is thus a priori without being conceptually analytic.

Unfortunately Malcolm has said very little more about the criteriological connection, and the little more is somewhat perplexing: that the connection is also necessary, and that it pertains to the very possession of the concept of the experience in question. The second point seems to be correct, but the necessity of the connection between behavior and experiences is not clear. Grant that Malcolm is right and that the criteriological connection is synthetic (i.e., not of entailment), necessary, a priori (i.e., not empirical), and has something to do with our having a certain set of concepts of experiences (i.e., is not merely a causal connection). Grant further that Malcolm's arguments show all of this. Then we have a problem: *We must account for the possibility of a certain synthetic necessary a priori connection.* Thus, we should begin almost precisely at the point Malcolm has ended his discussion.

It seems to me that the criteriological view is faced with an initial difficulty: all the evidence points to a lack of necessity in the connection between behavior and consciousness (or the phenomenal features of experiences), regardless of how a priori it might be. In the first place, there is the phenomenon of feigning. The possibility of successful feigning is an essential part of our mental concepts. To understand our concepts of the phenomenal types of experiences is to be prepared to bump into, unknowingly, of course, a case in which a most complete presentation of the criteria for an experience of a certain type ϕ is accompanied by the absence of an experience of type ϕ. So how can the connection be necessary? In the second place, we have all had "unexpressed" experiences. An experience or an "inward" state is in no need at all of an "outward" criterion. In the third place, more often than not we "know" what a person is feeling or thinking because he *tells* us, and we accept his word. But this is not to infer from his behavior that his thought or feeling is such and such. To take X's words as a true statement involves two logical steps, and only one of them involves a non-causal necessity: the step (a) from X's experience of feeling or thinking to his judgment that he is feeling or thinking, and the step (b) from X's judgment-in-words to one's own thought that X has had [or has, in a specious present] the thought or feeling in question. Sometimes there is a third "step" between the judgment and the judgment-in-words. The point is that by the postulates of direct access to one's own experiences, the only non-causally necessary step is from X's thinking or feeling together with both his attending to his mental goings-on and his ability to judge that he is thinking or feeling, to the judgment that he is so feeling or thinking. In the fourth place, the criteria for having an experience do not guarantee that two persons will have exactly the same type of experience when they fulfill the criteria. For suppose Y knows that X satisfies the criteria for pain. By the criteriological view Y knows that X is in pain, and Y ascribes to X a property which is necessarily connected with the criteria. But when Y knows that he is in pain, what he knows *cannot* be a conclusion from the criteria, and he knows that he has it by encountering certain properties in his experience. But then it remains an open question whether or not these properties he apprehends are necessarily connected with the criteria.* And the criteria for pain cannot, then, establish with necessity that what X experiences is the same as what Y experiences when both are correctly said by Y to experience pain.

These four considerations show that the connection between so-called criteria and the experiences they are criteria

---

* The criteriological view seems to have exactly the same problem that Malcolm finds in the traditional view of the mind, namely, that according to it "I cannot attribute pain to others *in the same sense* that I attribute it to myself." ("Knowledge of Other Minds," *op. cit.* 981.) On the one hand, if my utterances of the form "I am in pain" cannot ascribe anything to me, because they are not statements, then I cannot ascribe to myself what I ascribe to others in any sense at all. If they are statements, what I ascribe to myself is not a state inferred from my behavior, but a state which says nothing about my behavior, whereas my statement "X is in pain" ascribes to X an inferred state and some definite criterial condition.

for is either chimerical (i.e., conceptually impossible), or probabilistic, but not necessary.*

This concludes both my brief defense of my first set of assumptions and my setting-up of the preliminary issues between other philosophers and myself. If both the criteriological and the analogical views are incorrect, we must try to formulate a view which "saves the appearances": that we have no real knowledge of the existence or of the experiences of other minds; that we have an original certainty of their existence, which cannot be explained inductively; that the relation between consciousness and behavior is purely con-

---

* In his *Individuals: An Essay in Descriptive Metaphysics* (London: Methuen & Co. Ltd., 1959), Ch. 3, Strawson has written as if he were slowly working his way toward a criteriological view. He has offered some arguments purporting to show that our concept of *person* is logically primitive, not merely the concept of a complex of body and self. This concept is such that it is the proper subject for a set of predicates, whose distinctive characteristic is that they are self-ascribed without criteria and are other-ascribed on the basis of criteria. The criteria in question are sets of behavior and circumstances, and they are "logically adequate" for other-ascription. However, we cannot know what Strawson is aiming at as long as he is silent about the meaning of "logically adequate criteria." If this means "conditions which conceptually entail," we have behaviorism, indeed, an uneasy behaviorism because of the noncriteriological self-ascriptions. How does Strawson know that in a self-ascription of pain we are ascribing the same property as in an other-ascription? At any rate, the possibility of successful feigning and unexpressed experiences show that the connection is not one of entailment. If "logically adequate criteria" is meant in a sense in which the criteria are necessary (logical) even though neither conceptually entailing nor simply causal, then we have a criteriological view very much like Malcolm's. Finally, if the term means that the connection is neither necessary nor causal, yet a priori, Strawson has been confusing in his use of "logically" and "adequate." However, he is free from the objections against the claim of necessity. Then he has a synthetic a priori connection, though not a necessary one, and he can proceed to the philosophical task of accounting for it. Thus far, he has not.

For some of the difficulties in Strawson's views see Plantinga's paper cited in footnote 8 and B. O. Williams, "Mr. Strawson on Individuals," *Philosophy*, XXXVI (1961), 309–332.

tingent (aside from tautological relationships); that, nevertheless, there seems to be a non-empirical connection between the awareness of other minds and the awareness of
bodily behavior, but that such an a priori connection is not
a necessary one.

2. Two Fundamental Assumptions

Before outlining a philosophical theory concerning the
relationships between behavior and consciousness, I shall
present two other fundamental assumptions.

Section 6. PRIVATE LANGUAGE AND THE LEARNING OF CON-
CEPTS. In my view, experiences are private objects in several
senses. First, they are private in the sense that my postulates
of direct access and incorrigibility, express conceptually
necessary propositions; that is, one has, of necessity, a direct,
non-inferential, incorrigible access to one's own experiences
as they possess phenomenal properties. Second, experiences
are private in the sense that, *if* one is to learn one's concepts
from experiences one cannot learn each concept of a phenomenal property of experiences fully unless one experiences
instances of these properties. Third, they are private in the
sense that, *if* one is to learn one's indefinable concepts with
the help of instances, then one can get a workable idea of
the phenomenal properties of experiences from one's own
before knowing anything about another's experiences. But
I do *not* think that experiences are private objects in the
sense that no two persons can share experiences, i.e., that no
two persons can have identical experiences. I believe that this
just happens to be true of Earthians; it may even be an
Earthian psychological law just as well established as the law
of Earthian gravity, but it is not a conceptual necessity.

Now, on the assumption that the possession of a language
is, of conceptual necessity, required for having thoughts, it
has been recently argued that a private language is impos-

sible, where "private language" is a language all or some of whose "individual words refer to what can only be known to the person speaking, so that another person cannot understand the language."[11] The phrase "can only be known to the person speaking" is unclear, but it can be understood in such a way that in some of the senses in which I hold that experiences are private, experiences would turn out to be objects which "can only be known to the person speaking." If X believes attentively that he is in pain, X knows that he is in pain, while others can have only inconclusive opinions. Thus, inasmuch as I believe that judgments are expressible in private marks or noises, and that these marks or noises can be a language, I am committed to the view that a private language is conceptually possible. Here, however, I will not defend my commitment. Elsewhere[12] I have refuted each of the arguments in the literature which purports to show that a private language cannot satisfy some necessary condition for a language. Of course, a refutation of all the arguments for some proposition does not prove its denial, but there is at least an impasse, and my assumption that private languages are possible is as legitimate an assumption as its contradictory. There is, however, an argument outlined by Malcolm and called by him "Wittgenstein's external attack on private language,"[13] which is more insidious than the direct attack on private language. It tries to discredit private language by showing that the idea of private language is irrelevant to the analysis of the concepts of experiences. It attacks the assumption that "once I know from my own case what pain, tickling, or consciousness is, I can transfer these things to objects outside myself."[14] Thus, the attack is a set of arguments for each phenomenal property, all having essentially the form illustrated by the following:

> If I were to learn what pain is from perceiving my own pain then I would, necessarily, have learned that pain is something that exists only when I feel pain. For the

pain that serves as my paradigm of pain (i.e., my own) has the property of existing only when I feel it. That property is essential, not accidental; it is nonsense to suppose that the pain I feel could exist when I did not feel it. So if I obtain my *conception* of pain from pain that I experience, then it will be part of my conception of pain that I am the only being that can experience it. For me it will be a *contradiction* to speak of *another's* pain. This strict solipsism is the necessary outcome of private language. (his italics.)[15]

This argument is an enthymeme; and if it is completed, its premises are:

(1) If the language of pains is private, one can learn what pain is from the pains one feels (or experiences).

(2) If I learn what pain is from the pains I feel, all my paradigms of pain are pains which I feel.

(3) All the pains I feel, have, necessarily, the property of existing only when I feel them. So,
    (3A) the pains I feel have the essential property of existing only when I feel them.

(4) If all my paradigms of pain have an essential property P, then it is part of my conception of pain that all pains have, necessarily, P.

(5) If it is part of one's conception of pain that all pains exist only when one feels them, then one has not learned what pain is.

(6) If one learns what pain is from the pains one feels, one does learn what pain is.

From (2)–(6) it seems to follow that I do not learn what pain is from the pains I feel. Since, presumably, all of the above premises are conceptually necessary and the pronoun "I" is just an arbitrary variable, it seems to follow that:

(7) One cannot learn what pain is from the pains one feels. Clearly, this is a very important proposition. It certainly

contradicts one of my assumptions. Proposition (7) would prove that one cannot start by learning what pain is from one's own case and then know by empirical induction that there are pains one does not feel. Of course, *it would not refute the view that, one has an innate idea of pain, uses it in accumulating inductive generalizations based on one's own pains and then acquires inductive knowledge of other persons' pains.* Yet if Malcolm's argument is conclusive, and the parallel arguments for the other phenomenal properties are also conclusive, he has established the very important proposition that concept-empiricism (i.e., the view that one has to derive or learn the concepts of phenomenal properties from instances) is incompatible with the traditional empirical (i.e., analogical or inductive) view about one's knowledge of other minds.

But Malcolm's sample argument is not conclusive. As far as I can see: (i) Malcolm has no right to premise (4); (ii) there is an ambiguity in the term "learn" that the argument can be valid only at the cost of having a false premise in place of either (5) or (6); (iii) granting premise (4), the argument does not prove that one cannot start from a concept of pain which applies only to one's own and then arrive at a multi-personal concept of pain. The latter is all that a philosopher has to be committed to if he holds that the language of pains is private in any of the senses mentioned earlier. Elsewhere[16] I have established (i) and (ii); here I will be mainly concerned with (iii).

For me, premise (3) is not conceptually analytic. My concept of pain allows for the admittedly fantastic conceptual possibility that pains may be shared. Of course, if two persons share a pain *p,* each has direct and incorrigible access only to his having of *p:* by the argument in Section 2 above, each does not have real knowledge that his pain *p* is also felt by someone else. Likewise, for me pains may be transferable. As I see it, the universe might have been such that all muscular pains could be made to move to one's toes or fingers by pressing with one's thumb, and that one could transfer a finger pain to another person by pressing the finger on the other's body. But many philosophers have held that pains are private in that they cannot be shared, and for them Malcolm's argument would apply as it is. Furthermore, Malcolm could very well have employed some true premise instead of (3), for instance:

(3') All the pains I feel have, necessarily, the property of being pains that I feel; or

(3'') All the pains I feel have, necessarily, the property of being known by me to exist, if I know this at all, by feeling and attending to them, without the help of inference or perception.

There is a subtle equivocation in Malcolm's argument, which makes it appear more persuasive than it is. The term "learn what pain is" may be understood either (a) as "learn in part what pain is" or (b) "learn fully what pain is." It is easy to check that premise (5) is false if it is understood in sense (a), and that (6) is false if it is understood as "If one learns in part what pain is from the pains one feels, one learns fully what pain is." Let us, then, take "learn" as "learn fully" throughout the argument and accept all the premises. Thus, we are committed to

(7b) One cannot learn fully what pain is from the pains one feels.

This is really the *strongest* conclusion that Malcolm could derive from this argument. It would be an important result. It would establish that *the ordinary, multi-personal concept of pain is either innate or obtained by some procedure that goes much beyond ostensive learning,* which yields only the first person subconcept. Furthermore, it would establish that the defender of private language, in whatever sense this may be understood, cannot consistently hold premise (1). He can hold at most:

> (1a) If the language of pains is private, one can learn *in part* what pain is from the pains one feels.

All these results suit me perfectly well. I conclude, therefore, that in the senses in which I am committed to the possibility of a private language, I have nothing to fear from any of the existing arguments. This concludes my defense.

I now propose to investigate the possibility that the concept of pain is neither innate nor produced by a causal process that has absolutely nothing to do with what the concept is about. I propose to formulate an analysis of the concepts of experiences which shows that if I start with a partial concept of pain, tickling, etc., I can "transfer these things to objects outside myself."[17]

The fundamental thesis of the philosophical theory I adhere to is that knowledge of the consciousness of others is theoretical knowledge, while knowledge of one's own experiences is *like* observational knowledge. That is, I claim that the subconcepts of *my-pain, my-tickling, my-sensation-of-red, my-(mental)-image, my-feeling-thus-and-thus* (for any appropriate replacement for *thus-and-thus*) are *like* observational concepts, while the subconcepts *your-pain, his-pain, your-tickling, his-tickling,* etc. are theoretical concepts in a scientific theory.[18] Hence, I must explain what I take a theoretical concept to be.

Section 7. SCIENTIFIC THEORIES. A philosophical theory is a claim that a family of concepts has certain necessary connections. A scientific theory, on the contrary, is essentially the claim that there are certain entities linked by contingent relationships. Following Sellars,[19] I conceive of a scientific theory as a conceptual framework which (1) postulates or conjectures a "new" category of entities, (2) purports to explain why the "older" entities satisfy certain causal or functional laws or empirical generalizations, and (3) relates the "older" framework to the new in such a way that propositions (or facts) about the "older" entities constitute evidence in varying degrees for propositions (or facts) about the "new" entities. To accept a scientific theory is to add a new ontological dimension to, as well as to change one's view of, the world. In restatement, a scientific theory is constituted by: (a) a sub-universe of discourse made up of "new" entities; (b) a set of "new" predicates, perhaps some "old" predicates, and often a subset of "old" predicates with modified meanings; (c) a set of conceptually analytic propositions which characterizes these predicates by extending the meaning of some "old" ones, or by restricting their meanings, or by relating "old" predicates to "new" ones, or by relating "new" predicates to "new" ones; (d) a set of synthetic *a priori* propositions, which gives the theory its scientific character through its empirical content, but which is irrefutable by experience.

To illustrate, let us consider the earliest kinetic theory of gases. In it, the "new" entities are the molecules. The "old" predicates are the predicates already employed in classical mechanics; the "new" predicate is "being a molecule." The propositions which extend the meaning of the "old" predicates by making the molecules physical objects are, for instance: "The size of a molecule is so small that it can be disregarded," "The collisions of molecules are perfectly elastic," "The molecules are in perpetual and disorderly motion." These conceptually analytic propositions extend the meanings of the "old" predicates, "motion," "elastic," "size," etc. Other implicit conceptually analytic propositions restrict the meaning of "liquid," "solid," "hot," "cold," etc. Analytic propositions which relate "old" predicates to "new" ones are, e.g., "A gas is made up of molecules, all identical if the gas is pure or compound, different if the gas is a mixture." The characteristic synthetic proposition is the formula equating the temperature of the gas with the average kinetic energy of the molecules making up the gas. This proposition is not a logical consequence of the above mentioned propositions which resemble, instead, meaning-postulates. However, this formula is not an empirical proposition. There is no way in which one can verify, or falsify, by experience that the temperature of a gas is identical with an average of kinetic energy. This equation is an *a priori* proposition. Scientists have, of course, recognized this as is evidenced by their insistence that the formula *defines* "temperature" in the theory. This synthetic *a priori* proposition distinguishes this molecular theory from its possible alternatives, which have the same set of conceptually analytic propositions.

I claim that knowledge of one's own pains is like observational knowledge, while knowledge of others' pains is theoretical knowledge built upon this observational knowledge. Hence, I must set forth at least some of the conceptually analytic propositions governing the predicates "my-pain," "your-pain," and "his-pain," as well as the synthetic *a priori* propositions characteristic of this theoretical knowledge of other minds.

3. The Dialectic of Self-Consciousness

Section 8. THE GENERAL CHARACTER OF THE THEORY. These are the data for which we seek a rationale: we do not really have knowledge that there are selves different from oneself or that there are experiences different from one's own; nevertheless we firmly believe that there are other minds; the relationships between consciousness and behavior are purely contingent but there seems to be an *a priori* connection between the consciousness of other selves and consciousness of bodily behavior; however, the connection is not necessary but only probable.

It is well to repeat that the keystone of the underlying

rationale is the thesis that knowledge of self is like observational knowledge while the "knowledge" of others is like theoretical knowledge, which is knowledge in an extended sense. However, it is only a contingent fact that scientific theories are historical cumulative creations of the human mind. It is not conceptually impossible for a human being to be born with a complete battery of concepts, including the most sophisticated scientific theories. The logical or meaning connections among concepts are exactly the same, whether one learns his concepts experientially or by some other causal mechanism, or possesses them innately. Nevertheless, with a bow to empirical fact, and with an eye on Malcolm's premise (4), I will assume that one acquires one's concepts piecemeal. Thus, to accept a scientific theory is to undergo a conceptual revolution. If a being starts with knowledge of his own experiences and arrives at "knowledge" of experiences which are not his, he must undergo a fundamental conceptual adjustment, a change in his view of the world. Thus, we can formulate our philosophical view by discussing the "logical" structure of his conceptual framework, at each stage in the growth of his consciousness. This is precisely what I propose to do. I will consider the intellectual career of a being I will call *Privatus*. Privatus' history is simply the conceptually possible biography of any one of us.

However, unlike Privatus, we have learned from our elders the perfected conceptual framework, with the theory of other minds already embedded in it. We have learned from the very beginning to perform the moves in the observational as well as the theoretical subframework. Thus, we have discovered the *other* as early as the physical objects of our world. We have not lived through the conceptual revolution. But the conceptual framework we learned still has the scars of its struggles to produce such a rich world. Again, these scars may be made more apparent by considering Privatus' biography.

Each conceptual framework is a system of relationships of implication. I am concerned, however, much more with the meaning changes involved in the transition from one framework to another in which the former is embedded. I will refer to these meaning changes between frameworks as *dialectical*. I will speak of the *dialectic of self-consciousness* in referring to the conceptually possible transition from a pure consciousness of one's own experiences with no idea of others, to the consciousness of one's own experiences as contrasted with the experiences of others.

Section 9. ANALYSIS OF THE CONCEPTS OF EXPERIENCES. In this section I will discuss Privatus' conceptually possible development from concepts which apply to only himself to concepts which allow him to "transfer" the ideas of those things to "objects outside himself." In the next section I will discuss his coming upon the concept of other persons.

The crucial features of the concepts of the phenomenal properties of experiences is their disjunctive recursive structure. For instance, the concept of *pain* is constituted by three rules which can schematically be formulated as follows: (R1) Pain is this, that, that, . . . (ostensive rule); (R2) Pain is what exists when the honest statement is made that there is a pain which is apprehended directly; (R3) Pain is what exists as the cause (or causal factor) of behavior of sort . . . in circumstances . . . when there is no honest statement disrupting that course (or causal factor) as a pain. Clearly, (R1) entails neither (R2) nor (R3); on the other hand, (R2) and (R3) need (R1) as the nonrecursive step that breaks their circularity. (R1) by itself constitutes a subconcept of pain, the first person subconcept. The philosophical theory we endorse is simply the view that (R2) and (R3) are the schemata of the analytic propositions that in the "scientific" theory of other minds extend the "old" meaning of "pain" given by (R1). We proceed now to describe this in some detail.

For the present I will not challenge the dogma that it is conceptually impossible to think without possessing a language. I will assume that Privatus slowly develops a language to match the increasing complexity of his thoughts, a language to think about the physical objects of his environment as well as about his own experiences and states of consciousness. His concepts of the phenomenal properties of his experiences are not quite the same as ours, if we accept Malcolm's claim that one cannot learn fully what pain (tickling, etc.) is from the pains (ticklings, etc.) one feels. For simplicity, I will accept this contention. Thus, at this stage Privatus' concepts of pain, tickling, etc. are all first person. However, since Privatus has no idea of other persons (or selves), these are not exactly first person concepts; they are really impersonal. To avoid confusion, let us express his impersonal concepts with an extra "l" (to remind us of fee*l*ing). Thus, Privatus has the concepts of *plain, tlickling,* etc. These are purely ostensive concepts of the properties he directly apprehends in his pains, ticklings, etc. If he feels no pain or tickling (as we say), there is no plain or tlickling. And all his thoughts and statements about his own experiences or body are impersonal; they can be of forms like: "This leg (pointing to one of his legs, as *we* would say) has plains, but that leg (pointing or looking to a leg which is not his) never has a plain or tlickling"; "All pains and tlicklings and litchings (his itchings, as *we* would say) exist only in this object (his body)."

Gradually Privatus accumulates generalizations, correlations of the properties of physical objects, correlations between properties of physical objects and the properties which exist in that very peculiar body (which *we* call his body). He frames hypotheses and even scientific theories to explain these phenomena. He develops a scientific theory to explain the behavior of what we call animals: when an object behaves in certain specified ways, there is an entity inside the object called *prain.* For instance, Privatus sees a dog with a wounded paw suck his wound and moan, and immediately infers that there probably is a prain in that wound. That is, prains are theoretical entities, not physical objects, standing in causal relations to certain behavior, and resembling plains. It is conceptually analytic of prains that they are not directly apprehensible by Privatus but that they are inferrable with high probability. Since at this stage Privatus has no idea of his body as such, except as the very peculiar locus of plains, tlicklings, etc., he can also infer that this body has a prain. When he perceives the body reacting appropriately, he concludes that this body has both a plain and a prain. (This is intended as a paradigm description, applicable to all the phenomenal characteristics of experience.)

Soon Privatus develops the concept of *thlought* (i.e., the impersonal protoconcept of his-own-thoughts). At this stage Privatus still lacks the concept of self, so that even if he were surrounded by beings who spoke only about the external world, he would be unable to distinguish his thoughts or statements from the statements of his neighbors. If Privatus states, "It is raining," and another man, Secundus, asserts, "It is hailing," Privatus' comprehension of both statements will be essentially of the same impersonal form:

(a) There is a thlought that it is raining, and the utterance "It is raining" issued from this body (his own); and

(b) There is a thlought that it is hailing, and the utterance "It is hailing" issued from that body (Secundus').

Statement (a) may include conjuncts describing (his) bodily sensations connected with an act of uttering, but this is the only way in which Privatus can be aware of the difference between these first and second person thoughts, at this stage.

If Secundus' consciousness has been developing along similar lines, he, too, has got the corresponding subconcepts of pain. We may, for simplicity and without loss of generality, suppose that Secundus uses the same words as Privatus. Thus, Secundus' utterances of "prain" are on a par with Privatus' utterances of it. But Secundus cannot use the word "plain" to refer to his own pains, i.e., to the pains he feels *qua* felt by him. (I am grateful to A. J. Ayer for having pointed this out during the discussion.) Suppose, then, that he uses the word "splain." Since at this stage Privatus does not have the concept of self, he cannot attribute statements to Secundus, nor can he attribute pains to him on the mere ground that Secundus has asserted that he has them. Thus, an assertion by Secundus that some prain exists, say, in Tertius, appears in Privatus' consciousness as the content "There is a thlought that body X (Tertius' body) has a prain, and the noises 'There is a prain in body X' issued from body S (Secundus')." In cases like this, Privatus' contents of consciousness often includes the thlought "Body X is in conditions C, and there is a prain in body X." That is, there occurs in Privatus' consciousness a verification of the thlought which is (in our terminology) Privatus' apprehension of Secundus' statement. On the other hand, when Secundus utters out loud the statement that he has a splain, and Privatus overhears it, the contents of his consciousness do not allow for a verification. They can only be of a form like "There is a thlought that there is a splain in body S, whatever that is, and the noises 'There is a splain here' issued from body S." These thloughts perplex Privatus. And if he never had found a way of pinpointing splains, he would have never developed a multipersonal concept of pain. But slowly Secundus' utterances cause in Privatus' consciousness the appearance of thloughts that formulate properties of splains, e.g., location in space or in Secundus' body, intensity, and causal properties, so that their similarity to plains is established. Privatus accepts the existence of splains, and t-plains (namely, Tertius' own plains as described by him), and other x-plains (for other persons x).

These have many properties in common and differ essentially in that they are located only in certain bodies or spaces surrounding certain bodies. Thus, Privatus introduces a new type of theoretical entity: *peains,* which are characterized by having as part of their evidential "observational" basis a host of thloughts systematically caused by sentences uttered by bodies other than Privatus'. Again, the evidence does not conceptually, let alone logically, imply that there must be peains; but Privatus accepts, in a *theoretical decision,* that peains are probable in those conditions, and, indeed, as more and more probable the more his predictions come true and the more he systematizes his experiences with the help of the hypothesis that they exist.

Naturally, in many cases Privatus thinks that Secundus, or Tertius, has both prains and peains. Occasionally Privatus is also in the very peculiar position of saying that in a certain body (namely, his body, as *we* would say) there is a plain, a prain, and peain.

Privatus' world is now too rich, but he can trim his ontology with Occam's razor. His scientific theory then will include the following synthetic *a priori* propositions:

(P1) If X is a plain and Y is a prain, both at place and time *pt,* then $X = Y$:

(P2) If X is a prain and Y is a peain, both at place and time *pt,* then $X = Y$.

Privatus has, thus, achieved a reduction of particulars in his ontology, but not of properties. There are still cases in which a *prain* and not a *plain* or *peain* exists, for instance, when a dog behaves as if in pain (as *we* say). But Privatus is by now ready to pluck out some properties from his ontology. He introduces the concept of pain, which is to subsume his proto-concepts of plain, prain and peain:

X is a *pain* at place and time pt = Def. (1) X is a plain at pt; or (2) X is a prain at pt, or (3) X is a peain at pt.

At this stage Privatus simply drops his protowords, and speaks of pains. His talk of pains is indistinguishable from ours, except that he still has to form the concept of self and with it the distinction between first, second and third persons. So far, this story suffices to show how Privatus, with an ability to formulate scientific theories, can go successfully from ostensive characterizations of his own pains to a concept of pain which applies to pains he does not feel. Of course, my argument will break into pieces if it is shown by Malcolm or others that it is conceptually inconsistent for the speaker of a private language to frame scientific theories. Meanwhile, we can learn a lot about the *logic* of pain (as well as of the logic of experiences in general) by this consideration of a consciousness which stepwise reaches the conception of a community of persons.

The point is that our ordinary concept of pain has the disjunctive, recursive structure constituted by the above rules (R1), (R2), and (R3). These schematic rules, when filled out, provide only sufficient conditions for saying that a pain of some sort exists; they do *not* guarantee that in each case exactly the same property is called "pain." That we may be correctly and honestly using the same word "pain" for different qualities, is simply a conceptually necessary proposition about our concept of pain. Its explanation lies in that the basic layer of the concept is ostensive and the other layers are built upon it like parts of a scientific theory. The "old" predicate "pain," introduced by rule R1, changes meaning when the conceptually necessary proposition is introduced that pains are the unexperienceable entities which cause such and such behavior. A further change is registered by rule R3, with the change from peain to pain. The fundamental synthetic *a priori* proposition is that ostensive and theoretical pains possess exactly the same characteristics or properties; or, if it is preferred, that this identity between ostensive and theoretical pains is "defined" in the theory, just as the identity between temperature and average molecular kinetic energy is "defined" in the kinetic theory. Better perhaps, both identities are simply pious metaphysical postulates or conjectures, characteristic of scientific theorizing.

Section 10. THE CONCEPT OF SELF. Privatus does not have to acquire the idea of an unfelt pain (i.e., his concepts of prain and peain) before he acquires some idea of himself as a distinct being. Thus, the development to be discussed in this section is, in its beginning, somewhat independent of the development discussed in section 9. For simplicity of exposition, however, I will begin at the stage where Privatus has the concepts of plain, tlickling, etc., prain, trickling, etc., peain, teickling, etc., as well as the concept of thlought.

All that Privatus needs to get a crude idea of himself is simply to view all the *l*-particulars (i.e., all the plains, tlicklings, thloughts, etc.) as constituents of a "larger" particular he might call *"the slelf."* In principle, this peculiar particular would be extended throughout the whole universe, both in space and time, although a discontinuous particular, both in time and in space. The unity the slelf has (in Privatus' consciousness) is simply the unity of belonging to a system of items in the world, omnipresent and without physical or material particulars. But the unity of the slelf is arbitrary. With equal consistency, the unconscious powers of theorizing and concept formation that determine the contents of Privatus' consciousness might very well have determined that he would have developed the idea of quite a different particular. Privatus' mental "nature" could, in principle, have been such that he might conceive of particulars made up of both plains and puddles of water or of both tlicklings and wisps of smoke, rather than of plains and tlicklings and thloughts, in the way both he and *we* are prone to do.

However, the main point is that, armed with the concept of "the slelf," Privatus is able to modify his view of the world. Now all the *l*-particulars (his own experiences looked upon as impersonal objects by him) are no longer the independent entities they were; they become, so to speak, adjectival to the self. "There is a plain here" becomes "The slelf feels a plain here." The new terminological alternative is redundant, but it is not superfluous. It introduces an important change in Privatus' view of the world.

Privatus is still unaware of himself as a person. His body is simply a very peculiar physical object, the locus of particulars which constitute the slelf.

Let us suppose that Privatus thinks and speaks of *"The Body,"* referring to the peculiar body or set of bodies in which plains, tlicklings, etc. occur. The connection between The Body and the slelf is purely contingent. But when Privatus identifies the plains with the prains existing in The Body, he is moved to draw a tighter causal connection between the slelf and The Body. He may even build this causal connection into his idea of *the I,* the composite particular constituting the slelf together with those *r*-particulars (prains, tricklings, etc.) and *e*-particulars (peains, teicklings, etc.) which exist in or on The Body. This is not Privatus' full idea of himself as a self, since "the I" is still not the first person pronoun with its rich contrast to second and third person expressions. Furthermore, that there is a conceptually analytic connection between the I and the Body does not alter the contingency of the relationship between experiences and The Body's behavior.

Independent of his idea of the I, Privatus is in a position to frame the concept of *throught.* Suppose that Secundus thinks aloud and that Privatus hears the noises and has thoughts on hearing them. Suppose that he is aware of his thoughts. And suppose further that his thoughts on hearing the words (as is normally the case with Earthians) coincide with his hearing of the words so that there is no uttering involved. In situations such as this Privatus is aware of a thlought, of an utterance issuing from Secundus' body and of no utterance issuing from The Body, as well as of certain other features of the situation, which *we* may want to describe in the form "Secundus asserting such-and-such." To account for the constancy of these features (doubtless, of a set with a great disjunction of features) Privatus develops a scientific theory. According to it, there are certain entities called throughts, analogous to events, in general, and, in particular, to thloughts, but which are never directly present in the realm of experienceable objects like plains, perceptible things, etc. Throughts, according to the theory, are essential causal factors of the events of issuance of noises from material objects similar to The Body, whenever such noises are accompanied by thloughts. Again, there is no entailment going from issuances of noises to throughts, or vice versa, but only a postulated causal link. The phenomena of noises and thloughts, etc. are, by the very construction of the theory, evidence for the probability of the existence of throughts.

The concept of *throught* is thus developed in a way that parallels the formation of the concept of prain.

The crucial point, however, of Privatus' biography is that he conceive of the I as the totality of all *l*-particulars together with the *r*- and *e*-particulars (if any) causally related to events in The Body. From this it is a simple transition to the conception of other particulars which are the totality of all the *r*- and *e*-particulars (if any) introduced to explain, causally, certain behavioral events observed in another body. Let us call this the concept of *shelf*.

But either before or after *shelf* is introduced, Privatus identifies thloughts with the throught reactions of The Body. At any rate, after the theoretical framework of shelves is introduced, the body-related theoughts and the throughts are identified. And all of them are conceived of as *thoughts*. Thus, the concept of thought replaces the protoconcepts of thlought, throught, and theought, in essentially the same way (see section 9) the concept of pain (tickling, itching, etc.) replaces (because it is the fusion of) the protoconcepts of plain (tlicking, etc.), prain (trickling, etc.), and peain (teickling, etc.).

The fantasy of Privatus' biography is a device to bring out into the open the recursive character of the concept of thought and how it involves certain connections. Thoughts are ostensively characterized as this or that which one can apprehend directly, but this characterization is only sufficient, not necessary. Other sufficient characterizations of thoughts are: events of a peculiar kind, which are probable causes of action; and events which are causes of acts of speech. But, again as in the case of pain, these characterizations of thoughts *assume,* without proof, that ostensive and inferred thoughts exemplify the same property. This assumption is simply an unverifiable assumption, whose only justification lies in the way it (i) organizes and explains perceptible behavior, and (ii) allows further predictions and explanations by drawing consequences from the analogy with one's own thoughts. But, clearly, successful predictions do not guarantee that the assumptions are true.

Now Privatus' consciousness is ready for the ultimate stage in the knowledge of other minds: communication and the distinction between first and second persons. Earlier, even his own experiences and thoughts were, for Privatus, a sort of third person knowledge. There was no real communication. For this, it is necessary that Privatus become aware of the possibility of recursive chains of thought-causation: that he can do something to cause a thought which is not his and that this thought can, in turn, arouse a thlought and so continue reciprocally. Such recursive chains of thought-causation require the further enrichment of the idea of selves: they must be agents, or bundles of powers (dispositions and abilities), not merely collections of r- and e-particulars, or even l-particulars.

From the concept of shelf to the concept of *self* there is a simple transition. The shelves are entities connected with bodies (or systems of bodies) similar to The Body. Thus, when the noises and written tracks that issue from a certain body cause thloughts to exist they may be easily conceived by Privatus to be actions of the shelf connected with the body in question. Thus, Privatus may easily come to think that the thlought-causing noises and marks made by other bodies may also be purposeful, made because the shelves connected with the bodies want to accomplish something with those noises or marks. And in this way Privatus comes to ascribe to shelves the causal powers necessary for communication. And the shelves endowed with these powers he comes to call *selves*. These are the shelves that can engage in conversation, i.e., in recursive thought-causation.

To conclude these hints at the conceptually possible history of Privatus' consciousness, I want to soften the apparent emphasis on the causal associations between bodies and experiences. I allowed Privatus' view of the world to develop along the lines that experiences and thoughts are connected with events in a body (or system of bodies). This was to accord with empirical fact. But this sort of development is no more necessary than the historical, cumulative development of concepts is necessary. In fact, Privatus could have framed the idea of throughts to explain, scientifically, the thlought-causing noises or marks originating at some place in space, which was otherwise empty. He could have framed the concept of peain (teikling, etc.) in connection with throughts which claimed that there were events like plains, and he could have developed the idea of selves by grouping together throughts and other r-particulars with some sort of self-reference. This would allow the selves to avoid being permanently fixed at a given position in space. In sum, although I believe that communication would be impossible without selves (or minds) having a power to cause physical events that in turn cause thoughts in other selves, I do not think we are committed to the view that there is a necessary connection between thoughts and events occurring in a body. Of course, to say this is not to say (let alone show) that it is not one and the same entity which *in fact* has the property of being both a thought (pain, tickling, feeling of discomfort, sensation of red, etc.) and a certain specifiable state of a body or a brain. That such is the case may very well be another synthetic *a priori* proposition constituting a new and even more powerful scientific theory.

COMMENTS

Leonard Linsky

University of Illinois

PROFESSOR CASTAÑEDA discusses a great number of issues in his paper. I shall confine my comments to a very small part of what he has to say. Moreover, I shall confine my remarks to the negative side of Castañeda's paper, i.e., the part in which he prepares the way for his own account by a series of criticisms of view held by other philosophers.

It has been said that the last fifteen years have witnessed a revolution in philosophy. From this point of view, Professor Castañeda is a counterrevolutionary, and in many respects even a reactionary. I should myself be willing to defend many of the accomplishments of the revolution, if only from the point of view of one who is himself a revisionist.

1

First I want to look at what Castañeda has to say about one of the premises which he finds in an argument of Norman Malcolm's. It is the argument which he calls "Wittgenstein's external attack on private language." I do not wish to argue that Malcolm's argument is valid. I do not think that it is valid or even fully intelligible, but Castañeda's criticisms of it raise some interesting issues, and are themselves rather puzzling.

The third premise of Malcolm's argument, according to Castañeda, is this, "All the pains I feel have, necessarily, the property of existing only when I feel them." Castañeda objects to this. He says that this premise is not "conceptually analytic":

> My concept of pain allows for the admittedly fantastic conceptual possibility that pains may be shared. . . . As I see it, the universe might have been such that all muscular pains could be made to move to one's toes or fingers by pressing with one's thumb, and that one could transfer a finger pain to another person by pressing the finger on the other's body.

Now, suppose I have a stomach-ache. Is it possible, as Castañeda seems to imply, that this stomach-ache could be made to move to my thumb by pressing on my thumb? Then I would have a stomach-ache in my thumb. That really would be, to use Castañeda's phrase, "quite fantastic." Can I have a headache in my tooth? If pains are transferable, as Castañeda says, how does he avoid committing himself to these absurdities? Does Castañeda think that it is "conceptually possible," that a woman might transfer her labor pains to my forehead by pressing hard on my brow? (Is this what Zeus felt when Athena sprang full-grown from his brow?)

But how is this whole business about transferring pains relevant to Malcolm's third premise? Apparently Castañeda is trying to give some sense to the notion that someone else might feel my pains. If someone else could feel my pains then my pains might have the "property" of "existing" even when I do not feel them. But does this bit of science fiction about transferring pains help at all to show this? After all, I can give someone a pain if I press on some part of his body, especially if I press hard and on a tender part, like his eyeball. Still, if I do this I am certainly not giving him my pain nor is he feeling my pain. Suppose the pain in my eye stopped when I pressed on his eye. If this sort of thing happened often we might say that we had given another person our pain. But we might say instead that pressing on his eyeball had made the pain in my eye disappear. But isn't it bad practice in philosophy to construct these science fiction cases and then try to figure out what we would say if confronted with them? In the cases we are considering, wouldn't it perhaps depend on unforeseen advances in physiology as to what we would say?

It would perhaps be useful to go into this matter of identifying sensations, especially pains. One thing that comes out is that it makes perfectly clear sense for one to say, e.g., "I'm now having the same pains in my legs which you used to have in your legs." One does not need to resort to Castañeda's fantasies in order to establish this. It is perfectly obvious, and we all know what cases of this sort are like. Though I can give you my stomach-ache or my itch, I can't give you the pain in my stomach or the pain in my head. But you and I can have the same headache, and you can have the same pains in your stomach that I have in mine. (A comparison will reveal this.)

I might say, "My pains and yours are identical." I might say, "Your cup and mine are identical." That does not mean that you and I share one cup between us. I might have your cup in my pocket; but even if my pain and your pain are identical, I could not have your pain in my stomach. If you ask me whether the cup which is now on my table is the same cup as was there yesterday, I might reply, "No, it is not the same cup but it is identical with it." But if I ask you whether the pain you now feel in your head is the same pain you felt last week, you could not reply, "No, it is not the same pain, but it is identical with it." What would this difference be? With pains, unlike cups, there is no difference between "the same," and "identical." There is no difference between my having the same pains I used to have and my having pains just like the ones I used to have. But there is a difference between my having shoes just like the ones I used to have, and my having the same shoes I used to have. None of these considerations go to show that I can have pains which I do not feel, or that I can feel your pains. On at least one very natural interpretation of what Malcolm is saying, this is all he wished to maintain in what Castañeda calls his third premise. Why quarrel with these truisms?

2

Castañeda rests a great deal of weight on the notion of a conceptually necessary proposition. But he really does not give us much help toward understanding what sort of a beast this is. The sailing is smooth enough until we get to the main item in his definition, category (d). Castañeda himself says that the category is "'obscure." One can certainly agree with him on that. "But," he says, hopefully, "the following examples may help." Presumably Castañeda thinks that the examples which follow have something in common by which they are all conceptually analytic. Presumably he thinks that by studying the examples we should be able to get the idea of what this is and thus get the idea of what conceptual analyticity is. But I cannot. One source of difficulty is that some of the propositions offered do not even seem to be true on any natural interpretation of what they say. Consider the first of them. "Everything red is colored." The juice of a cherry is red. Would anyone say that the juice of a cherry was colored? Margarine is colored, but butter is not. A banana isn't colored yellow unless it is in a coloring book or made of wax. The Soviet flag is red, the Mediterranean Sea is blue, the lily of Florence is red, and the sky is blue. Would anyone say that any of these were colored?

Another of Castañeda's examples of a conceptually analytic proposition which gives me trouble is this, "Everything colored is extended." We have just been told that everything red is colored; so my arm, if red, is colored. Is it a conceptual necessity then, that my arm is extended? And what about the sky? It is blue, so according to Castañeda it is colored and *a fortiori,* extended. Is the Mediterranean extended? It is blue.

I suppose it will be said that "extended" just means something like "occupies space." I think it perfectly fair to ask in reply why that was not said if that was what was meant. But in any case this will not help very much, for the same kind of difficulties will now arise over "occupies space." Smoke, for example, is white, and therefore according to Castañeda, colored. But is smoke extended? Does it occupy space? Can one plausibly maintain that to say that a rainbow is extended means that it occupies space? It is just plain nonsense to say that a rainbow is extended.

There are other locutions in Castañeda's examples which muddy the waters. Would anything ever be called an "instance of red," for instance? The locution "an instance of red" simply does not exist. Again, do we ever judge, "while attending to our experiences," that we are in pain? Do we "judge" we are in pain at all?

But the tides of language rise even higher here. Consider this example of a conceptually analytic proposition: "If X judges at t that he judges that p, then at t X judges that p." Have you ever judged that you were judging that something was the case? Is this even possible? With example like these, we get nowhere toward explaining what it is for a proposition to "express a connection constitutive of the connected concepts."

Now I do not mean to imply that all of Castañeda's examples are in some way or other obscure or problematic. One could hardly ask for anything clearer than two of them. "If X is larger than Y, Y is not larger than X." "If X is heavier than Y and Y is heavier than Z, X is heavier than Z." These are utterly clear. Well, certainly that shouldn't count against their being conceptually analytic. The problem is to try to find something which all of the examples have in common. I cannot see what Castañeda's examples have in common, and I cannot get the idea of what a conceptually analytic proposition is by examining them. These are not carping criticisms. Over and over Castañeda appeals to what he considers to be conceptually necessary propositions in order to make his arguments go through. But he leans, I fear, on a very weak reed.

In closing this section of my remarks I want to say something about one proposition which Castañeda calls conceptually analytic and which he works rather hard. "X knows that p, conceptually implies that p is true, and X believes that p and X has conclusive reasons for p." Suppose a student asks me to raise a grade on an examination in order to keep him in good standing with his fraternity. I say, "You know that I can't just raise a grade in order to keep you in good standing with a fraternity." It is absurd to claim that when I say this I am implying he believes what I say. It is equally absurd to suggest that I imply that he has "conclusive reasons" for the proposition, "I can't just raise a grade. . . ." Is this the sort of thing one *could* have "conclusive reasons" for? Do *I* imply that *I* have these reasons when I say, "I know you can't just raise a grade . . . ?" Far from its being the case that "I know that p" implies that "I believe that p," it seems to me that these two are actually imcompatible with each other. After all, we do say, "I don't *believe* p, I *know* p."

3

Castañeda holds the view that "experiences are private objects." By way of giving an explanation of these dark words he says:

> . . . they are private in the sense that, *if* one is to learn one's concepts from experience one cannot learn in full each concept of a phenomenal property of experiences unless one experiences instances of these properties.

I suppose that the kind of view which Castañeda is here advocating is that, e.g., a man born blind could never fully acquire color concepts. The reasons which are usually given are these: some terms can only be defined ostensively. If a man does not know what "red" means, no amount of talk will get him to understand that word. One will simply have to resort to examples. It is sometimes then said that the meaning of color words has to be learned through acquaintance with their instances.

Are these claims true? As soon as one looks at them a little closer one sees that it is very difficult indeed even to make out what exactly the claims are. Does a man born blind have color concepts? Does he have the concept of red? What exactly is at issue when we ask these questions? First of all they assume that at least some people *do* have the concept of red; but it is not at all clear to me that there even is such a thing. Philosophers have come to use this word "concept" very loosely. Would we ever normally talk about the concept of red? If your conception of democracy, or education, or philosophy, is different from mine, I can understand that. But what am I to consider in considering whether or not we have the same concept of red (or pain for that matter)?

Again, what is it for one to *have* the concept red (fully or at all)? I am not at all clear about these matters, consequently I find it difficult to consider whether the blind man has the concept of red or whether he has the *same* concept I have.

One thing seems clear to me and that is that the blind man (*some* blind men) can use color words perfectly correctly. He can tell you that the flag is red, white and blue. In fact he can tell you anything about colors I can, so why shouldn't that count for his having the concept of color? What the blind man cannot do is to identify something as red. But neither can I if my eyes are closed. Is this any reason for saying that he does not know what red is? It is perhaps worth remarking that according to the dictionary the word "concept" as used in these examples is used in a sense proprietary to logicians and philosophers.

Sometimes the discussion of these matters is carried out in terms of "meaning" rather than "concepts." Then the question becomes, "Does the man who is blind from birth know the meaning of the word 'red'?". As soon as one thinks about the matter, it is apparent that one cannot sensibly ask for the meaning of just any word. What does "of" mean, or "and" or "to"? It seems to me that philosophers often talk about the meaning of words which cannot in any clear sense even be said to have a meaning. Is the question, "What is the meaning of the word 'pain'?" really sensible? Do you think that you know the meaning of the word "red"? Another thing which is often enough said here is that these words cannot be defined. But they can be defined and are defined in my dictionary. It seems to me that the questions which can be asked here are these: "What is heliotrope?" or "What is pain?" (Assume that the latter question appears as a chapter heading in a book on physiology.) In answer to the former question one might supply a definition, e.g., "The shade of purple of flowers of the genus *Heliotropium.*" Or one might produce an example. (Shouldn't this dispose of the queer dogma that color words can only be defined "ostensively"?)

I cannot identify a color as "mauve" when I see it. Do I have the concept "mauve"? Do I know what the word "mauve" means? I have no idea what to say here except that these are queer questions. That explains my embarrassment with them.

4

In this section I shall try to come to grips with something at the center of Castañeda's way of looking at his problems. He holds that we have certain and incorrigible knowledge of our own states of mind and feelings but not those of others. Castañeda is fully aware that his account of these matters is at variance with our ordinary ways of speaking. But he thinks that these considerations about ordinary talk do not really support the views often taken by the philosophers whom he criticizes. These views are radically opposed to his own. But I find his way of dealing with some of these arguments unconvincing.

Castañeda is undisturbed by considerations such as these: We do not ordinarily say, e.g., "I know that I am in excruciating pain." (Although it is possible to imagine circumstances in which one might say this; the words might be ironical.) On the other hand we might say of a third person, "I know that he is in excruciating pain." (And here one does not need to imagine anything special about the circumstances which make this remark intelligible.)

These considerations certainly seem to be incompatible with Castañeda's views. Remember that Castañeda claims to be defending the plain man's ideas about these things. How does he explain the fact that the plain man often enough claims (and at times with considerable emphasis) to *know* what others think, believe, and feel? On Castañeda's view we can never know, but are confined to making inferences about these things. Well then, why, if we believe what Castañeda says we believe, do we so commonly say what we do not believe?

He does offer an explanation why I would not ask a person, "How do you know that you are in excruciating pain?".

> Since one cannot be mistaken about one's pains, the senselessness of the question lies in asking for an answer the respondent knows is already known. The only answer to, "How do you know?" is, "By having the pain" or "By attending to my feelings."

According to this view, the answer to the question, "How do you know that you are in excruciating pain?" is, "I know by having the pain" or "I know by attending to my pain." But would we ever say these things? It is strange to suggest that the obvious answer to an obvious question should be an utterance which a speaker of our language would never produce. We would not say either, "I know I have pains by having them" or, "I know I have pains by attending to them."

Consider the principle upon which Castañeda rests his

explanation. Suppose he is right in saying that if I ask a person how he knows that he has a headache, I am asking him a question to which I already know the answer and to which he knows that I already know the answer. Will that explain what Castañeda acknowledges to be the senselessness of the question? Not at all. Often on examinations I ask students questions to which I know the answers. And the student knows that I know the answers to these questions. I ask them because what I do not know is whether *they* know the answers. But does that make my question senseless? Not at all. I may even ask them questions to which I know that they know the answers, e.g., in order to be able to show others they know the answers. But that does not make my question senseless.

Castañeda thinks that the words, "By having the pain," "By attending to my feelings" constitute perfectly satisfactory answers to the question, "How do you know that you are in pain?" These are, he says, "ways of knowing" and if one were making an "'inventory of the ways of knowing" one would list them. The difficulty here is that the very idea of an "inventory of the ways of knowing" is queer. It is like making an inventory of the kinds of things. What counts as a kind? Again, do we ever actually talk about "ways of knowing"? We do, of course, talk about ways of finding out, ways of telling, ways of determining, etc.; but not "ways of knowing." We say, "There is no way of knowing," but not, "There are no ways of knowing." And in contradicting the former we would say, "There is a way of finding out (or telling)" not, "There is a way of knowing." But would it make sense at all to try to make an inventory of ways of finding out? Would looking through keyholes be on the list, along with reading the newspaper? The earlier question which needs to be answered here is, "What kind of thing are you interested in finding out about?"

Let us look again at the answers proposed to the question, "How do you know that you are in pain?" Surely it is obvious that this question is just plain silly, and so are the answers. Take the answer, "By attending to my feelings." Is Castañeda suggesting that this is one way of finding out among others? Might I also have found out by listening to the news? Does he imagine me attending to my feelings, (I suppose there *is* such a thing) and suddenly discovering with amazement that they are my own feelings rather than yours, as I might, by examining "your" book, suddenly discover that it was the one stolen from me?

REJOINDER
Hector-Neri Castañeda

1. Linsky is correct in asserting that the views I am defending here make me a sort of "reactionary." This does not disturb me. My devotion to truth is stronger than my desire for popularity. I am comforted by the fact that Linsky had no additional objection to offer to those views, even if he finds some of my criticisms of opposing views objectionable.

2. Linsky is correct in saying that the transferability of pains need not be mentioned in order to establish that two persons can have the same numerical pain. It has been, however, a persuasive device for many people with whom I have discussed the matter. But Linsky's alleged counterexamples to the transferability of pains involve a confusion. He challenges: "Then I would have a stomach-ache in my thumb." But surely nowhere in my paper did I suggest that the transferability of a pain requires the transferability of the bodily parts in which it exists. Whether or not you can transfer your stomach, or tooth, to my thumb is beside the point. All I have claimed is that the pain that was in your stomach, or tooth, may *leave* it and go to my thumb.

3. Apparently Linsky and I have a different concept of pain. In his, it is senseless to speak of pains being numerically the same, but in mine it is not senseless (whatever this may be).

4. Linsky is again right in emphasizing that my notion of conceptual necessity is not clear. This is a serious charge, for

which I have no answer. But this charge applies to *all* philosophers. And I at least can claim that my definition, or definition-schema, of "conceptually necessary propositions" demarks the areas of clarity, from the crucial area (d), which is unclear. I also grant that my ten examples are not sufficient for the apprehension of a common feature, although some philosophers find the examples useful as a guide. This is, of course, a personal matter, and Linsky has the right to say he gets nothing from them.

5. It is not true that "some of the propositions offered do not even seem to be true on *any* natural interpretation" (my italics). Linsky himself has provided a perfectly natural interpretation for "Everything colored is extended." At any rate, simply because the "natural" interpretations Linsky chose to discuss are false, it certainly does not follow that *no* natural and true interpretation exists. As a matter of fact, the sentences, "Everything red is colored" and, "Everything colored is extended" do have the natural interpretations discussed *ad nauseam* in the philosophical journals during the last thirty years, precisely in discussions of analyticity and necessity.

6. Linsky offers counterexamples to the claim that "X knows that *p*" conceptually implies "X believes that *p*." They miss the target. If Linsky tells the student, "You know that I can't just raise a grade to keep you in good standing with a fraternity" and exclaims, "It is absurd to claim that when I say this I am implying he believes what I say," I do not know exactly what Linsky wants to say to his student but I am sure that if I were to make such a statement, I would imply that he *believes* that the University rules do not allow me to change his grade, and would thereby inform him that I am a rule-biding instructor, which perhaps he did not believe before.

On the same topic Linsky adduces a true fact of ordinary language: that we often use the word "believe" in the sense of "merely believe." I insist that "X knows that p" is incompatible with "X merely believes that p." But here again, Linsky is deliberately forgetting that philosophers have for a long time employed the word "believe" in its generic sense, and not in the sense of "merely believe." I cannot but assume that my readers have some acquaintance with the standard terminologies.

7. Linsky attacks the view that one must learn one's concepts from experience. I agree with everything he says in this connection. He seems to think that he is refuting a claim I made; he is not. The claim I made is a conditional one, and to emphasize this I underlined the word "if." I agree with Linsky: the antecedent of the conditional is obscure, and in my view it is also false.

8. In his final comment Linsky is also right in asserting that people do not ordinarily say that they know that they are in pain. He is also right in noting that I offered an explanation of this fact. But for the life of me I cannot see why he believes that the fact in question refutes my views about pain. Linsky surely knows that the reasons why certain statements are not ordinarily made are of very many different sorts, so that the mere fact that something is not asserted is not a proof that a certain view is mistaken. We must dig into the reasons why it is not said and we must separate the reasons which are based on pervasive, but empirical, facts from those which are based on necessary facts, conceptually or otherwise.

Linsky's only relevant discussion is his attempt to refute my explanation. My explanation was that it is silly to ask a person, "How do you know that you are in pain?" because there is only one way of knowing one is in pain, and whoever knows what pain is knows this and whoever knows that another person knows what pain is knows he knows this. Linsky argues that this explanation won't do because "often on examinations I ask students questions to which I know the answers," etc. Clearly this does not refute my explanation, which has nothing to do with examinations. All that this establishes is that the type of explanation I gave for the case of pains does not apply to examinations. I never suggested that they would. Indeed, his mention of examinations helps my case. If one were examining a child, or adult, on his grasp of the meaning of the word "pain," or on his concept of pain, one could very well ask him "How do you know that you are in pain?"

Linsky is, of course, right in claiming that ordinary language contains all the philosophical clues. But he errs by excluding the ordinary language that philosophers employ in their professional pursuits. And he errs, further, in his apparent belief that ordinary language presents those clues naked, so that the philosophical task consists of merely listing them. Ordinary language has all the philosophical clues, but they are mixed with empirical beliefs and superstitions, and they must be mined, and sometimes subjected to elaborate processes of refinement and distillation. This is my reaction to the so-called ordinary language revolution.

NOTES ON CASTAÑEDA ESSAY

1. I am grateful to Professor J. Findlay for having read the original version and suggested improvements.
2. This clause has been added on a suggestion of my student, George Landrum.
3. For a detailed discussion of the uses of the first-person pronoun, both in *oratio recta* and in *oratio obliqua,* see my "Indicators and Quasi-indicators," *The American Philosophical Quarterly,* IV (April 1967).
4. Here I am adopting an argument of A. J. Ayer's against a similar argument for the sentence "I am dreaming." See his "Professor Malcolm on Dreams," *The Journal of Philosophy,* LVII (1960), 517–535.
5. Rush Rhees, "Can there be a private language?" *Proceedings of the Aristotelian Society,* Supp., XXIV (1954), 77–94.
6. Premise (1) in *"Lenguaje, pensamiento y realidad,"* *Humanitas* (yearly publication of the University of Nuevo Leon, Monterey,

Mexico), III (1962), 199–217; and premise (2) in *La dialectica de la Conciencia de Si Mismo* (Guatemala: University of San Carlos Press, 1960), 64–70; and in "The Private Language Argument" and "Rejoinders" to valuable comments by V. C. Chappell and J. F. Thomson in C. D. Rollins (ed.), *Knowledge and Experience* (Pittsburgh: Univ. of Pittsburgh Press, 1963) 88–132.

7. For a complete characterization of the traditional analogical view see my "Criteria, Analogy, and Knowledge of Other Minds," *The Journal of Philosophy*, LIX (1962), 533–546.

8. I have reached this conclusion after discussing problems in the philosophy of mind with my colleagues: Edmund Gettier, Alvin Plantinga, George Nakhnikian and Robert Sleigh. It is impossible to determine how much I owe them in the reaching of this conclusion. For criticism on some attacks on the analogical view by Strawson and Malcolm, see Alvin Plantinga, "Things and Persons," *The Review of Metaphysics*, XIV (1961), 515–519; for criticism of other arguments by Malcolm see the paper mentioned in footnote 7, and my "The Private Language Argument"; for criticisms of Strawson, Malcolm, Rhees, Heidegger and Sartre, see my *La Dialéctica de la Conciencia de Si Mismo (op. cit.)*. Robert Sleigh has been working on a paper refuting the arguments which purport to show that the inductive arguments for other minds are necessarily weaker than normal inductions.

9. *Op. cit.,* p. 517.

10. Norman Malcolm, "Knowledge of Other Minds," *The Journal of Philosophy*, LV (1958), 969 ff.; *Dreaming* (London: Routledge & Kegan Paul; New York: The Humanities Press, 1959), pp. 10, 15, 23, *et al.;* "Discussion of Wittgenstein's *Philosophical Investigations*," *The Philosophical Review*, LXIII (1954), 542–555. This will be cited as "Disc" followed by page number.

11. L. Wittgenstein, *Philosophical Investigations* (Oxford: Basil Blackwell, Ltd., 1953), I, No. 243.

12. See the papers mentioned in footnote 6.

13. "Disc.," 537 (see footnote 6).

14. *Loc. cit.,* 537.

15. *Ibid.,* 538.

16. In "Knowledge and Certainty," *The Review of Metaphysics,* XVIII (1965), 529–535. For other criticisms of Malcolm's views see other parts of this study.

17. "Disc." 537. I owe to Edmund Gettier the realization that my analysis of our ordinary concept of pain may be viewed as a counterexample to this contention behind Malcolm's argument.

18. I owe this idea essentially to Wilfrid Sellars, for whom all mental concepts regardless of whether they are first person, third person or second person, are like theoretical concepts. For him, I take it,

the whole language of the mind is a theoretical language introduced on the basis of an observational language constituted by the language of bodies, behavior and circumstances. As soon as I read his "Empiricism and the Philosophy of Mind," in H. Feigl and M. Scriven (eds.), *Minnesota Studies in the Philosophy of Science,* Vol. I (Minneapolis: University of Minnesota Press, 1956), 253–329, it dawned on me that the correct way of looking at our concepts of experiences and of states of consciousness is the one that Sellars suggested, but drawing the line between the theoretical and observation-like within the psychological concepts themselves. I think that this adjustment does more justice to the "logical" structure of self-knowledge.

19. See Sellars' "The Language of Theories," in H. Feigl and G. Maxwell (eds.), *Current Issues in the Philosophy of Science* (New York: Holt, Rinehart & Winston, 1961), 57–77. But I stop following Sellars sometime before he claims that "correspondence rules would appear in the material mode as statements to the effect that the objects of the observational framework *do not really exist—there really are no such things.* They envisage the *abandonment* of a sense and its denotation." (p. 76; his italics throughout.)

THE MENTAL LIFE OF SOME MACHINES

Hilary Putnam

Harvard University

(The following paper makes use of the notion of a "Turing Machine," the conception of the English mathematician and logician, A. M. Turing. A Turing Machine is essentially an effective computational *procedure* for problem-solving. However, since a Turing Machine is, in principle, physically realizable, it is commonly spoken of as if it were an unspecified computer, described by a set of rules in its *machine table,* and operating in a finite number of internal configurations or *states* while scanning, erasing, and printing a fixed number of symbols on an infinite tape. For details see Putnam's essay "Minds and Machines," cited in footnote 1—Editor.)

1

IN THIS PAPER I want to discuss the nature of various "mentalistic" notions in terms of a machine analog. In an earlier paper,[1] I tried to show that the conceptual issues surrounding the traditional mind-body problem have nothing to do with the supposedly special character of human subjective experience, but arise for any computing system of a certain kind of richness and complexity, in particular for any computing system able to construct theories concerning its own nature. In that paper I was primarily interested in the issues having to do with mind-body identity. In the present paper the focus will be rather in trying to shed light on the character of such notions as preferring, believing, feeling. I hope to show by considering the use of these words in connection with a machine analog that the traditional alternatives—materialism, dualism, logical behaviorism—are incorrect, even in the case of these machines. My objectives are not merely destructive ones; I hope by indicating what the character of these words is in the case of the machine analog to suggest to some extent what their character is in application to human beings.

One question which I shall not discuss, except for these remarks at the outset, is the question to what extent the application of such terms as "preference" to Turing Machines represents a change or extension of meaning. I shall not discuss this question because, as will become clear, it is not too relevant to my undertaking. Even if the sense in which the Turing Machines I shall describe may be said to "prefer" one thing to another is *very* different in *many* ways from the sense in which a human being is said to prefer one thing to another, this does not run contrary to anything that I claim. What I claim is that seeing why it is that the analogs of materialism, dualism, and logical behaviorism are false in the case of these Turing Machines will enable us to see why the theories are incorrect in the case of human beings, and seeing what these terms might mean in the case of Turing Machines will at least suggest to us important logical features of these terms which have previously been overlooked by philosophers.

In this paper, then, I am going to consider a hypothetical "community" made up of "agents," each of whom is in fact a Turing Machine, or, more precisely, a finite automaton. (Of the many equivalent definitions of "finite automaton," the most useful for present purposes is the one that results if the definition of a Turing Machine is modified by specifying that the tape should be *finite*.) The Turing Machines I want to consider will differ from the abstract Turing Machines considered in logical theory in that we will consider them to be equipped with sense organs by means of which they can scan their environment, and with suitable motor organs which they are capable of controlling. We may think of the sense organs as causing certain "reports" to be printed on the tape of the machine at certain times, and we may think of the machine as being constructed so that when certain "operant" symbols are printed by the machine on its tape, its motor organs execute appropriate actions. This is the natural generalization of a Turing Machine to allow for interaction with an environment.

The fundamental concept we want to discuss will be the concept of *preference*. In order to give this concept formal content with respect to the behavior of these "agents," we will suppose that each of these agents is described by a rational preference function, in the sense of economic theory.* We will suppose that our Turing Machines are sufficiently complex so as to be able to make reasonably good estimates of the probability of various states of affairs. Given the inductive estimates made by a machine, the behavior of the machine will then be completely determined by the fact that the machine is to obey the rule: act so as to maximize the estimated utility.

The reader should note that the term "utility" is completely eliminable here. What we are saying is that there is associated with each machine a certain mathematical function, called a utility function, such that that function together with another function, the machine's "degree of confirmation" function, completely determines the machine's behavior in accordance with a certain rule and certain theorems of the probability calculus.[2] In short, our machines are *rational*

---

* John Von Neumann and Oskar Morgenstern, *A Theory of Games and Economic Behavior* (3rd ed.; Princeton, N.J.: Princeton University Press, 1953) pp. 26 f., 83 *et al.* Von Neumann and Morgenstern think of such a function as an assignment of coordinates (in an n-dimensional space) to objects, the sum of the coordinates being the "value" of the object. Here it will be convenient to think of it as a function assigning a "utility" to "possible worlds" (or "state descriptions" in the sense of Carnap).

agents in the sense in which that term is used in inductive logic and economic theory. If the rational preference functions of these machines resemble the rational preference functions of idealized human beings, and the computing skills of the machines are approximately equal to the computing skills of human beings, then the behavior of these machines will closely resemble the behavior of (idealized) human beings. We can complicate this model by introducing into the behavior of these machines certain irrationalities which resemble the irrationalities in the behavior of actual human beings (e.g., failure of the transitivity of preference), but this will not be attempted here.

What then does "prefer" mean as applied to one of these machines? As a start it simply means that the function which controls the behavior of the machine (more precisely, the function which together with the machine's inductive logic controls the behavior of the machine) assigns a higher weight to the first alternative than to the second. Even at the outset we can see that the relation of preferring to behavior is going to be quite complicated for these machines. For example, if one of these machines prefers A to B, it does not necessarily follow that in any concrete situation it will choose A rather than B. In deciding whether to choose A rather than B, the machine will have to consider what the consequences of its choice are likely to be in the concrete situation, and this may well bring in "values" of the machine other than the preference that the machine assigns to A over B. We might say that if the machine prefers A to B then that means that *ceteris paribus* the machine will choose A over B, and we might despair of ever spelling out in any precise way the *ceteris paribus* clause. In an analogous way, Miss Anscombe[3] has suggested that if someone intends not to have an accident then that means that, *ceteris paribus,* he will choose methods of driving from one place to another that are likely to minimize the chance of having an accident. She has suggested that in this kind of case the *ceteris paribus* clause could not *in principle* be spelled out in detail. On this basis she has gone on to suggest a fundamental difference between what she calls practical reason and scientific reason. This conclusion should be viewed with some suspicion, however. The fact is that she has shown that certain proposed methods of spelling out the *ceteris paribus* clause in question would not work; but these methods would not work in the case of our machines either. It hardly follows that our machines exhibit in their ordinary "behavior" a form of reasoning fundamentally different from scientific reasoning. On the contrary, given a rational preference function, always acting so as to maximize the estimated utility is exhibiting scientific reasoning of a very high order.

Miss Anscombe might reply that actual human beings do not have rational preference functions. However, Von Neumann and Morgenstern have shown, and this is the fundamental result in the area, that any agent whose preferences are consistent always does behave in a way which can be interpreted in terms of at least one rational preference function. Miss Anscombe might reply that actual human beings do not have consistent preferences; but this would be to say that the difference between practical reason and scientific reason is that practical reason is often in fact more or less irrational—that everyone's practical reasoning is irrational in some areas. This is like saying that deductive logic is different in principle from the logic contained in any textbook because everyone's deductive reasoning is bad in some areas. The fact is that Miss Anscombe's remarks on intentions are supposed to apply not only to the intentional behavior of more or less irrational human beings but just as much to the intentional behavior of an ideally rational human being with a rich and complex system of values. I think this is quite clear from reading her whole book. But for such an agent one of her major conclusions is just false: the practical reasoning of such an agent would be, as we have seen, not at all unlike scientific reasoning.*

The point in a nutshell is that practical reasoning *is* fundamentally different from scientific reasoning if we think of scientific reasoning as consisting of syllogisms, the premises of which can in principle be spelled out exactly, and we think of practical reasoning as consisting of so-called "practical syllogisms" whose premises must in all interesting cases contain ineliminable *ceteris paribus* clauses. However, actual scientific reasoning involves modes of connecting premises and conclusions much more complex than the syllogism, and decision making, either actual or idealized, involves modes of reasoning which are depicted much too inexactly by being forced into the traditional mold of the "practical syllogism."

---

* Some of the differences between practical and theoretical reasoning pointed out by Miss Anscombe do hold. For instance, that the main premise must mention something wanted, and that the conclusion must be an action (although "there is no objection to inventing a form of words by which he *accompanies* this action, which we may call the conclusion in a verbalized form." *Ibid.*, p. 60). What I challenge is the claim that the conclusion (in "verbalized form") does not follow *deductively* from the premises (at least in many cases—cf. her n. 1 on p. 58) and cannot be made to follow, unless the major premise is an "insane" one which no one would accept. This leads Miss Anscombe to the view that Aristotle was really engaged in "describing an order which is there whenever actions are done with intentions" (p. 79). This comes perilously close to suggesting that engaging in practical reasoning is merely performing actions with intentions. Mary Mothersill, in "Anscombe's Account of the Practical Syllogism," *Philosophical Review*, LXXI (1962), 448–461, criticizes Miss Anscombe on this same point but seems to miss the force of her argument. To say, as Mothersill does, that "do everything conducive to not having a car crash" has a *"non*insane" interpretation is surely true but no help, since *on the noninsane interpretation,* "Do *this"* does not follow deductively from the major premise together with *"this* is conducive to not having a car crash"—*this* may not be an *appropriate* action, and "do everything" means (on the "noninsane" interpretation) "do everything appropriate" (*Ibid.*, p. 455). Mothersill seems to assume that "assuming appropriate conditions" could be spelled out, but this is just what Anscombe is denying.

The complex weighing of multitudinous conflicting alternatives and values does admit of deductive schematization; but not the type of deductive schematization considered by Miss Anscombe (and Aristotle).

Before going on, I should like to make one comment which may perhaps prevent some misunderstandings. A Turing Machine is simply a system having a discrete set of states which are related in certain ways. Usually we think of a Turing Machine as having a memory in the form of a paper tape upon which it prints symbols; however, this can be regarded as mere metaphor. Instead, in the case of a finite automaton, i.e., a Turing Machine whose tape is finite instead of potentially infinite, the tape may be thought of as physically realized in the form of any finite system of memory storage. What we mean by a "symbol" is simply any sort of *trace* which can be placed in this memory storage and later "scanned" by some mechanism or other. We can generalize further by allowing the "machine" to "print" more than one symbol at a time and to scan more than one symbol at a time. Turing has shown that these generalizations leave the class of Turing Machines essentially unchanged. Note then that a Turing Machine need not even be a *machine*. A Turing Machine might very well be a biological organism. The question whether an actual human being is a Turing Machine (or rather, a finite automaton), or whether the brain of a human being is a Turing Machine, is an empirical question. Today we know nothing strictly incompatible with the hypothesis that you and I are one and all Turing Machines, although we know some things that make this unlikely. Strictly speaking, a Turing Machine need not even be a physical system: anything capable of going through a succession of states in time can be a Turing Machine. Thus, to the Cartesian dualist, who likes to think of the human mind as a self-contained system in some sort of causal interaction with the body, one can say that from the point of view of pure logic it is entirely possible that the human mind is a Turing Machine (assuming that the human mind is capable of some large but finite set of states, which seems certainly true). To the person who believes that human beings have souls and that personality and memory reside in the soul and survive bodily death, one may say again that from the standpoint of pure logic it is entirely possible that the human soul is a Turing Machine, or rather a finite automaton.

Although it is likely that human brain states form a discrete set and that human mental states form a discrete set, no matter what meaning may be given to the somewhat ambiguous notion of a mental state, it is somewhat unlikely that either the mind or the brain is a Turing Machine. Reasoning *a priori* one would think it more likely that the interconnections among the various brain states and mental states of a human being are probabilistic rather than deterministic and that time-delays play an important role. However, empirical evidence is scarce. The reason is that an automaton whose states are connected by probabilistic laws and whose behavior involves time-delays can be arbitrarily well-simulated by the behavior of a Turing Machine. Thus, in the nature of the case, mere empirical data cannot decide between the hypothesis that the human brain (respectively, *mind*) is a Turing Machine and the hypothesis that it is a more complex kind of automaton with probabilistic relations and time-delays.

There is another respect in which our model is certainly oversimplified, however, even if the human brain and mind *are* Turing Machines. As has already been remarked, the necessary and sufficient condition that someone's behavior at a given time should be consistent with the assignment of some rational preference function is that his choices be consistent—e.g., if he prefers A to B and he prefers B to C, then he prefers A to C. But even this very weak axiom of transitivity is violated by the preferences of very many, perhaps all, actual people. Thus, it is doubtful that any actual human being's pattern of choices is consistent with the assignment of a rational preference function. Moreover, even if someone's pattern of preferences is consistent with the assignment of a rational preference function, it is doubtful that people consistently obey the rule: maximize the estimated utility.

And, finally, our model is not dynamical. That is to say, it does not allow for the change of the rational preference function with time—although this last feature can be modified. Thus our model is an overly simple and overly rationalistic one in a number of respects. However, it would be easy, in principle, although perhaps impossible in practice, to complicate our model in all these respects—to make the model dynamical, to allow for irrationalities in preference, to allow for irrationalities in the inductive logic of the machine, to allow for deviations from the rule: maximize the estimated utility. But I do not believe that any of these complications would affect the philosophical conclusions reached in this paper. In other words, I do not believe that the philosophical conclusions of this paper would be changed if we replaced the notion of a Turing Machine by the notion of a K–machine, where the notion of a K–machine were made sufficiently rich and complex so that human brains and minds were, literally, K–machines.

Besides saying that they are Turing Machines and that they have rational preference functions, I shall say nothing about my hypothetical "agents." They could be artifacts, they could be biological organisms, they could even be human beings. In particular then, I shall nowhere specify in this paper that the "agents" in my "community" are alive or not alive, conscious or not conscious. There is, however, a sense in which we may say of these agents, regardless of their physical realization, that they are *conscious of* certain things and *not conscious of* others. Moreover, if they have periods of what answers to sleep, then there is one use of "conscious" and "unconscious" in which we may say that they are "conscious" at certain times and "unconscious" at others.

2 Materialism

It does not, I think, have to be shown that Cartesian dualism is untenable as a description of the "inner life" of these machines and of the relation of that inner life to their behavior. The "agents" are simply certain systems of states in certain causal interrelations; *all* of their states are causally interrelated. There are not two separate "worlds," a "world" of "inner" states and a "world" of "outer" states in some peculiar kind of correlation or connection. They are not ghosts in Turing Machines, they *are* Turing Machines.

But what of materialism? If materialism as a philosophical doctrine is correct as an account of the mental life of *any* organism, then it should *certainly* be correct as an account of what corresponds to the "mental life" of *these* agents—at least if we imagine the agents to be realized as automata built out of flip-flops, relays, vacuum tubes, and so forth. But even in this last case I shall argue that traditional materialism is incorrect.

Traditional materialism (which is pretty much of a philosopher's straw man by now) holds that mental conduct words are definable in terms of concepts referring to physical-chemical composition. If this is right, then the predicate "T prefers A to B" should be definable in terms of the physical-chemical composition of our Turing Machines. But in fact there is no logically valid inference from the premise that one of our Turing Machines has a certain physical-chemical composition to the conclusion that it prefers A to B, in the sense explained above, nor from the premise that it prefers A to B to the conclusion that it has a certain physical-chemical composition. These are logically independent statements about our Turing Machines even if they are *just* machines.

Let us quickly verify this. Suppose we are given as a premise that T_1 prefers A to B. We can then infer that T_1 must have been programmed in a certain way. In particular, its program must involve a rational preference function which assigns a higher value to A than to B. Suppose that we are given not just this information, but are given the specific machine table of the machine T_1. We can still draw no inference whatsoever to the physical-chemical composition of T_1, for the reason that the *same* Turing Machine (from the standpoint of the machine table) may be physically realized in a potential infinity of ways. Even if in fact a machine belonging to our community prefers A to B when and only when flip-flop 57 is on, this is a purely contingent fact. Our machine might have been exactly the same in all "psychological" respects without consisting of flip-flops at all.

What of inferences in the reverse direction? Suppose that we are given the information that machine T_1 has a certain physical-chemical composition, can we infer that it has a certain rational preference function? This reduces to the question: can we infer the machine table of the machine from its physical-chemical composition? As an empirical matter, there is no doubt that we *can,* at least in simple cases. But we are concerned here with the question of logically valid inferences, not empirically successful ones. In order to know that a machine has a certain machine table, we must know how many significantly different states the machine is capable of and how these are causally related. This cannot be inferred from the physical-chemical composition of the machine unless, in addition to knowing the physical-chemical composition, we also know the *laws of nature*. We don't have to know all the laws of nature, we only have to know some relevant finite set; but there is no way of specifying in advance just what finite set of the laws of nature will have to be given in addition to the physical-chemical composition of the machine before we are able to show that the machine in question has a certain machine table. From the single fact that a machine has a certain physical-chemical composition it does not follow either that it has or that it does not have any particular rational preference function and hence that it does or does not prefer A to B.

Given a description of the physical-chemical composition of a machine *and* a statement of all the laws of nature (for simplicity we will assume these to be finite), can we infer that the machine prefers A to B? Suppose, for the sake of definiteness, the laws of nature are of the classical atomistic kind; that is, they describe how individual elementary particles behave, and there is a composition function which enables us to tell how any isolated complex of elementary particles will behave. Finally, the physical-chemical composition of the machine is described by describing a certain complex of elementary particles. Even in this case, we cannot as a matter of *pure logic* deduce from the statements given that the machine has a particular machine table, or a particular rational preference function, unless in addition to being given the physical-chemical composition of the machine and the laws of nature, we are given the additional premise (which from the formal point of view is a logically independent statement) that we have been given a description of *all* of the machine. Suppose, for the sake of an example, that there exist in addition to elementary particles, entities unknown to physical theory—"bundles of ectoplasm"—and that the whole machine consists of elementary particles and some "bundles of ectoplasm" in some complex kind of causal interrelationship. Then when we give the physical-chemical composition of the machine, in the usual sense, we are only describing a *substructure* of the total machine. From this description of the substructure plus the laws of nature in the ordinary sense (the laws governing the behavior of *isolated systems* of elementary particles) we can deduce how this substructure will behave *as long as there are no interactions with the remainder of the structure* (the "bundles of ectoplasm"). Since it is not a fact of pure logic that the physical-chemical description of the machine is a description of all of the machine, one cannot by pure logic deduce that the machine has any particular machine table or any particular rational preference function from a description of the physical-chemical composition of the machine and the laws of nature.

Logically, the situation just discussed is analogous to the situation which arises when certain philosophers attempt to treat universal generalizations as (possibly infinite) conjunctions, i.e., the proposal has been made to analyze "all crows are black" as "(a_1 is a crow $\supset a_1$ is black) & (a_2 is a crow $\supset a_2$ is black) & (a_3 is a crow $\supset a_3$ is black) . . ." where $a_1, a_2, \ldots$ is a possibly infinite list of individual constants designating all crows. The mistake here is that although this conjunction does indeed follow from the statement that all crows are black, the statement that all crows are black does not follow from the conjunction without the additional universal premise: "$a_1, a_2, \ldots$ are all the crows there are." It might be contended that the possibility that there exist causal agents unknown to modern physics and not consisting of elementary particles is so remote that it should be neglected. But this is to leave the context of logical analysis altogether. Moreover we have only to reflect for a moment to remember that today we know of a host of causal agencies which would have been left out in any inventory of the "furniture of the world" taken by a nineteenth century physicist. Atoms and their solar system-like components, electrons and nucleons, might possibly have been guessed at by the nineteenth century physicist; but what of mesons, and what of the quanta of the gravitational field, if these turn out to exist? No, the hypothesis that any inventory includes a list of all ultimate "building blocks" of causal processes that there are is a synthetic one and cannot be regarded as true by pure logic.

Materialism, as I admitted before, is today a philosopher's

straw man. Modern materialists (or "identity theorists," as they prefer to be called) do not maintain that the *intensions* of such terms as "preference" can be given in physical-chemical terms but only that there is a physical referent. Their formulation would be, roughly, that preferring A to B is *synthetically identical with* possessing certain more or less stable features of the physical-chemical composition (e.g., "preferring A to B is a fairly lasting state of the human cerebral cortex."). This runs into the difficulty that *preference* is a universal, not a particular—preferring A to B is a *relation* between an organism and two alternatives—and the "is" appropriate to *universals* appears to be the *"is" of meaning analysis.* We say, e.g., *"solubility* is the property that something possesses if and only if it is the case that if it were in water it would dissolve." We *don't* say, "solubility is a certain physical-chemical structure," but rather that the solubility of those substances that are soluble is *explained* by their possession of a certain physical-chemical structure. Similarly, in the case of our machines what we would say is that preferring A to B is possessing a rational preference function which assigns a higher value to A than to B. If we say, in addition, that preferring A to B is "synthetically identical with" possessing a certain physical-chemical structure—say, a certain pattern of flip-flops—then we let ourselves in for what seem to me to be remarkable and insufficiently motivated extensions of usage. For instance, if the same Turing Machine is physically realized in two quite different ways, then even though not only the rational preference function but the whole machine table is the same in the two cases, we shall have to say "preferring A to B is *something different* in the case of machine 1 and machine 2." Similarly, we shall have to say that "belief" is something different in the two cases, etc. It would be much clearer to say that the realization of the machine table is different in the two cases. There are a number of subtleties here of which it is well to be aware, however.

First of all, what has been said so far suggests the incorrect view that two properties can only be *analytically* identical, not *synthetically* identical. This is false. Let "a_1" be an individual constant designating a particular piece of paper, and suppose I write the single word "red" on the piece of paper. Then the statement, "The property *red* is identical with the property designated by the only word written on a_1," is a synthetic statement.* However, this is the *only* way in which properties can be "synthetically identical" and the statements, "Solubility is a certain molecular structure," "Pain is stimulation of C-fibres," are not of this kind, as one can easily convince oneself.

So far I have suggested that, apart from the kind of synthetic identity statement just cited, the criterion for the *identity* of two properties is *synonymy,* or equivalence in some analytical sense, of the corresponding designators. In my earlier paper I pointed out that for certain other kinds of abstract entities—e.g., situations, events—this does not seem to be correct, and that there might be reasons for giving this up even in the case of properties. I cited in that paper the *"is" of theoretical identification* (i.e., the "is" exemplified by such statements as "water *is* H_2O," "light *is* electromagnetic radiation") and I suggested that some properties might be connectible by this kind of "is." But this would not be of help to the identity theorist. (This represents a change of view from my earlier paper.) Even if we are willing to say "being P *is* being Q" in some cases in which the designators 'P' and 'Q' are not synonymous, we should require that the designators be equivalent and that the equivalence be *necessary,* at least in the sense of *physically necessary.* Thus, if *one* particular physical-chemical composition should turn

* More simply, "blue is the color of the sky" is a synthetic identity statement concerning properties. This example is due to Neil Wilson of Duke University, to whom I am indebted for enlightenment on the subject of identity of properties.

out to explain *all* cases of solubility, it would not be a wholly unmotivated extension of ordinary usage to say that solubility *is* the possession of this particular physical-chemical composition. There is an argument in my earlier paper for the view that this would not necessarily be a "change of meaning." This sort of thing cannot happen in the present case. We *cannot* discover laws by virtue of which it is physically necessary that an organism prefers A to B if and only if it is in a certain physical-chemical state. For we already know that any such laws would be false. They would be false because even in the light of our present knowledge we can see that any Turing Machine that can be physically realized at all can be realized in a host of totally different ways. Thus there cannot be a physical-chemical structure the possession of which is a necessary and sufficient condition for preferring A to B, even if we take "necessary" in the sense of *physically* necessary and not in the sense of logically necessary. And to start speaking of properties as "identical in some cases" because they happen to be coextensive in *those cases* would be not only a change of meaning but a rather arbitrary change of meaning at that.

So far we have ascribed to our machines only "multi-tracked" dispositions such as preference and belief but not such more or less transient states as states of feeling. Of course, we have equipped our machines with sense organs, and if we suppose that these sense organs are not perfectly reliable, then, as I argued in my earlier paper, it is easy to see that the distinction between appearance and reality will automatically arise in the "life" of the machine. We can classify certain configurations of these machines as "visual impressions," "tactile impressions," etc. What of such feelings as pain?

By suitably adapting Stuart Hampshire's discussion in his *Feeling and Expression*,[4] we can introduce into our model a counterpart of pain. Hampshire's idea is that the feelings are states characterized by the fact that they give rise to certain inclinations. For instance, pain is normally, although not invariably, occasioned by damage to part of the body and gives rise to inclinations to withdraw the part of the body that seems to be damaged and to avoid whatever causes the painful damage in question. These inclinations are in a certain sense *spontaneous* ones—a point that has to be emphasized if this account is not to be open to damaging objections. That is, when X hurts my hand, the inclination to withdraw my hand from X arises at once and without ratiocination on my part. I can answer the question, "Why do you draw your hand away from X?" by saying, "X is hurting my hand." One does not then go on to ask, "But why is that a reason for drawing your hand away from X?" The fact that X's hurting my hand is *ipso facto* a reason for drawing my hand away from X is grounded on and presupposes the spontaneity of the inclination to draw my hand away from X when I am in the state in question.

Let us then equip our machines with "pain signals," i.e., signals which will normally be occasioned by damage to some part of the machine's "body," with "pain fibers," and with "pain states." These "pain states" will normally be caused by damage to some part of the machine's body and will give rise to spontaneous inclinations to avoid whatever causes the pain in question. I think we can see how to introduce the notion of an inclination into our model: inclinations are naturally treated as more or less short-lasting modifications of the rational preference function of the machine. Temporarily, the machine assigns a very high value, as it were, to "getting its arm out of there." This *temporary* change in the machine's rational preference function should not, of course, be confused with the long term change in the machine's behavior occasioned by learning that something it did not previously know to be painful is painful. This last can be built into the machine's rational preference function to begin with, and need not be accounted for by supposing that the pain experience changed the long term rational preference function of the machine (although, in a dynamical model, it may have). In a sense this is a complication of Hampshire's model:* pain states are characterized both by the momentary and spontaneous inclinations to which they give rise and by the negative weight assigned by the machine's basic rational preference function to things which the machine has learned from experience put the machine into these states.

The above remarks against identifying preference with a particular physical-chemical composition apply equally strongly now against identifying pain with a particular physical-chemical composition. Suppose that the pain fibers of the machines are made of copper and these are the only copper fibers in the machines. It would still be absurd to say, "Pain is stimulation of the copper fibers." If we said that, then we would have to say that pain is something different in the case of machine 1 and the case of machine 2, if machine 1 had copper pain fibers and machine 2 had platinum pain fibers. Again, it seems clearer to say what we said before: that "pain" *is* a state of the machine normally occasioned by damage to the machine's body and characterized by giving rise to "inclinations" to . . . etc., and to eschew the formulation, "Pain is synthetically identical with stimulation of the copper fibers" in favor of the clearer formulation, "The machine is physically realized in such a way that the 'pain' pulses travel along copper fibers."

3 Logical Behaviorism

We have seen that statements about the preferences of our machines are not logically equivalent to statements concerning the physical-chemical composition of these machines. Are

---

* Other aspects of Hampshire's model are, however, omitted here: the role of *unconditioned* responses; the "suppression" of inclinations; and the role of imitation.

they perhaps logically equivalent to statements concerning the actual and potential behavior of these machines? In answering this question, it is convenient to widen the discussion and to consider not only statements about the preferences of our machines but also statements about their "knowledge," "belief," and "sensory awareness." When we widen the discussion this way, it is easy to see the answer to our question is in the negative. Consider two machines T_1 and T_2 which differ in the following way: T_1 has "pain fibers" which have been cut, so T_1 is incapable of "feeling pain." T_2 has uncut "pain fibers" but has an unusual rational preference function. This rational preference function is such that if T_2 believes a certain event to have taken place, or a certain proposition to be true, then T_2 will assign a *relatively infinite weight* to concealing the fact that its pain fibers are uncut. In other words, T_2 will maintain its pain fibers have been cut when asked, will contend that it is incapable of "feeling pain," and suppress its inclination to give behavioral evidence of feeling pain. If T_2 does not believe that the critical event has taken place or that the critical proposition is true, then T_2 will have, as it were, no reason to conceal the fact that it is capable of "feeling pain" and will then behave quite differently from T_1. In this case, we can tell that a machine is a physical realization of T_2 and not of T_1 by observing its behavior.

However, once T_1 and T_2 have both been informed that the critical event has taken place or that the critical proposition is true, there is then no distinguishing them on behavioral grounds. That is to say, the hypothesis that a machine is an instance of T_1 believes that the critical event has taken place leads to exactly the same predictions with respect to all actual and potential behavior as the hypothesis that a machine is an instance of type T_2 which believes that the critical event has taken place or that the critical proposition is true. In short, certain combinations of beliefs and rational preference functions which are quite different will lead to exactly the same actual and potential behavior.

I have argued in another paper[5] that exactly the same thing is true in the case of human beings. That is to say, two human beings may be inclined to behave in the same way under all possible circumstances, one for the normal reason and the other for a quite abnormal combination of reasons. Once we allow the computing skills or the intelligence of the machine to vary, the point becomes even more clear. Consider the problem of distinguishing between a machine with a normal rational preference function but rather low intelligence and a machine quipped with very high intelligence but with an abnormal rational preference function, which assigns relatively infinite weight to concealing its high intelligence. It is clear the difference is not a wholly untestable one. If we are allowed to take the machines apart and to see what goes on inside them, we can tell whether a given machine is an instance of the first type or an instance of the second type, but it is easily seen that there is no way to tell them apart without examining the internal composition of the machines in question. That is, quite different combinations of computing skills, beliefs, and rational preference functions can lead to exactly the same behavior, not only in the sense of the same actual behavior but in the sense of the same potential behavior under all possible circumstances.

Let T_1 be the machine of low intelligence and let T_2 be the machine of higher intelligence which is simulating the behavior of T_1. It might be asked in what precisely the greater intelligence of T_2 consists. Well, it could consist in two things. First of all, T_2 may be printing many things on its tape which do not contain operant signals and which, therefore, constitute mere interior monolog. T_2 may be solving mathematical problems, analyzing the psychology of the human beings with which it comes in contact, writing caustic comments on human mores and institutions, and so forth. T_2 need not even contain any subsystem of states which at all resembles the states or computations of T_1. T_2 may be sufficiently intelligent to determine what T_1 would do in any particular situation without actually reconstructing the thought processes by which T_1 arrives at the decision to do it. This would be analogous to the case of a human being whose behavior was in no way out of the ordinary but who, unknown to everyone else, enjoyed a rich and unusual inner life.

It will be observed that the machines we have been considering all have, in a sense, *pathological* rational preference functions, i.e., rational preference functions which assign a relatively infinite weight to something. Assigning a relatively infinite weight to something simply means preferring that thing over all alternatives, come what may. Suppose we call a rational preference function *nonpathological* if it does *not* assign a relatively infinite weight to anything except possibly the survival of the machine itself. Let T be the theory that all actually existing intelligent systems possess nonpathological rational preference functions. Then it can be shown that the statement that a machine with fixed computing skills has a particular rational preference function is equivalent under T to saying that it has a certain kind of actual and potential behavior. In fact, to say that a machine has a particular rational preference function is equivalent under T to saying that it behaves under all circumstances exactly as a machine with that particular rational preference function would behave. This does not, however, vindicate logical behaviorism, although it constitutes a kind of "near miss." Logical behaviorism in the case of our machines would be the thesis that the statement that a machine has a particular rational preference function is logically equivalent to some statement about the machine's actual and potential behavior. This is not correct. What is correct is that there is a theory T, which is very likely true (or whose analog in the case of organisms is very likely true), such that in the theory T every statement of the form "T prefers A to B" is equivalent to a statement about T's actual and potential behavior. But there is all the difference in the world between equivalence as a matter of logic alone and equivalence within a synthetic theory.

In a sense the situation with respect to logical behaviorism is very similar to the situation with respect to materialism. In connection with materialism, we saw that although the statement that a machine has a certain machine table is not logically equivalent to the statement that it has a certain physical-chemical composition, it follows from the latter statement within a synthetic theory, namely the theory consisting of the laws of nature together with the completeness statement, i.e., the statement that there do not exist any causal agencies other than the elementary particles and combinations of elementary particles, and that these possess only the degrees of freedom ascribed to them in physical theory. Indeed, it is easily seen that there is a class C of physical compositions such that the statement that a machine has a particular machine table is equivalent, within the synthetic theory mentioned, to the statement that its physical-chemical composition belongs to the class C. Since the statement that the machine prefers A to B, or that it has a certain belief, or that it "feels pain," etc. is true only if a suitable conjunction of two statements is true, the first of which says that the machine has a certain machine table, while the second describes the total configuration of the machine at the present instant, and since some such conjunction can be true, assuming the synthetic theory alluded to, only if the physical composition of the machine belongs to a very large class C* of physical compositions, we can see that the statement, whatever it may be, will be equivalent within the synthetic theory alluded to, to the statement that the physical composition of the machine is in such a class C*.

Similarly, assuming the synthetic theory alluded to in connection with logical behaviorism—the theory that no machine has a pathological rational preference function—any statement about the "mental life" of one of our machines will be equivalent to some statement about its actual and potential behavior.

Given an "agent" in our hypothetical "community," this is our situation: with enough information about the actual and potential behavior of the agent, we may infer with relative certainty that the agent prefers A to B, or again, with enough information about the physical-chemical composition of the agent (and enough knowledge of the laws of nature), we may infer with relative certainty that the agent prefers A to B. But the two inferences do not support the claims of logical behaviorism and materialism, respectively. Both inferences are synthetic inferences carried out within synthetic theories.

But, it may be asked, how can we even know that either the assumption of the nonexistence of pathological rational preference functions or the completeness assumption with respect to physical theory is correct? I believe that the answer is much the same in both cases. Each assumption is justified as long as there is no good reason to suppose that it might be false. If this is right, then inferences to the mental life of any empirically-given actual system may be perfectly justified; but they are never analytic inferences if the premises only give information about the actual and potential behavior of the system and about its physical-chemical composition. Such inferences are always "defeasible": there are always far-fetched circumstances under which the premises might be retained and the conclusion might be overturned.

On looking over what I have written, I must confess to a certain sense of disappointment. It seems to me that what I have said here is too obvious and trivial to be worth saying, even if there are indeed certain philosophers who would disagree. But at the same time, it seems to me that these remarks, even if they do seem obvious, might suggest something about the nature of our mentalistic concept which it is not at all usual to point out. What is suggested is this: It seems that to know for certain that a human being has a particular belief, or preference, or whatever, involves knowing something about the functional organization of the human being. As applied to Turing Machines, the functional organization is given by the machine table. A description of the functional organization of a human being might well be something quite different and more complicated. But the important thing is that descriptions of the functional organization of a system are logically different in kind either from descriptions of its physical-chemical composition or from descriptions of its actual and potential behavior. If discussions in the philosophy of mind are often curiously unsatisfying, I think, it is because just this notion, the notion of functional organization has been overlooked or confused with notions of entirely different kinds.

COMMENTS

Alvin Plantinga
Calvin College

MR. PUTNAM proposes to show that the traditional alternatives
with respect to the mind-body problem—Cartesian dualism,
logical behaviorism and materialism, both ancient and modern—are incorrect. He proposes to do this by showing that
none of them is an adequate account of the "mental lives" of
a hypothetical community of Turing Machines; his claim is
that "seeing why it is that the analogs of materialism, dualism
and logical behaviorism are false in the case of these Turing
Machines will enable us to see why the theories are incorrect
in the case of human beings." What I have to say concerns
only his discussion of Cartesian dualism and modern materialism.

Putnam evidently thinks it obvious that Cartesian dualism
is untenable as an account of the inner life of his hypothetical agents; I do not find this at all obvious. Is it possible for a
certain kind of ordered pair of Turing Machines to be itself
a Turing Machine? This is relevant in the following way:
Putnam points out that a Turing Machine need not be a
physical system at all; to the Cartesian dualist "one can say
that from the point of view of pure logic it is entirely possible
that the human mind is a Turing Machine." What Putnam
says here, I take it, entails that it is logically possible for
something to be both a Turing Machine and a Cartesian
Mind, where a Cartesian Mind is anything which has all the
properties that on the Cartesian view are necessary and suffi-

cient for something's being a human mind. But I should guess that it is also possible for something to be both a Turing Machine and a Cartesian Body. Further, nothing in Putnam's characterization of the Turing Machine seems to preclude the possibility that a Turing Machine which is a Cartesian Mind bears to one which is a Cartesian Body the relation—call it R—in which, on Descartes' view, the human mind stands to the human body. Now let us suppose that an ordered pair, whose elements are a Cartesian Mind and a Cartesian Body standing in R, can itself be a Turing Machine. If so, then for all Putnam tells us, every member of his hypothetical community might be just such an ordered pair; and then each of them would be precisely the sort of thing of which Cartesian dualism is a correct description. So if it is possible that such an ordered pair be a Turing Machine, then Cartesian dualism might very well be a correct description of the inner life of Putnam's agents.

Suppose, on the other hand, that it is impossible for an ordered pair whose members are a Cartesian Mind and a Cartesian Body related by R to be a Turing Machine. Then it would indeed follow that Cartesian dualism is not a correct description of Putnam's agents. But how would seeing that the analog of Cartesian dualism is false in the case of these machines enable us to see that this theory is false in the case of human beings? Perhaps no *Turing Machine* can be an ordered pair of the sort I mentioned above; but from that it does not follow either that there are no such ordered pairs or that persons are not such ordered pairs. What follows is only that if persons are ordered pairs of this sort, they are not Turing Machines. And this conclusion the Cartesian can accept with equanimity. Since Putnam himself thinks it unlikely that persons are Turing Machines, I am inclined to conclude that he has given us no reason whatever for rejecting Cartesian dualism as a theory about human beings.

My second comment concerns Putnam's discussion of mod-

ern materialism or identity theory. Putnam sets out to show
that this theory is not a correct account of the "mental life"
of his machines, and hence, presumably, not a correct account
of the mental life of human beings either. With an exception
I shall mention later, the arguments he advances against the
identity theory involve no premises mentioning or referring
to Turing Machines; so far as Putnam's case against the
identity theory goes, Turing Machines appear to be irrelevant.

According to the identity theory, Putnam says, there is some
physical state S such that *preferring A to B* is contingently
identical with *possessing S*. Putnam then points out that *preferring A to B* is a universal; and so is *possessing S*.
But, he argues, universals U and U' are contingently
identical only under certain very special conditions; and
such universals as *preferring A to B* and *possessing S* do
not meet these conditions. I find this argument altogether
puzzling, for I am unable to see what the special conditions
referred to above might be. I doubt, however, that the identity
theorist would wish to dispute Putnam's conclusion; for I am
inclined to think that when he says *being in pain is really
being in a certain neurological state S',* the identity theorist
does not mean to assert the identity of any universals at all.
What he means to assert is that every instance of the universal
being in pain is contingently identical with some instance of
the universal *possessing neurological state S';* and that every
instance of the universal *preferring A to B* is contingently
identical with some instance of the universal *possessing S*.
On this theory, then, the universal *preferring A to B* need
not be identical, contingently or otherwise, with *possessing S;*
but *Jones' preferring A to B at time t* is contingently identical with *Jones' possessing S at t*. More generally, of course, the
theory holds that for every mental state M there is a bodily
state B such that, for any person P and time t, P's being M at
t is contingently identical with P's being B at t. This theory

is not open to any of the objections Putnam deploys against modern materialism. I may be wrong in supposing that this is the theory the modern materialists mean to put forth; nonetheless, Putnam should have considered it, for the words in which he himself states the identity theory are plainly open to this interpretation. Someone might conceivably hold that the identity theory is true only if it is causally or physically necessary that someone prefers A to B if he is in some physical-chemical state S. Putnam suggests this view. But he declares:

> We *cannot* discover laws by virtue of which it is physically necessary that an organism prefers A to B if and only if it is in a certain physical-chemical state. For we already know that any such laws would be false. They would be false because even in the light of our present knowledge we can see that any Turing Machine that can be physically realized at all can be realized in a host of totally different ways. Thus there cannot be a physical-chemical structure the possession of which is a necessary and sufficient condition for preferring A to B, even if we take "necessary" in the sense of *physically* necessary and not in the sense of logically necessary.

Now what Putnam has shown here is that (a) there is no physical-chemical state S such that it is physically necessary that a *Turing Machine* prefers A to B if it is in state S. But, of course, this doesn't entail that (b) there is no physical-chemical state S' such that it is physically necessary that an *organism* prefers A to B if, and only if, it is in S'; nor does it entail (c) there is no physical-chemical state S such that it is physically necessary that a *human being* prefers A to B if and only if it is in S. Upon superficial reflection it looks to me as if any premise which is such that its conjunction with (a) entails (b) is either flagrantly question-begging or such that its conjunction with (a) entails the false proposition that it is necessary that every Turing Machine be an organism. Hence there seems to be no hope at all for this argument.

We might ask ourselves whether there is any other line of objection which could plausibly be brought against the identity theory. An approach sometimes suggested is as follows: consider a mental state such as Jones' belief that p. That belief could have, for example, the property of being supported by all the available evidence. Suppose that it does. No physical-chemical state, however, ever has the property of being supported by all the evidence. But for any x and y, if x is identical with y, then x has all and only those properties y has. Hence there is no physical-chemical state with which Jones' belief that p is identical.

This argument has a certain plausibility; but unfortunately one of its premises—that for any x and y, if x is identical with y, then x has all and only those properties y has—is false in that unrestricted form. We may see that it is as follows: Let us say that x is *necessarily red,* if and only if, *x is not red* is contradictory. The red thing on my desk is necessarily red, since the proposition *the red thing on my desk is not red* is contradictory. The red thing on my desk, however, is identical with the ashtray on my desk. But the proposition *the ashtray on my desk is not red* is not contradictory; hence the ashtray on my desk is not *necessarily* red. And hence the ashtray on my desk, though identical with the red thing on my desk, does not have all and only those properties which the latter has; so the principle is false in this unrestricted form. Perhaps there is some qualification or restriction of this principle which will serve in the argument and be clearly true. I don't know of any, however, and hence know of no sound argument along these lines against the identity theory. On the other hand, of course, I know of no sound argument in favor of the theory either.

REJOINDER

Hilary Putnam

MR. PLANTINGA'S "COMMENT" is a pleasure to read for its lucidity and for the briskness with which it gets down to the discussion of the central arguments in my paper. I am grateful to him for giving me an opportunity to emphasize further one or two points that appear to require it.

Plantinga appears to understand "dualism" differently than I did in my paper. As far as I can make out, "Cartesian dualism," as Plantinga understands it, is only a slight variant of the ordinary common sense view of the nature of living human organisms. On the ordinary common sense view, the "seat of the higher faculties," to employ the charming old language, is the brain. According to the variant view, this is wrong. The seat of the higher faculties is an organ which I shall call the "Sbrain" (otherwise "the soul," or "the Mind," with a capital "M"). The "Sbrain" is supposed not to be a "physical object," or anyway not to consist of elementary particles, not to have mass, etc. (It *is* supposed to be a "substance," according to Descartes, and this rather suggests that it *might* be "physical" in one of the recently proposed wider senses of that term.) Descartes thought that the "Sbrain" was immortal; but Plantinga fortunately does not bring this issue into our discussion.

I call this view a *slight* variant of the common sense view, because it does not seem to make any philosophical difference whether the seat of the higher faculties is the brain, or the stomach, or the Sbrain, or the foot. Also it does not make any difference, as far as I can see, whether the brain *or* Sbrain consists of elementary particles or of "mental substance." It would make considerable difference scientifically, of course. For example, if the seat of the higher functions is not the brain but the Sbrain, then what is the brain for? And why does damage to the brain, but not the stomach, cause loss of memory, speech, and other psychological functions? Again, if the Sbrain consists of a "substance" which is in time but not in (ordinary) space, then what sort of mathematics is going to be needful for a proper description of this unique organ? Should we, perhaps, think of Sbrains and similar entities (e.g., angels) as existing in some suitable topological "space" with mathematical properties of its own, in terms of which the laws obeyed by "mental substance" admit of a simple and revealing formulation? Clearly, the serious Cartesian dualist is going to have his work cut out for him.

One possibility might be that human beings have *two* brains and not one: the brain ordinarily so named, and the ghostly immaterial counterpart that we are calling the "Sbrain." This intriguing suggestion even has some explanatory value: one might, for example, explain various psychological disorders in terms of brain-Sbrain conflict. Fascinating as it would be to dwell further on the hypothesis that people have Sbrains, I must get back to philosophy. For, of course, there is not the slightest reason to think that people *do* have Sbrains in addition to brains, or Sfeet in addition to feet, or Sguts in addition to guts. And in any case it is not the job of the philosopher either to advance or to refute irresponsible empirical hypotheses.

In my paper, as the reader can quickly verify, I spoke throughout of "dualism," contrasting it throughout with "materialism" and "logical behaviorism" as *theories of the meaning* of such words as "prefers" and believes." There was only one passing reference to Cartesian dualism—the bizarre doctrine just discussed—and then only for the purpose of clarifying the notion of a Turing Machine, and *not* for the purpose of refuting this bizarre doctrine. If Plantinga wishes to stress that the bizarre doctrine thus remains unrefuted by me, I cheerfully agree.

What doctrine was I then concerned to refute? The doctrine that the peculiar character of the concepts of preference, belief, etc., *requires* us to assume the existence of ghostly causal agencies. The doctrine that the very semantical analysis of such words as these presupposes some such account as the bizarre doctrine lately alluded to. "Dualism" so understood is a conceptual claim; and the refutation of this sort of conceptual claim is eminently the business of the philosopher. But this is A, B, C. . . .

Plantinga brings three separate criticisms against my discussion of the identity theory, and concludes with a brief discussion of his own. I turn now to these criticisms.

(1) *Under what conditions would I allow that universals U and U' are contingently identical?* "I find this argument altogether puzzling, for I am unable to see what the special conditions referred to above might be," writes Plantinga. The conditions I had in mind are just that the identity statement $U = U'$ should be deducible from premises that we can admit to be true (without recourse to dubious philosophical doctrine), where "deducible" may be understood in the sense of any standard system of higher order logic.

For example, we would all admit "a_1 is blue" to be true, where a_1 is any suitable blue object. But from "a_1 is blue," we can deduce "Blue = the one and only F such that F is a color and $F(a_1)$," given the premise "Nothing has two colors at once," and, say, the logical symbols and rules of *Principia Mathematica*. Thus, for example, "Blue = the color of the sky" is a philosophically unpuzzling synthetic identity statement. It is unpuzzling, even though it asserts the identity of universals, because it follows from "the sky is (normally) blue" and "the sky has only one (normal) color," which, while they might puzzle a painter, are not premises that trouble a philosopher. However, "Anger = such and such a brain state" is not this sort of identity statement. It cannot be deduced from any known facts about brains and about anger— or, at any rate, if it can be deduced, the "deduction" is not one that can be validated in *Principia Mathematica*. It appears to be not a logical consequence of ordinary or garden variety empirical facts, but a proposed new way of speaking in the light of those facts. And just the distinction that Plantinga finds puzzling—between the synthetic identity statements about universals that we all ordinary make ("Blue is the color of the sky") and the ones I wish to reject ("Anger = such and such a brain state") is already drawn for us by the deductive formalism of modern logic.

(2) But all this is beside the point, argues Plantinga, because what the identity theorist "means to assert" is that every *instance* of the universal *being in pain* is contingently identical with some *instance* of the universal *possessing neurological state S'*. "P's being M at t is contingently identical with P's being B at t." Now then, the "instances," or members of the extension ("instance'" is normally restricted to one-place predicates) of a two-place predicate are the ordered pairs $<X, Y>$ such that X bears the relation in question to Y. Thus the "instances" of "P is angry at t" are just the pairs $<P, t>$ such that P is an organism and t is a temporal instant and such that the organism which is the first member of the ordered pair is angry at the instant which is the second member of the ordered paid.

> (I) For every P, t, $<P, t>$ is an instance of "being in M" if and only if $<P, t>$ is an instance of "being in B."

—which asserts the "contingent identity" of the *instances* of the two-place predicates M and B (*not* of the universals themselves), is logically equivalent to the "parallelism statement":

(II) For every P, t, P is in M at t if and only if P is B at t.

—thus, on Plantinga's interpretation, the "identity theorist" would be making a straightforward empirical claim, and moreover just the claim that the "psycho-physical parallelist" is making. Clearly, this cannot be right.

Instead of "instances," Plantinga might have tried "facts." Consider the claim "the fact of P's being in M at t is identical with the fact of P's being B at t." This claim could be objected to on linguistic grounds similar to those that I used to argue against the "synthetic identity" of universals. "Facts," in philosophical usage, appear to be one-one associated with true statements. On this usage, the claim above would reduce to "the statement that P is in M at t is the very same statement as the statement that P is B at t," and this is clearly false. Indeed, "synthetic identity" of facts appears to make no more sense than synthetic identity of universals. And if we take "fact" in the idiomatic sense of, roughly, what can be established beyond dispute, then we are even worse-off, since clearly it could be the case that a man's psychological state was established beyond dispute but not his brain state, *or* that his brain state was established beyond dispute but not his psychological state. Thus the fact that Jones is angry is simply *not* the same fact as the fact that Jones is in brain state B.

The fact is, I simply do not see what Plantinga means by an "instance" of *being in pain,* or how the "contingent identity of instances" can possibly be of help here.

(3) In his comments, Plantinga declares:

"Upon superficial reflection it looks to me as if any premise which is such that its conjunction with (a) entails (b) is either flagrantly question-begging or such that its conjunction with (a) entails the false proposition that it is necessary that every Turing Machine be an organism. Hence there is no hope at all for this argument."

I shall employ (a), (b), (c) to refer to the propositions so denoted in Plantinga's Comment.

(c) appears to me to be irrelevant. Even if there is a physical-chemical state S such that it is physically necessary that a *human being* prefers A to B if and only if it is in S, the proposal to say (for this reason) that the universal "preference" is identical with the universal "being in S" is completely unacceptable. For, supposing that Martians have a quite different physical constitution than we do, it would make it *analytically false* that Martians sometimes prefer A to B although they are never in S. But, I claim, we do in fact use "prefer" in such a way that creatures whose behavior sufficiently resembles ours may correctly be said to "prefer A to B" under certain conditions, whether or not they are in the same physical-chemical states as we are. (Cf. Wittgenstein's: ". . . now look at a wriggling fly and at once these difficulties vanish and pain seems able to get a foothold here, where before everything was, so to speak, too smooth for it." *Philosophical Investigations* [Oxford: Blackwell, 1953], p. 98).

For (b) one needs only the premise "Any naturally evolved physical system which is functionally isomorphic to an organism is an organism." I restrict this premise to "naturally evolved" systems in order to exclude robots, etc. In my paper I illustrated the notion of functional isomorphism (sameness of functional organization) in this way: I said that two Turing Machines (or even two probabilistic automata, which is what organisms probably are) with the same machine table are functionally isomorphic (have the same functional organization). To avoid the language of automata theory altogether, let us put the same notion in the following way: let P be an organism, and let $M_1, M_2, \ldots$ be all of the states of P that we wish to recognize as "psychological." Here $M_1, M_2, \ldots$ may be psychological states *either* in the lay sense (e.g., being angry at something, being in love) or in some technical sense (having a high "inhibitory potential," being "fixated at the oral level"). Let $B_1, B_2, \ldots$ be the corresponding physical states. Let P′ be a system which is capable of *physical* states B_1^*, B_2^* . . . which are different (in terms of physics and chemistry) from B_1, B_2, . . . , but which have the same causal-probabilistic relations to one another and to behavior. So, if M_1 is "being angry at the psychologist," when P′ is in state B_1^* it behaves just like an organism which is angry at the psychologist. Moreover, if P is quietly thinking, and going through a series of states B_{i_1}, . . . , B_{i_n}, then P′ when going through the corresponding states $B_{i_1}^*$, . . . , $B_{i_n}^*$ will also sit quietly (as if in thought), and will have the same behavior *dispositions* as P. Thus P′ is *isomorphic* to P———*up to* whatever makes a "psychological" difference to behavior.

The thrust of my paper was that, under the above conditions, we would *call* P′ an organism just as much as P, and we would *say* P′ when it is in state B_1^*, "is angry at the psychologist," etc. In short, if a *psychological* predicate applies to one organism P, then it applies to every organism which is functionally isomorphic to P, and which is in the states which correspond (under the isomorphism) to the states that P is in. Here the vagueness of "psychological" and "functional" does not matter. For this is a *grammatical* point, and however we take the notion of "psychological predicate," we must take the notion of "functional organization" in such a way that a difference in what psychological predicates are applicable corresponds to a difference in the functional organization and vice versa.

To complete the argument, it suffices to point out that any physical-chemical system which possesses a "functional organization" which can be represented by a machine table or a probabilistic machine table (and I cannot envisage what sort of functional organization would not be) is functionally isomorphic to a denumerable infinity (at least) of systems with quite different physical-chemical constitutions. But, if (b) is false, then there is a physical-chemical state which is the counterpart of "preference" in the case of all *possible* organisms,—say the presence of certain electrical intensities in a certain distribution. Then it would follow that no physical system exists—in principle, not just in fact—which is functionally isomorphic to an organism which prefers A to B, and which is nonelectrical in nature and naturally evolved. But this is just false. And if it be argued that we could modify the notion of a "physical-chemical state," so that "physical-chemical state" is preserved under *functional* isomorphism, then this is just to say that what all possible organisms which prefer A to B have in common is *not* physical-chemical state, in the sense in which that term is understood at present, but *psychological* state.

NOTES ON PUTNAM ESSAY

1. Hilary Putnam, "Minds and Machines," in New York University Institute of Philosophy, *Dimensions of Mind* [Sidney Hook, ed.] (New York: New York University Press, 1960) pp. 148–179.
2. Cf. Rudolf Carnap, *Logical Foundations of Probability* (Chicago: University of Chicago Press, 1950) esp. pp. 253–279.
3. G. E. M. Anscombe, *Intention* (Ithaca, N.Y.: Cornell University Press, 1957), esp. pp. 59–61. I wish to emphasize that the view I am criticizing occurs in only three pages of what I regard as an excellent book.
4. Stuart Hampshire, *Feeling and Expression* (London: H. K. Lewis and Co., Ltd., 1961).
5. Hilary Putnam, "Brains and Behavior," in *Analytical Philosophy* [R. J. Butler, ed.] (Oxford: Basil Blackwell & Mott, Ltd., 1965), pp. 211–235.

PHENOMENALISM

Wilfrid Sellars
University of Pittsburgh

THE TREND in recent epistemology away from what I shall call
classical phenomenalism ("physical objects are patterns of
actual and possible sense contents") has become almost a
stampede. Once again, as so often in the history of philosophy, there is a danger that a position will be abandoned
before the reasons for its inadequacy are fully understood,
with the twin results that (a) it will not be noticed that its
successor, to all appearances a direct contrary, shares some of
its mistakes; (b) the truths contained in the old position will
be cast aside with its errors. The almost inevitable result of
these stampedes has been the "swing of the pendulum"
character of philosophical thought; the partial truth of the
old position reasserts itself in the long run and brings the rest
of the tangle with it.

I believe that this is exactly what is happening with respect
to the phenomenalistic account of physical objects. On the
other hand, I also believe that the tools are at hand for a
decisive clarification of traditional puzzles about perceptual
knowledge, and that the pendulum can be brought to a stop.
This essay is an attempt to do just that by submitting phenomenalism to a thorough review in the light of recent
achievements in the logic of conceptual frameworks. I hope
to isolate the important insights contained in recent phenomenalism, so that they can remain as abiding philosophical

achievements no longer periodically obscured by the confusions with which they have been associated.

In the early stages of the argument, devoted to an initial survey of the ground, I shall be distinguishing a number of "phenomenalisms," all of which are variations on a common theme. This theme is the idea that the physical objects and processes of the "common sense" world (i.e., physical objects as contrasted with "scientific objects" such as electrons and electro-magnetic fields) actually do have the kinds of quality they seem to have. Some physical objects are *red*, even though other physical objects, viewed in abnormal circumstances, merely seem to be red. Notice that this common theme is an ontological one. It says nothing about the "direct" or "indirect," "inferential" or "noninferential," character of perceptual experience. On the other hand, the reasons which philosophers have offered to support one or other variation on this ontological theme (or which have led them to reject it *in toto*) have stemmed largely from perceptual epistemology, meaning theory, and reflection on the bearing of the sciences, in particular physics and psychology, on the problem of what there *really* is.

The simplest form of phemomenalism would be that "naive" realism which holds that while the verb "to see" has many uses—including, perhaps, that in which Macbeth "saw" a dagger which wasn't there—its primary use is one in which a person is said to see a physical object and to see that it is of a certain color, e.g., green, where this implies that the physical object in question exists and that it is in fact green. According to "naive" realism, seeing that a leaf is green is a special case of knowing that a leaf is green. Indeed, it is a special case of direct, i.e., noninferential, knowing. One *can* infer from the fact that the leaf looks black when one is viewing it in a red light that the leaf is green. To do so, however, is not to *see* that the leaf is green. Nor does seeing that the leaf is green consist in inferring that it is green from the fact, say, that it looks green and one knows oneself to be viewing it in daylight. This is not to say that such an inference cannot occur, but simply that it is not an analysis of seeing that the leaf is green.

"Naive realism," thus understood, is not committed to the paradoxical view that "O appears red to S" has the force of "S knows (sees) that O is red"—thus implying that things are everything they seem to be—though the label "naive realism" has often been used in this sense. To avoid confusion—and the paradox of calling anything as sophisticated as an ably defended philosophical position "naive," I will use the phrase "direct realism" instead. According to direct realism, then, seeing that a leaf is green is not a matter of seeing that it *looks* green and inferring from this, together with the character of the circumstances of perception, that it is green. Nor, the direct realist goes on to say, is seeing that the leaf is green a matter of (directly) seeing that a certain item, not a physical object, is green and inferring (or taking for granted) that the item "belongs to" a green leaf. My immediate purpose, however, is not to explore the merits of direct realism—though I shall be doing so shortly. For before this increasingly popular view can be evaluated, we must turn to the announced task of examining classical phenomenalism.

Direct realism and classical phenomenalism share what I have referred to as the "phenomenalistic theme." For both are inclined to say that physical objects and processes actually do have the various sorts of quality which they can also merely seem to have. The extent of this agreement, however, must not be exaggerated, since, of course, they give quite different accounts of what it is for a physical object or process to have (or, for that matter, to seem to have) a certain quality, e.g., red. The point is a familiar one. Direct realism takes as the basic grammar of predicates: O is (was, will be) red at place p, e.g., "This apple is red on the surface (but white inside)." It faces the problem of explaining statements of the form "O looks (looked, will look) red at place p to S" in terms of this "basic" statement form. Classical phenomenalism, on the other hand, introduces in one way or another a set of entities, not themselves physical objects, which are more "basic" than physical objects and characterized by color in a sense more basic than that in which physical objects are colored.* Let us call these entities, following Ayer, "sense contents." We can then say that according to the classical phenomenalist the fact that a physical object is red in the appropriate sense of "red"—is constituted by the fact that the actual sense contents which would "belong" to it if it were viewed in standard conditions are red in the appropriate sense of "red"—red ϕ_s. On the other hand, the object merely looks red ϕ_p to S if the red ϕ_s sense contents which S is directly seeing occur under relevantly abnormal circumstances of perception.

Another way of looking at the difference between the two positions is to note that according to classical phenomenalism, whenever an object *looks* ϕ_p to someone, whether or not it is ϕ_p, a ϕ_s sense contents exists; also, that all sense contents the direct seeing of which is ingredient in the seeing of a physical object, whether as it is (say, red ϕ_p) or as it merely seems to be (say, black ϕ_p), are constituents of the object. Thus a black ϕ_s sense content can be a constituent of an object which is red ϕ_p through and through and through (e.g., a piece of sealing wax). By contrast, the direct realist typically holds that the only entities characterized by color which are involved in the perception of physical objects are the physical objects themselves and their *publicly observable* "parts" and that only those colors belong to a physical

---

* What, exactly, is meant by "more basic than" in this connection is by no means clear. Certainly it is not claimed that expressions for these entities and the colors which characterize them are learned before expressions for physical objects and their colors. Whether or not the same is true of the corresponding "concepts" or "recognitional capacities" is less clear.

object or one of its "parts" which it would be seen to have by a standard observer in standard conditions. He may be prepared to say, as we shall see, that for a physical object to *be* red ϕ_p is for its "surface" to *be* red in a more basic sense prepared to say, as we shall see, that for a physical object to *look* red is for its "surface" to *look* red. But, as is well known, he rejects the inference from "x looks ϕ "to" (Ex) x is ϕ" with its correlative distinction between ϕ_p and ϕ_s.

I pointed out above that according to the direct realist (*dit* "naive") the basic grammar of color predicates is illustrated by "This apple is red on the surface, but white inside." We can, indeed, say, "This surface of the apple is red"; but if by "surface" is meant, e.g., the skin, we would merely have another statement about the color of a physical object. Perhaps we wish to say that the skin itself is red "on the surface" (and pinkish underneath). Well and good; we can still handle this in terms of the proposed basic grammar. We can even introduce in terms of this form the idea that, however thin a "skin" we take, that "skin" would be red. We must, however, beware of making the move (which has often been made) from "This apple is red at the surface because it has a skin which is red," to "This apple (or skin) is red at the surface because it has a 'surface' which is red," where the quoted "surface" no longer means a physical object (e.g., a skin) nor sums up a reference to "no matter how thin a paring were taken," but introduces an entity of a new category, a particular without thickness. If one makes this move, he is committing himself to the idea that "O is red at the surface," entails "O has x and x is red," where x is a "surface" or "expanse," and while this is an ontological thesis, it is difficult, in view of the fact that we don't see inside things (most things, that is) to avoid concluding that "seeing" an apple consists in *seeing* the "surface" of the apple and "believing in" the rest.

Notice that the "color surfaces" of the philosopher who

makes the above move from an initial position of direct realism are not yet the counterparts of the sense contents of the classical phenomenalist. For these "surfaces," like the physical objects to which they belong, are *public* entities which presumably can *look* other than they *are*. In other words, a direct realist could reasonably be expected to apply to them the distinction between *being* of a certain color and *seeming to be* of that color which was originally drawn in connection with physical objects, and to do the same with the numberless color surfaces which would be exposed by slicing the apple in all possible ways. The direct realist who has embarked on this path might use some such formula as "the object consists of actual and potential color 'surfaces'"—which has a verbal similarity to the thesis of classical phenomenalism. Yet there would remain one essential difference. The direct realist would insist that each "surface" is a public object which can look other than it is. Thus, a certain exposed "surface" could be red, and yet, because of differing circumstances of perception, look red to S, black to S′ and purple to S″. For classical phenomenalism, on the other hand, there would be as many actual sense contents as there were experiences of the exposed surface: a red one sensed by S, a black one sensed by S′ and a purple one sensed by S″.

It is worth pausing to note that the direct realist can scarcely hold that the remainder of the apple, over and above its exposed "surface," consists of actual "surfaces" waiting, so to speak, to be disclosed. After all, the apple can be sliced in many ways, and the resulting "surfaces" have equal claim to be *the* constituents of the apple. Surely the only plausible forms of the view that physical objects *qua* colored "consist of actual color through and through" are those which either think of objects *qua* colored as "colored solids" and of "surfaces" as dependent colored particulars which have a merely potential existence until the object is "sliced," or conceive of color points as basic realities, physical objects *qua* colored being three-dimensional and "color surfaces" being two-dimensional sets of color points. Of these two views the second alone would be fully consistent with the idea that "O is red at the surface" is analyzable into "O has a 'surface' which is red," for one who thinks of color solids as the basic mode of being of color is unlikely to make the mistake of thinking of the surfaces of such solids as particulars. The idea, however, that our common sense conception of physical objects is analyzable into that of a three-dimensional (solid) continuum of color points is a dubious one, to say the least. While if "surfaces" are highly derived abstractions pertaining to the solids of which they are the "surfaces," then so far from "O is red at the surface" being explained in terms of "O has a 'surface' which is red," the converse would have to be true.

Not only is his move an ill-considered one, but the direct realist who analyzes the red apple into a red "surface" the seeing of which involves no supplementation by "belief," and a "core" which is "believed in," has stepped on the slippery slope which leads to classical phenomenalism. For if the "surface" is one particular related to others, there is no contradiction in supposing it to exist without the others. Why, then, shouldn't there be *unattached* color "surfaces"? And if the object of *pure*-seeing (seeing which contains no "supplementing belief") is always "surfaces," what inductive reason could there be for supposing that there are "cores" to which they belong? It is, perhaps, a synthetic *a priori* truth that every "surface" covers a "core"? At this point the existence of hallucinations and double vision is likely to suggest that it isn't even true.

Here we must be careful. The direct realist who eschews "surfaces" will simply say that there seemed to Macbeth to be a dagger in front of him or that it seems to Jones that there are two candles on the table. But one who is sliding down the slippery slope will be tempted to say that although there *merely seemed* to Macbeth to be a dagger, there *really was* a dagger-shaped "surface" which Macbeth was pure-seeing, and that although it merely seems to Jones as if there were two candles on the table, there really are two curved white "surfaces" which Jones is pure-seeing. He *need* not, of course, make this move. It is open to him to say that there merely seemed to Macbeth to be a dagger-shaped "surface"; that there merely seems to Jones to be two curved white "surfaces." These would be the "existential seeming," counterparts of the "qualitative seeming" he has already extended to his "surfaces." He could, in other words, stop his drift in the direction of classical phenomenalism by keeping his "surfaces" what they were to begin with, namely *publicly-observable closed* "surfaces" only part of which can be seen at one time (without the use of mirrors) and which always contain a "core" though one may be mistaken as to just what kind of "core" it is. Where there is no "core," he will insist, there merely seems to be a "surface." "Surfaces," as originally introduced, include *back* "surfaces" as well as *front* or *facing* "surfaces." To limit "surfaces" to facing "surfaces" is to take a decisive step in the direction of equating "surface" with "seen color surface," preparing the way for the identification of "surfaces" with the sense contents of classical phenomenalism.

Perhaps the most important single outcome of the above discussion is the recognition that there are *two* radically different trains of thought which might lead one to distinguish between a "basic" and a "derivative" sense of "seeing x," and, correspondingly, of "seeing that x is ø." One of them is rooted in a distinction between physical objects and their public "surfaces." It is, in essence, a misinterpretation of the fact that we can see a book without seeing its back cover or its insides, and amounts to a distinction between what we see without supplementation by belief or taking for granted (i.e., a public "surface") and what we see in a sense (*see* 2) which consists of seeing in the former sense (*see* 1) a "surface" and believing or taking it to belong to a physical object of a certain kind. It is worth insisting once again that this reification of surfaces into objects of perception is a mistake. It is simply not the case that we *see* "surfaces" and *believe in* physical objects. Rather, what we see is the physical object, and if there is a sense in which "strictly speaking" what we see *of* the physical object is that it is red on the facing part of its surface and rectangular on the facing side, nevertheless the physical object as having *some* color all around (and all through) and some shape on the other side is the object seen, and not an entity called a "surface." This mistake, however, has been endemic in modern perception theory and has led to a distinction between two senses of "see" each with an appropriate kind of object: the *see* 1 and *see* 2 characterized above. Notice that according to the above train of thought, items which are *seen* 1 (public "surfaces") as well as items which are *seen* 2 (physical objects) can seem to be other than they are.

On the second train of thought, what is basically seen (*seen* 1) is a sense content, sense contents being *private* and at least as numerous as the facts of the form "There seems to S to be a physical object in a certain place," with which they are supposed to have an intimate, but variously construed, connection. Here, also, *seeing* (2) a physical object is explicated in terms of *seeing* (1) an item—in this case a sense content—and "believing" or "taking" it to "belong" in an appropriate sense to a physical object.

If one confuses between these two ways of distinguishing (correctly or not) between a "basic" and a "derivative" sense of "see," melting them into a single contrast between what is *directly* seen and what is *seen but not directly seen,* one is bound to be puzzled (as was, for example, Moore) as to whether or not what is directly seen can be the surface of a physical object, and as to whether or not what is directly seen can look other than it is.

Before embarking on the next stage of my argument, let me pause to emphasize that I do not intend to deny that when Macbeth saw (i.e., seemed to see, thought he saw) a dagger, there existed as an element in his visual experience something that might well be called a dagger-shaped color expanse. Indeed, I think (and shall argue) *that all things considered,* it is as certain as anything can be that there was. The point I wish to stress, however, is that unless one locates correctly the idea that there are such "expanses," one runs the risk of other mislocations and confusions, the net result being to lessen seriously the chances of getting out of the morass of traditional perception theory.

2. Sense Contents

My exploration of classical phenomenalism will be built around a study of the key terms in the slogan "physical objects are patterns of actual and possible sense contents." I shall begin by examining the ways in which philosophers have used the expression "sense content" and related technical terms. I think that three major traditions can be distinguished which differ radically in spite of verbal similarities in their formulations. I shall begin by considering the approach which is in many respects the simplest of the three, a virtue which springs from its use of a thoroughly familiar model for its technical language. This model is ordinary perception talk. Such perception—expressions as "directly see," "directly hear," etc. are given a logic which parallels, in significant respects, the logic of the verbs "to see," "to hear," etc., as they occur in everyday perceptual discourse. Thus, to such statements as "Jones *saw* a book and *saw that* it was blue," there correspond such statements as, "Jones *directly* saw a bulgy red expanse and *directly saw that* it was bulgy and red." And just as *seeing that* is a specific form of *knowing that,* a variety of observational knowledge, of *observing* or *perceiving that,* so *directly seeing that* is construed as a variety of *directly observing* or *perceiving that,* and hence, as a specific form of *directly knowing that.* Again, just as *seeing* x is a form of *perceiving* x, so *directly seeing* x is introduced as a specific form of *directly perceiving* x, or, as the term is introduced, *sensing* x.

The fact that "sensing x" is introduced on the model of "perceiving x" as ordinarily used brings with it a number of implicit commitments not all of which can be dodged without cutting the theory off from the roots of its meaning. One such commitment rests on the fact that in ordinary perceptual discourse the consequence from "Jones saw a book," to "There was a book" (i.e., the one that Jones saw), is valid. The theory, thus introduced, brings with it, therefore, as commitment to the consequence from "Jones sensed a red and triangular expanse," to "There was a red and triangular expanse" (i.e., the one that Jones sensed).

Another commitment rests on the fact that in ordinary perceptual discourse the objects of perception typically exist before they are noticed and after we have turned away; in short they can and do exist unperceived. The theory, introduced on this model, brings with it the implication that the red and triangular item which Jones sensed is capable of existing unsensed. Other implications are that items which are sensed can appear to be other than they are, and that the fact that a sensed item is red and triangular, can no more depend on the fact that someone *senses that* it is red and triangular, than the fact that a table is round and brown depends on the fact that someone *perceives that* it is round and brown.

But before further exploration of this first approach, it will be useful to describe the second approach, which has a quite different background and orientation. It is a sophisticated approach, and if the influence of ordinary perception talk is clearly there, it is often curiously indirect, mediated by the influence of a certain interpretation of conceptual thinking.

Indeed, it would not be amiss to say that the fundamental model of this second approach is the framework of categories traditionally used to explain the status of the objects of thought. But the point of saying this will emerge as the view itself is described.

According to this second approach, then, the *esse* of the red and triangular item of which one has an "idea" or "impression" on a particular occasion is *percipi*. By this is meant, fundamentally, that the inference from "S has a sensation of a red and triangular expanse," to "There exists a red and triangular expanse," is illegitimate. Why it should be construed as invalid will be taken up shortly. For the moment it will be useful to set down beside it as a supposed parallel the invalidity of the inference from "S has an idea of" (i.e., is thinking of) "a golden mountain," to "There exists a golden mountain." Notice that the thesis we are considering is to the effect that the *esse* of the red and triangular expanse of which one is having a sensation, *qua being that of which one is having a sensation,* is *percipi.* This must not be confused with the claim that the *esse* of color expanses *in general and without qualification* is *percipi.* It is perfectly possible to claim that the *esse* of a triangular expanse of which one is having a sensation is *percipi,* while insisting that there are triangular expanses the *esse* of which is not *percipi.* Thus, Locke would surely have agreed with Berkeley that the *esse* of the (red) triangular expanse of which, on a particular occasion, he is having a perception is *percipi,* while denying that the *esse* of all triangular expanses is *percipi.* And Locke who avoided bifurcating nature would say the same of red triangular expanses as well.

In this second framework, the general claim that the *esse* of all color expanses is *percipi* might be formulated—somewhat anachronistically—as the claim that expressions such as "a red triangle"—in the sense in which they refer to what is "immediately" or "directly" perceived—can properly occur only in the context "S has a sensation of. . . ." Thus, "S has a sensation of a red triangle," or, as we shall see, in derivative contexts which are introduced in terms of it. This is a stronger thesis than the above, according to which "S has a sensation of a red triangle" doesn't entail "There exists a red triangle." For, with a qualification to be developed in a moment, it insists that the latter statement is ill-formed.

In the material mode of speech, this more radical thesis might be put by saying that there are no red triangles, only sensations of red triangles. It is easy to see, however, that if one were to introduce the term "sense content" in such a way that "There exists a red and triangular sense content," had the force of "Someone is having a sensation of a red triangle," then, of course, one could say, "There are red and triangular *sense contents,*" as well as "There are sensations of red triangles." But, then, these would be simply two ways of saying the same thing, and the inference from "S is having a sensation of a red triangle," to "There exists a red and triangular sense content," would be analytic.

We are now in a position to see that, whereas a philosopher who takes the *first* approach might claim that red triangles cannot exist unsensed, and put this by saying that their *esse* is *percipi,* he would (in addition to doing violence to his model) be making a quite different claim from the above. He would, indeed, be claiming that "(Ex) x is a red triangle" entails "(ES) S senses x," and this claim would be a puzzling one, for it is difficult to see why the existence of an item (a red triangle) should entail a relational fact about it which is not included in its definition. The entailment would have to be *synthetic,* and either *a priori* or *inductive,* and both alternatives are not without their difficulties. However this may be, the point I wish to stress for the moment is that on the second approach, the idea that the *esse* of color expanses is *percipi* is not the claim that "x is red" entails "(ES) S has a sensation of x." Rather, it is the claim that "x is red"—unless it has the sense of "x is red *sense content*,"—is ill-formed. And, however paradoxical it may seem to say that "red triangle" doesn't properly occur apart from the context "sensation of (a red triangle)," it must be remembered that the second approach does not have as its model only ordinary perception talk. For it would indeed be paradoxical to make the parallel claim with respect to "green tree" and the context "perception of (a green tree)" as ordinarily used.

Another significant difference between the second and first approaches concerns the fact that whereas on the first approach *sensing x* has a close logical connection with *sensing that*–p—a connection which parallels the connection with sensing between statements of the form "S saw x," e.g., "Jones saw the table," and the statements of the form "S saw that–p," e.g., "Jones saw that the table was brown"—the *second* approach doesn't even contain the form, "S has a sensation *that*. . . ." This difference accounts for the fact that proponents of the *first* approach characteristically speak of sensing as a form of *knowing* whereas those who take the *second* line characteristically deny that having a sensation is a form of knowing. They grant, of course, that one may know that he is having a sensation of a red triangle. But this knowing is supervenient to the sensation, whereas on the *first* approach, "S senses that x is red and triangular," is a special case of "S knows that–p." And just as in the model (ordinary perception talk), "Jones sees x," implies that Jones has singled out x in terms of some *fact* about it and is in a position to ascertain by vision *more facts* about it (*see that* x is f, g, h, etc.), so in the approach built on this model there is a commitment to regard the form "sensing x" as logically tied to the form "sensing that x is f."

Let us leave the first and second approaches aside for a moment, and turn our attention to a third. A relative newcomer to the scene, it equates "S has a sensation of a red triangle," with "There appears to S to be a red and triangular physical object in a certain place." It follows immediately that it agrees with the second approach that "S has a sensation of a red triangle," does not entail "A red triangle exists," for the "appears" statement to which it is equivalent in sense does not entail the latter. Once again, however, it must be noted that the category expression "sense content" can be so introduced that "A red and triangular *sense content* exists," has the force of (ES). There appears to S to be a red and triangular physical object in a certain place, in which case "S has a sensation of a red triangle," does entail "A red and triangular *sense content* exists."

But the important thing about this *third* approach is that according to it, while the fact that there appears to me to be a red and triangular physical object over there is not itself a *knowing*, it is facts of this kind which are *directly known* in sense perception.* Or, to put the same point in the language of sensation, what one directly knows in perception is that one is having sensations (e.g., of a red triangle).

New facts of the form "there appears to S to be a red and triangular physical object over there," entail (or, perhaps, presuppose) the existence of S and of *there* (and hence space). Of these commitments the latter is, for our purposes, the more interesting, inasmuch as it implies that, whereas there may *merely* appear to be a red and triangular object in a certain place, the place itself is not something which might *merely* appear to be. This commitment can, however, be eliminated by rephrasing the above form to read "There

---

* Notice that whereas on the *second* approach having a sensation does not seem to imply (as it does on the *first* account) that the subject has any knowledge, this does not seem to be true of the account we are now exploring. For while the fact that there appears to someone to be a red and triangular physical object in a certain place is not itself a *knowing*, it does seem to imply that the person in question has *some knowledge* (*knowledge* that –p). But this point will be discussed shortly.

appears to x to be a space (or, perhaps, a spatial system) at a certain place in which a red and triangular physical object is located." But if we leave aside this refinement, and others which might be introduced, the essence of the third account can be stated as the claim that to know that one is having a sensation of a red triangle is to know that there appears to one to be a red and triangular *physical object* at a certain place. And while there is nothing absurd in the idea that one could directly know such a fact, it does seem absurd to combine this third conception of *sensations* with the thesis of classical phenomenalism. For, one is inclined to expostulate, how can physical objects be patterns of actual and possible sense contents, if to say that a ϕ sense content exists is to say that there appears to someone to be a ϕ physical object somewhere?

It would seem clear that if classical phenomenalism is to get off the ground, it must give a different interpretation of sense contents than that offered by the third approach. It is surely reasonable to say that "Whenever there appears to S to be a red and triangular physical object somewhere, then it is also true that S has a sensation of a red triangle." But if classical phenomenalism is to be a live option, this cannot be taken to express an identity of sense.

Now I want to suggest that once the above statement is taken as synthetic, it is true (though as we shall see, its converse is not). Whether or not its truth gives support to phenomenalism will emerge in the course of the discussion. But if sensations are not "existential appearings," what are they? Let me say at once that it is a form of the *second* approach which I would wish to defend. I shall begin to sharpen distinctions by exploring the differences between approaches *two* and *three*. On neither approach is *having a sensation* a form of *knowing*. On the third approach, however, *but not on the second as I propose to defend it, having a sensation* is a form of *thinking*. For having it appear to one that there is a red and triangular physical object over there is a case of thinking in that broad sense in which wondering, wishing, resolving, etc., as well as judging, reasoning, etc., are modes of thought.

Thus, just as *resolving to do A* is a mode of thought, even though it is not a mere matter of thinking that something is the case, so having *it appear to me that there is a red and triangular physical object over there* is a form of thinking, even though it is not a mere matter of thinking that something is the case. Just as *resolving to do A* involves having the idea of oneself doing A, so the *appearing* requires that the person appeared to have the idea of there being a red and triangular physical object in that place. Clearly the appearing isn't simply the having of the idea; but, then, no more is the resolving simply the having the idea of oneself doing A. *Being appeared to* is a *conceptual*—though not a merely conceptual—state of affairs. One can't be *appeared to* unless one has the conceptual framework of physical objects in space and time.

Now on the second view, the form in which I wish to defend it, having a sensation is *not* a conceptual fact.* Nor does the ability to have sensations presuppose the possession of a conceptual framework. To bring out the force of this claim, let us consider the following objection:

How can "S has a sensation of a red triangle," fail to entail "There is a red triangle," unless having a sensation of a red triangle is a matter of there *appearing to be* (and hence, possibly, *merely* appearing to be) a red triangle?

To this challenge the answer, in general terms, is that if "S has a sensation of a red triangle," had the sense of "S is in

---

* Knowing that one has a sensation would, of course, be a conceptual fact. I would agree with Kant that one couldn't know that one has a sensation unless one had not only the conceptual framework of *persons* and *sensations,* but also that of physical objects in space and time. My grounds for saying this will come out later.

that state which is brought about in *normal circumstances* by the action on the eyes of a red and triangular physical object," then, "S has a sensation of a red triangle," would not entail "There is a red triangle," though it would, of course, entail that there are such things as red and triangular physical objects.

This fact enables me to make the additional point that if the second approach to the status of sensations made the above move, it would be precluded from holding that the *esse* of red and triangular items *generally* is *percipi,* for the status of "red triangle" in "sensation of a red triangle" would be derivative from that of "red and triangular" in the context of statements about physical objects.

Let us suppose, however, that instead of contextually defining "sensation of a red triangle" in terms of "red and triangular physical object" as suggested above, and by so doing *explaining* the failure of the existential inference,* we simply said that it is an *irreducible fact* about sensations that the existential inference is invalid.** Classically, the "nonextensionality" of the context "S has a sensation of (a red triangle)," the irreducible impropriety of the "existential inference", was interpreted on the model of the logical nonextensionality of the context "x is thinking of a red triangle." With a proper commentary, one which discounts the *conceptual* character of the latter context, while highlighting its nonextensionality, the model is a useful one. Unfortunately, in its classical use the conceptual character of the model was not discounted.† Thus it is worth noting that Aristotle seems

---

* The inference, that is, from "S has a sensation of a red triangle" to "(Ex) x is red and triangular."

** It will be remembered that the inference from "S has a sensation of a red triangle" to "(Ex) x is a red and triangular *sense content,*" would be valid, but trifling.

† The idea that colors have only being-for-sense was grounded in the idea that mechanics doesn't need to mention the colors of things in explaining why they move as they do. Berkeley saw that no object,

to have conceived of sensation as, for example, the awareness of this white thing *as white* (*and as a thing*) thus introducing into sensation the "form of judgment" S is P. To do this, of course, is to treat sensation as cognitive and conceptual, and to construe the difference between sense and intellect, not as that between a "raw material" which involves *no* consciousness of anything *as thus and so* on the one hand, and any consciousness of something *as thus and so* on the other, but rather as that between *perceptual* consciousness of *individual* things as *determinately thus and so,* and consciousness in terms of the general (*All S is P*), the generic (*S is an animal*) and the abstract (*Triangularity is complex*).

Whether or not the "irreducible nonextensionality" form of the second approach is lured by its model into conceptualizing sensation, it is not precluded, as was the form discussed above which defined sensations of red triangles as states brought about in normal circumstances by the action of red and triangular physical objects on the eyes, from holding that the *esse* of all red triangles is *percipi,* and that except in *derivative* senses, thus as referring to the powers of physical objects to cause sensations of red triangles, "red triangle" occurs properly only in the context "S has a sensation of (a red triangle)" or contexts which unpack into this.

Such a view would be closely related to the claim, so characteristic of modern philosophy, that the *esse* of colors is *percipi.* The distinction between "primary" and "secondary" qualities would turn on the idea that whereas colors have *only* "being-for-sense," shapes, in addition to having "being-

---

pace Descartes, can have merely the metrical and structural properties studied by geometry. Either these nongeometrical qualities are such sense qualities as color, or we must postulate qualities which we do not sense. Classical concept empiricism precluded the latter alternative, and taking the former, Berkeley was committed to either abandoning the *esse-percipi* principle for colors, or extending it, as he did, to geometrical properties.

for-sense" *qua* immediately perceived, would have being *simpliciter* in the physical world as well.

But the idea that it is a basic or underivative fact about sensations that the "existential inference" is invalid need not be combined with the idea that the *esse* of all colors or shapes is *percipi*.* And if it is not, then we get a version of the second approach to sensation, according to which the statement "Sensations of red triangles are those states of perceivers which are brought about in normal circumstances by the action of red and triangular physical objects on the eyes," would not be an *analytic* statement, resting on a contextual definition of "sensation of a red triangle," but would either be a *synthetic* statement, or, if *analytic,* would be so by virtue of the definability of "red and triangular physical object" as the sort of physical object which in normal circumstances causes perceivers to have sensations of red triangles.

A few paragraphs back I made the point that if sensation-talk is logically—and not merely historically or genetically—built upon the framework of physical objects, then classical phenomenalism cannot get off the ground. This consideration eliminates, as materials for a phenomenalist construction, sense contents as construed by the third—or "appearing" —approach to sensation. It also eliminates that form of the second approach which *equates* "S has a sensation of a red triangle," with "S is in that state which is brought about in normal circumstances, etc." Of the alternatives we have examined, then, the phenomenalist is left with (a) the form of the second approach which rejects the above equation and takes the category of sensation to be an *irreducible* category for which the inference from "S has a sensation of a red

---

* *Vide* the Cartesian classification of sensations, feelings, images, etc. as *cogitationes.* The influences of this model can readily be traced through 17th and 18th century thought (and subsequently) in both "empiricism" and "rationalism." Kant's rejection of this assimilation of the manifold of sense to the conceptual was part of his Copernican revolution.

triangle" to "(Ex) x is a red triangle" does not obtain; and (b) the first approach, i.e., the sense datum theory.

According to the first approach, it will be remembered, there simply are such things as red and triangular expanses. They are "directly perceived" and it is directly perceived *that* they are *thus and so,* i.e., red and triangular. (That it may take skill and a special "set" to discriminate these expanses and the direct perception of them within the larger context of naive experience is granted.) It has already been pointed out above that this approach, having as it does ordinary perception talk as its model, does not readily permit of an *esse est percipi* interpretation of the objects of direct perception. The closest approximation to such a principle it can accommodate would involve a distinction between "S directly sees x; S directly sees that–p," as *cognitive* facts and, to stipulate a new use for the verb "to sense," so that "S senses x," would stand for the fact that x stands in a certain *non-cognitive* relation to S. To say that the *esse* of sense contents is *being sensed* would be to say that sense contents occur only in this *non-cognitive* relation to S. Thus, it might be held that sense contents occur only in the context of a certain kind of cortical process, or only as elements of a system of sense contents, for example in what H. H. Price has called "somato-centric bundles." Notice that to claim that the *esse* of sense contents is in either of these ways *being sensed* is compatible with saying that these are or might be sense contents which are not directly perceived or "sensed" in a cognitive use of this term.

3. *Possible Sense Contents*

Let us grant then, provisionally, that there is available for the phenomenalist an account of sense contents which does not rule out his enterprise *ab initio.* The next step, as specified by our program, is to explore what might be meant by the phrase "possible sense content." Here the essential point can be made quite briefly, though its implications will require careful elaboration. A "possible" sense content, in the desired meaning of "possible," would be more aptly referred to as a *conditional* or (to use Mill's term*) *contingent* sense content. The logical structure of this concept can best be sought by an analogy. Suppose we use the phrase "conditional skid" to refer to a skid which *would* take place if a certain driver *were* to do something, e.g., swerve. A beginning driver is constantly aware of the "existence" of conditional skids, collisions, etc., relatively few of which, fortunately, become actualized. (Notice that the contrasting term to "possible skid" in the sense of *conditional* or *contingent skid* will be "actual skid" *not* in the sense of *actually existing skid,* but simply as used to refer to skids *in the ordinary sense of the term* as contrasted with the conditional skids which are contextually defined in terms of them. Thus "actual skid" differs from "skid" only by calling attention to the contrast between skids and conditional skids.) Let us therefore, explore what it would mean to say that at a certain time and place there was a conditional skid. Obviously a conditional skid does not exist merely by virtue of the fact that the statement "Such and such a motion of such and such a car on such and such a surface occurred at this time and place," is both logically and physically self-consistent. "Conditional" involves a reference to *existing circumstances,* to *alternative courses of action* and on the *outcome* of these courses of action in the existing circumstances. The sense of "possible," i.e., "conditional," which we are exploring must also be carefully distinguished from the *epistemic* sense of "possible" illustrated by "It is possible that it will rain tomorrow." This

---

* J. S. Mill, *An Examination of Sir William Hamilton's Philosophy,* Appendix to chapters XI and XII (appearing in the third and later editions). Ironically, this appendix is such a clear formulation of the phenomenalists' position that it fails by a hairsbreadth to refute itself along the lines of the following argument.

sense, like the one we are defining, is also not simply a matter of the logical and physical self-consistence of the statement "It will rain tomorrow." It is a cousin of "probable" and the above statement has, roughly, the sense of "The presently available evidence is compatible with the idea that it will rain tomorrow." The sense we have in mind, on the other hand, is, so to speak, ontological rather than epistemic. It says how things stand, not how we stand with respect to evidence about how things stand.

Consider the following statements, where x is a piece of salt: (1) "x is soluble"; (2) "It is possible that x will shortly dissolve"; (3) "A possible dissolving of x exists." The first statement says simply that if x were put in water, it would dissolve. It is compatible with the idea that x is in an inaccessible place miles away from water. The second statement, which involves the *epistemic* sense of "possible," claims that the available evidence is compatible with the idea that x will shortly dissolve, and hence rules out the idea that the *evidence points* to the above description of the circumstances. The third statement—a contrived one, obviously, *but so is the language of possible sense contents*—claims that the circumstances of x are such as to leave open to us at least one course of action which would eventuate in the dissolving of x, and hence rules out the above description of the circumstances.

Notice that in statements of the kind we are considering agents and circumstances do not come into the picture in the same way. Roughly, circumstances come in as *actualities*, agents come in as *having powers*. Thus, returning to the example of the skid, we have "The circumstances of the driver are such and his capacities to move his limbs are such that there is at least one move he can make which would result in a skid." We are clearly in the region of difficult problems pertaining to the conceptual framework of conduct. What is an action? What is the scope of "circumstances"? Could a person ever have done something other than what he actually did? etc., etc.* Fortunately these problems are tangential to our investigations. For our purposes the significant feature of the above analysis of a "possible" or "conditional" skid is the implied reference to general principles (laws of nature) about what circumstances are consistent with the performance of what actions and about what would eventuate if the agent were to do an action of a certain kind which he is able to do in his circumstances. For, to bring the matter to a head, to say that E would eventuate if X, who is in circumstances C were to do A, is to imply that it is a general truth that: When A is done in C, E eventuates. This general truth may be either "strictly universal" or "statistical." The important thing is that it is *factual*, i.e., that it is not *logically* true. Thus, if the belief in such a generalization is to be a *reasonable* one, the reasons must be of an inductive character. This points to inductive arguments of the form: In observed cases of A being done in C, E has invariably (usually) eventuated. So, (in all probability) doing A in C invariably (usually) eventuates in E.

If we transfer these considerations from the case of the possible skid to the case of the possible sense content, a number of points can be made at once. To begin with, we must distinguish between: (a) the fact that the circumstances of perception are of kind C; (b) the fact that the perceiver can do A; and (c) the fact that doing A in C (usually)

---

* It is worth noting in this connection that when we say of Jones, who in fact did A, that he could have done otherwise, A', where A and A' are *minimal* actions (roughly, actions which are bodily actions under voluntary control) we mean that though Jones did A, he was able at the time to do A-like and A'-like actions, and the circumstances are compatible with his doing either. Where A and A' are not minimal actions we mean that there was a minimal action which Jones was able to do which the circumstances did not rule out, and which in those circumstances would have constituted his doing of A'. Clearly "circumstances" in this connection is a practical concept and does not refer to the total state of the universe at the time Jones did A.

eventuates in having a sense content of the kind in question. Now we can readily imagine that someone who, though a friend of sensations and sense contents, is not engaged in defending classical phenomenalism, might well illustrate these distinctions by putting himself in a position in which he can truthfully say, (a′) "I am standing, eyes closed, facing a fireplace in which a fire is burning." (b′) "I am not blind and can open my eyes." (c′) "Opening my eyes when facing a fire usually eventuates in my having toothy orange and yellow sense contents." He might well say in these circumstances that a possible or conditional toothy orange and yellow sense content exists.

Suppose, however, that he undertakes to defend the idea that "physical objects are patterns of actual and conditional sense contents" where "conditional sense content" has the sense we have been explicating. What moves can he be expected to make? The simplest move would be to start with the above model for interpreting the existence of conditional sense contents, but claim that each of the three statements, (a′), (b′) and (c′), can be reformulated in terms of sense contents. But what sort of sense contents? Actual? or both actual and conditional? This question probes to the heart of the matter. For if the presuppositions of statements asserting the existence of conditional sense contents are such as are ordinarily formulated in terms of physical objects, persons, sense organs, etc., as above, then the claim that physical objects are patterns of actual *and conditional* sense contents implies that, when reformulated in terms of sense contents, these presuppositions refer to conditional as well as actual sense contents. But if so, then an obvious difficulty arises. For these conditional sense contents *in their turn* presuppose generalizations, and if these generalizations are also such as are ordinarily formulated in terms of physical objects, persons, sense organs, etc., then we are faced with the absurdity of generalizations which are such that their own truth is presupposed by the very meaning of their terms. This vicious circularity finds its partial expression in the fact that if the reformulation from the language of physical objects to the language of sense contents were carried on step by step it would not only be an endless regress, but would involve a *circulo in definiendo,* "eye," for example, being explicated in terms of "eye."

The assumption that the general truths presupposed by the existence of conditional sense data are such as are ordinarily formulated in terms of physical objects, eyes, etc., also has for a consequence that those generalizations could never be supported by instantial inductions of which the premises referred to actual sense data only. For since the terms of the supported generalizations refer to actual and conditional sense contents, the premises would have to do so as well. Indeed, the truth of the premises for such a generalization would presuppose the truth of such generalizations.

The preceding argument has been based on the assumption that the general truths presupposed by the existence of conditional sense contents are such as are formulated in ordinary language by statements relating sensations to the physical and physiological conditions of perception. This consideration suggests that all the classical phenomenalist need do by way of reply is to insist that there are *independent** general truths about sense contents the terms of which involve no reference to conditional sense contents, and which can therefore be supported by instantial inductive arguments of which the premises refer to actual sense contents only. To probe more deeply into classical phenomenalism we must examine this new claim. Are there inductively establishable generalizations about the occurrence of sense contents which make no reference to either physical objects or conditional

---

* By calling them "independent," I mean simply that they are not supposed to be the "translated" counterparts of common sense or scientific propositions about perception.

sense contents? Can we, in short, explain conditional sense contents in terms of actual sense contents?

Now there is no contradiction in the idea that there are (perhaps statistical) uniformities which specify the circumstances in which sense content of a certain kind occurs in terms of actual (i.e., not conditional) sense contents. Are there any such? Here we must be careful to distinguish between two radically different kinds of generalization.* Let me call them *accidentally autobiographical* (A-generalizations) and *essentially autobiographical* (E-generalizations) respectively. If one fails to distinguish between them, the fact that there are true generalizations of one kind may deceive him into thinking that there are true generalizations of the other.

The difference between the two kinds of generalization is that between: "Whenever (or for the most part, whenever) I have such and such a pattern of sense contents, I have a sense content of the kind in question," (1) where it makes good sense to suppose that the generalization remains true if "anybody" is substituted for "I," and (2) statements of the same form where it is clear that the generalization would not remain true if the substitution were made. The former are A-generalizations; the latter E-generalizations.

Now it is reasonably clear that there have been uniformities in my immediate sense history. It is notorious that the antecedents must be very complex in order to discount the circumstances (e.g., blinks, getting ones hand in the way, etc., etc.) which upset simple applecarts. But if I am guarded enough in my conception of the antecedent, it will indeed have been followed (for the most part) by the consequent in my past experience. Before we ask ourselves whether such

---

* For present purposes it is unnecessary to break up the antecedents of these generalizations into a phenomenally characterized circumstance and a (supposed) phenomenal act of the perceiver (e.g., a setting oneself to open ones eyes) which jointly eventuate in the sense content in question.

uniformities in a person's sense history can serve as premises for an inductive argument, and whether, if they can, the evidenced generalizations can do the job required of them by the phenomenalist, let us imagine someone, Mr Realist, to comment on the above as follows:

> I grant that such past uniformities can be discovered, but surely I have come to discover them while conceiving of myself as a person, having a body, and living in an environment consisting of such and such physical objects (my house, this fireplace, the road out front, the wallpaper, etc.). I cannot even imagine what it would be like to discover them without operating within this conceptual framework.

To which we can imagine someone, Mr Phenomenalist, to reply:

> I grant that in the "context of discovery" your coming to notice these uniformities transpired within the framework you mention; but surely in the "context of justification" these uniformities stand on their own feet as evidence for inductive generalizations about sense contents.

Mr Realist is likely to retort:

> Surely it is paradoxical to grant that the noticing of the uniformities occurs within the conceptual framework of persons and things in space and time, while insisting that this framework is one in which physical objects are patterns of actual and conditional sense contents. For, *ex hypothesi*, the notion of a conditional sense content is to be explicated in terms of the kind of uniformity which is discovered while using the framework.

and Mr Phenomenalist to counter with:

> The *historical* or *genetic* fact that a child is taught the conceptual framework of persons and things in space and time and later uses this framework in the discovery

of the complex uniformities which are presupposed by conditional sense contents is not incompatible with the logical claim that this framework is reducible to the framework of sense contents, actual and conditional. Surely the common heritage of countless generations can embody a wisdom which the individual must scratch to acquire . . .

It is at this point that the distinction drawn above between the two kinds of generalization about actual sense contents becomes relevant. For if we ask, "Are the uniformities we have found to obtain in our past experience such that if they could serve as inductive evidence for sense content generalizations, the conditional sense contents they would make available would serve the phenomenalist's purposes?" the answer must be a simple "No." For the uniformities each of us finds are not only autobiographical; they are expressions of the fact that each of us lives among *just these individual physical objects*. The uniformities I find are bound up with the fact that my environment has included wall-paper of such and such a pattern, a squeaky chair, this stone fireplace, etc., etc. My having had *this* pattern of sense contents has usually eventuated in my having had *that* sense content, because having *this* pattern of sense contents guarantees, for example, that I am awake, not drugged, wearing my glasses and looking at the fireplace. And a generalization which is an expression of the contingencies of my existence can scarcely be one of the generalizations which, in the intersubjective conceptual heritage of the race, support the phenomenally conditional sense contents postulated by the phenomenalist. Thus, even granting that there are inductively warranted generalizations which permit the definition of phenomenally conditional sense contents, the latter will be logically tied to the peculiarities of my environment in such a way that they cannot be transferred to other things in other places.

What the phenomenalist obviously wants are generalizations which will serve the same purpose as the familiar principles about what people generally experience in various kinds of circumstance, but which will not lead to circularity or vicious regress when put to phenomenalistic use. But these principles are *impersonal,* applying, with qualifications which allow for individual, but in principle repeatable, differences to all perceivers. In other words, what the phenomenalist wants are generalizations, in sense content terms, which are *accidentally* autobiographical, generalizations in which the antecedent serves to guarantee, *not* that I am in the presence of the *this individual* thing, e.g., my fireplace, but rather that my circumstances of perception are of a certain *kind.* What he wants for his antecedents are patterns of sense contents which are the actual sense content counterparts of the kinds of perceptual circumstance which common sense expresses in the language of persons, sense organ and physical things. The best he can get, however, are essentially autobiographical uniformities in which the antecedents, however complex, are the actual sense content counterparts of the presence to *this* perceiver of *these individual things.*

In pinpointing our argument to the effect that the phenomenal uniformities we actually can put our fingers on cannot serve the phenomenalist's purpose, we have had to neglect equally telling considerations. Thus, we have permitted the phenomenalist to refer to perceivers and their personal identity in stating his phenomenal uniformities, without raising the objection that these concepts are part and parcel of the framework of physical things in space and time. We could do this because it is clear that the phenomenalist would simply retreat to the idea of an actual-phenomenal counterpart of a person, and there would have been no point in criticizing this notion until we had explored his account of the framework of phenomenal possibilities (conditionalities) which the actual-phenomenal is to be supplemented in the reconstruction of the framework of persons and physical things alike. We are now in a position to press our offensive on a broader front. For if we are correct in asserting that autobiographical generalizations of the sort which could find support in the uniformities which have occurred in our sense histories could not authorize conditional sense contents required by the phenomenalist's analysis, we can now make the stronger point that these uniformities are precluded from serving as instantial evidence for these putative autobiographical generalizations. For these uniformities come, so to speak, with dirty hands. Once it is granted that the framework of physical things is not reducible to that of actual and conditional sense contents, and, in effect, this is the burden of our argument of date, we see that the very selection of the complex patterns of actual sense contents in our past experience which are to serve as the antecedents of the generalizations in question presuppose our commonsense knowledge of ourselves as perceivers, of the specific physical environment in which we do our perceiving, and of the general principles which correlate the occurrence of sensations with bodily and environmental conditions. We select those patterns which go with our being in a certain perceptual relation to a particular object of a certain quality, where we know that being in this relation to an object of that quality normally eventuates in our having the sense content referred to in the consequent. Thus, the very principles in terms of which the uniformities are selected carry with them the knowledge that these uniformities are *dependent* uniformities *which will continue only as long as these particular objects constitute one's environment,* and hence preclude the credibility of the generalization in sense content terms which abstract consideration might lead us to think of as instantially confirmed by the past uniformities.

The fact that the noticing of complex uniformities within the course of one's sense history presupposes the conceptual picture of oneself as a person having a body and living in a

particular environment of physical things will turn out, at a
later stage of the argument, to be but a special case of the
logical dependence of the framework of private sense contents on the public, intersubjective, logical space of persons
and physical things.

One final remark before closing this section: It should be
noticed that although the uniformities we have been considering are biographical facts about individual persons,
there is a sense in which they imply impersonal truths about
all perceivers. For we know that if *anybody* with a similar
perceptual equipment were placed in our environment,
(roughly) the same uniformities would obtain in his immediate experience. As is made clear by the preceding argument,
however, this knowledge is not an induction from uniformities found in our immediate experience, but simply one more
consequence of our framework knowledge about persons,
physical things and sense perception.

4. The New Phenomenalism

Classical phenomenalism has been explicitly abandoned by
many of its most ardent proponents, including most of those
who brought it to its present state of intricate sophistication
by their successive attempts to strengthen it against evermore
probing criticism. And these defections have by no means
been offset by new recruits. One might therefore be tempted
to conclude that the above tortuous argument was a waste of
time, and that the task of exploring the whys and wherefores
of classical phenomenalism should be left to the historian.
There might be something to this contention if philosophers
had abandoned classical phenomenalism for the right reasons
and with clear understanding of its inadequacies. That this is
not the case is the burden of the present section.

The point can best be introduced by noting that the
decline of the claim that the framework of physical objects is

"in principle" *translatable* into the framework of sense contents has been accompanied by the rise of the claim, often by the same philosophers, that even if such a translation is "in principle" impossible, nevertheless there is a sense in which only sense contents *really* exist. This new phenomenalism can best be understood by comparing it with a form of realism which is almost its twin.

In the early years of the century, certain philosophers in the Lockean tradition were wont to argue that the framework of physical objects is analogous to a *theory*. Just as it is reasonable to suppose that there are molecules although we don't *perceive* them because the hypothesis that there are such things enables us to explain why perceptible things (e.g., balloons) behave as they do, so, they argued, it is reasonable to suppose that physical objects exist although we don't directly perceive them, because the hypothesis that there are such things enables us to understand why our sense contents occur in the order in which they do.

This neo-Lockean approach responded to the venerable challenge, "How can evidence in terms of sensations alone provide inductive reasons for supposing that sensations are caused by material things?" by granting that *instantial* induction cannot do the trick and appealing, instead, to that other mode of inductive argument, so central to modern physical science, the "hypothetico-deductive method." I shall shortly be arguing that this appeal was in principle misguided, and that, to put the matter in the form of a paradox, a necessary condition of the success of the appeal is the viability of classical phenomenalism. Hypothetico-deductive realism can get off the ground only by granting all the premises of classical phenomenalism; which would mean, of course, that it only *seems* to get off the ground.

But before making a frontal attack on hypothetico-deductive realism, I shall first show how closely related it is to what I have called the new phenomenalism. The point is a simple one. The new phenomenalism can be regarded as that variant of hypothetico-deductive realism which accepts the claim, characteristic of positivistic philosophies of science, that theoretical entities are "calculational devices" and do not exist in the full-blooded sense in which observables exist. Just as certain philosophers of science were prepared to say that:

> Atoms, electrons, etc. don't really exist. Frameworks of so-called scientific objects are pieces of conceptual machinery which enable us to derive observational conclusions from observational premises. Frameworks of scientific objects cannot be translated into the framework of observable fact, not, however, because they refer to *unobservable* entities, but because the very idea that they refer to *anything* is an illegitimate extension to theoretical terms of semantical distinctions appropriate to the language of observable fact,

so there is a current tendency, particularly among ex-phenomenalists of the "classical" variety to argue that:

> Although the framework of physical objects is not translatable into the framework of sense contents, this is not because it refers to entities over and above sense contents. It is merely a conceptual device which enables us to find our way around in the domain of what we directly observe, in a manner analogous to the role played by scientific objects with respect to the domain of the observable in a less stringent sense of this word.

It is my purpose to argue that this won't do, *not,* however, on the ground that "real existence" should not be denied to theoretical entities—though, indeed, I agree that it should not[1]—but rather on the ground that the relation of the

---

[1] See Chapter 4 of my *Science, Perception and Reality* (London, 1963); also "Scientific Realism or Irenic Instrumentalism," *Boston Studies in the Philosophy of Science,* ed. Robert Cohen and Marx Wartofsky (New York, 1965).

framework of physical objects to the framework of sense contents cannot be assimilated to that of a micro-theory to its observation base. To see that this is so requires no more than a bringing together of certain themes from the preceding section of the paper with the standard account of the relationship between theoretical and observational frameworks.[2]

According to what I have referred to as the "standard" account of the role of theories, a theoretical framework is an uninterpreted deductive system which is coordinated with a certain sector of the framework of observable things in such a way that *to each inductively established generalization in this sector there corresponds a theorem in the calculus, and that to no theorem in the calculus does there correspond a disconfirmed inductive generalization in the observation framework.* The co-ordination is done by "correspondence rules" which are in certain respects analogous to definitions in that they correlate defined expressions in the theoretical framework (e.g., "average momentum of a population of molecules") with empirical constructs in the framework of observation (e.g., "pressure of a gas"). The correspondence rules provide only a partial co-ordination (a "partial interpretation") in that they are not strong enough to permit the derivation of rules co-ordinating the primitive expressions of the theory (e.g. "molecule") with observational counterparts.

There are many interesting facets to this account of the tie between theoretical and observational discourse. The one which is directly relevant to our argument, however, is expressed by that part of the above summary statement which has been put in italics, according to which the tie between

---

[2] This "standard" account is the one associated with N. Campbell, H. Reichenbach, R. Carnap and many others. A clear formulation is presented in C. G. Hempel, *Fundamentals of Concept Formation in Empirical Science* (International Cyclopedia of Unified Science, Vol. II, No. 7 [Chicago: Univ. of Chicago Press, 1952]). For our purposes it will be sufficient to note certain formal features of the relationship. That the standard philosophical commentary on these formal features involves serious mistakes is the burden of Hempel's paper.

theoretical and observational discourse is a matter of coordinating inductive generalizations in the latter with theorems in the former. The significance of this point should be obvious. To claim that the relationship between the framework of sense contents and that of physical objects can be construed on the above model is to commit oneself to the idea that there are inductively confirmable generalizations about sense contents which are "in principle" capable of being formulated without the use of the language of physical things. If the argument of the preceding section was successful, this idea is a mistake.

A few paragraphs ago I made the point that the new phenomenalism can be construed as that form of hypotheticodeductive realism which denies that theoretical entities "really exist." To this it can now be added that the success of the new phenomenalism presupposes the success of the old. Hence the new phenomenalism is either mistaken or superfluous; and if it is mistaken, neither classical phenomenalism nor hypothetico-deductive realism is available as an alternative.

5. Direct Realism: Causal versus Epistemic Mediation

What, then, is the alternative? Surely to scrap the premises that led to this impasse by affirming that physical objects are really and directly perceived, and that there is no more basic form of (visual) knowledge than *seeing* physical objects (including public flashes of light, and other publicly perceptible visual phenomena) and *seeing that* they are, for example, red and triangular on this side. But to make this affirmation stick, it is essential to realize that it doesn't commit one to the view that the only items in visual experience which can be *directly known* are physical matters of fact. Thus it is perfectly compatible with the idea that people can *directly know* that there seems to be a red and triangular physical object in a certain place, and, I shall argue, with the idea that people can *directly know* that they are having a certain visual impression (e.g., an impression of a red triangle).

What can properly be meant by speaking of a knowing as "direct"? Clearly the use of the modifier is intended to imply that the knower has not *inferred* what he knows. But this is no mere psychological point. For one only knows what one has a right to think to be the case. Thus to say that someone directly knows that–p is to say that his right to the conviction that–p is not simply a matter of the availability to him of *same level* evidence which would justify the inference that–p. To abandon the "giveness" of "facts" as extra-conceptual entities is to recognize that the rightness of some convictions that–p essentially involves the fact that the idea that–p occurred to the knower in a specific way. I shall call this kind of credibility "trans-level credibility," and the inference schema to which it refers, as trans-level inference:

> X's thought that–p occurred in context C
> So, (probably) p

The problem of spelling out the principles of trans-level inference and explaining their authority is a difficult one which far transcends the scope of this paper. The above remarks are at best an indication of the direction in which a discussion of the "directness" of direct knowledge would move. I cannot pass up the opportunity, however, to emphasize once again the inextricable mutual involvement of trans-level and same-level inference in the justification of empirical statements.[3]

The distinction within visual perception between what is directly known and what is not must be carefully drawn if one is not to backslide into representationalism. Thus, the

[3] See "Empiricism and the Philosophy of Mind," Herbert Feigl and Michael Scriven (eds.), *Minnesota Studies in the Philosophy of Science,* Vol. I (Minneapolis: Univ. of Minnesota Press, 1956), pp. 253–329; reprinted as Chapter 5 of *Science, Perception and Reality.*

fact that there is a sense in which my knowledge that this is a book and in all probability red and rectangular on the *other* side, is an *inference* from my perception that this *physical object* is red and rectangular on *this* side, must not be confused with the idea that my knowledge that this is a book, etc., is an inference from a "direct seeing" of a red flat and rectangular "surface." We saw in section 1 that the perception that this physical object is red, flat and rectangular on this side is a direct but limited perception of a *physical object*. Its limitations are characteristic of most visual perception, though they are minimized in such cases as the perception of a cube of pink ice.

Again, the fact that my knowledge that I am having a sensation of a red triangle, or that there seems to me to be a red and triangular object over there, is more *secure* than my perception that this physical object is red and rectangular on this side, does not impugn the latter's status as direct knowledge. For (a) the fact that on occasion *I can* infer that there *is* a physical object in front of me which *is* red and triangular on this side from the fact that there *seems* to me to be a physical object in front of me which is red and triangular on the facing side, or from the fact that I am having a sensation of a red triangle, by no means requires that such knowledge is always a conclusion from such premises; and (b) the frameworks of qualitative and existential appearings and of sense impressions are parasitical upon discourse concerning physical things. The latter is obvious in the case of the framework of appearings; it is equally true, if less obviously so, in the case of the framework of sense impressions, as I shall shortly attempt to show.

But before reviewing the status of sense impressions and sense contents in the light of the above remarks, let us remind ourselves that while the direct realist rejects the view we have called classical phenomenalism, it is nevertheless phenomenalistic in the broad sense characterized in the opening paragraphs of this paper. For it holds that although things frequently appear other than they are, they *are* as they appear to be under advantageous circumstances. Thus, to take an example we have already used, a pink ice cube is a directly perceived, public, cold, solid, smooth, pink physical object having the familiar thermal and mechanical causal properties of ice. In advantageous circumstances it (a) appears to perceivers to be pink and cubical; (b) is responsible for the fact that there appears to these perceivers to be a pink and cubical physical object in front of them; and (c) causes these perceivers to have sensations of a pink cube.*

Again, the phenomenal world, thus conceived, of public physical objects, sounds, flashes, etc., exhibits a lawfulness which is formulable in phenomenal terms, i.e., in terms of the directly perceptible qualities and relations of these objects. (Generalizations which are in this sense phenomenal must not, of course, be confused with the generalizations in sense content terms which we found to be snares and delusions.) And since there are such generalizations, it is here, rather than at the level of sense contents, that we find a *pou sto* for the apparatus of hypothetico-deductive explanation, the introduction of theoretical entities to explain why observable (phenomenal) objects behave as they do.

At this point it is imperative that our direct realism be sufficiently critical. And to make it so requires three steps which will be seen to be closely related as the argument

---

* Much can be learned about the grammar of sense impression talk by reflecting on the fact that we speak of Jones and Smith as having sensations of *a* red triangle. Could it be the *same* red triangle? The fact that it doesn't make sense to say that the sensations are of the *same* red triangle (except as an odd way of saying that they are having sensations of the same kind) is partly responsible for the doctrine of essences. We shall see that the logical form of sensations is not, to use a crude schematism,

$$x \; Ry \quad \text{i.e., (sensation) } R \text{ (a red triangle)}$$
$$\text{but}$$
$$fx \quad \text{i.e., sensation of the } \textit{of-a-red-triangle} \text{ kind}$$

proceeds. The *first* step is the abandonment of the abstractive theory of concept formation in all its disguises. In its simplest form this theory tells us that we acquire our basic equipment of concepts from the direct perception of physical objects *as* determinately red, triangular, etc. Thus, we come to be able to think of an *absent* object as red by virtue of having directly perceived *present* objects *as* red. Having the concept of red presupposes the direct perception of one or more objects *as* red, the direct perception *that they are red*. This is at best a misleading half-truth. For while one doesn't have the concept of red until one has directly perceived something *as* red, *to be* red,* the coming to see something as red is the culmination of a complicated process which is the slow build-up of a multi-dimensional pattern of linguistic responses (by verbal expressions to things, by verbal expressions to verbal expressions, by nonlinguistic behavior to verbal expressions, by metalinguistic expressions to object-language expressions, etc.) the fruition of which as conceptual occurs when all these dimensions come into play in such direct perceptions as that this physical object (not that one) over here (not over there) is (rather than was) red (not orange, yellow, etc.). Thus, while the coming to be of a basic empirical concept coincides with the coming to be of a direct perception that something is the case, the abstractive theory, as Kant saw, makes the mistake of supposing that the logical space of the concept simply transfers itself from the objects of direct perception to the intellectual order, or, better, is transferred by the mind as Little Jack Horner transferred the plum. The idea that this logical space is an evolutionary development, culturally inherited, is an adaptation rather than a rejection of Kant's contention that the forms of experience are a priori

---

* A more careful formulation would be "unless it has appeared *that* there is a red object in front of one": for a child *could* be taught the use of color words by showing him objects of the wrong colors under conditions of abnormal illumination.

and innate. We are now able to see that his conception of the forms of experience was too narrow, and that nonformal patterns of inference are as essential to the conceptual order as the patterns explored by formal logic, Aristotelian *or* mathematical.

To nail down this point, we must take the *second* step towards an adequately critical direct realism. This step consists in the recognition that the direct perception of physical objects is mediated by the occurrence of sense impressions which latter are, in themselves thoroughly noncognitive. Furthermore, this mediation is causal rather than epistemic. Sense impressions do not mediate by virtue of being known. With these remarks, we pick up once again the discussion of sensations and sense contents which was interrupted that we might lay the ghost of classical phenomenalism.

6. Sense Impressions Again

From the point of view we have now reached, sense impressions can, as a *first approximation,* be construed as entities postulated by a theory (at first commonsensical, then more and more refined) the aim of which is to explain such general truths as that when people look at green objects in red light, the objects seem to be black, and that when people look in mirrors in front of which there is a red object, there seems to them to be a red object "behind the mirror," and other facts of this kind.

The significance of the phrase "as a first approximation" will come out in a moment. But before I make any other moves, I must emphasize that the following argument presupposes that the "calculational device" interpretation of theoretical entities is mistaken.[4] As I see it, to have good reason for holding a theory is ipso facto to have good reason for holding that the entities postulated by the theory exist. Thus, when I say that, as a first approximation, sense impres-

[4] I have argued this point in "The Language of Theories" (*op. cit.*)

sions can be construed as theoretical entities, I am not implying that sense impressions don't "really" exist. Indeed, I
should argue, not only do they really exist (since the theory is
a good one), but we can directly know (not merely infer by
using the theory) on particular occasions that we are having
sense impressions of such and such kinds. This ability directly
to know that one is having a sense impression of a certain
kind, however, presupposes the intersubjective logical space
of sense impressions as an explanation of such perceptual
phenomena as those referred to in the first paragraph of this
section. This fact about the logic of sense impressions also
finds its expression in the fact that the training of people to
respond conceptually to states of themselves which are not
publicly observable requires that trainer and trainee alike
(they may be identical) share *both* the intersubjective framework of public objects and the intersubjective theory of
private episodes, autobiographical sentences of which (in the
present tense) are to acquire the additional role of *Kon-
statierungen* by becoming symptoms (through conditioning)
of inner episodes and are recognized as such.*

The crucial step in understanding the logic of sense impressions talk, however, is a reprise of a point made early in
the paper when, in the course of discussing the "of-ness" of
sense impressions, it was pointed out that if (a) "S has an
impression of a red triangle," had the sense of (b) S is in that
state brought about in normal circumstances by the influence
of red and triangular physical objects on the eyes, then the

---

* A fuller treatment of this topic would tie it in with the discussion
of trans-level inferences in the preceding section. Furthermore, since
the "theory" of sense impressions presupposes not only the framework of public physical objects, but also that of perceivers and perceptual episodes, it is clear that an adequate account of the logical
status of sense impressions and our knowledge of them presupposes an
account of such private episodes as seeing or seeming to see that there
is a red and triangular physical object in front of one. For a discussion of these topics the reader is referred to my "Empiricism and
the Philosophy of Mind" cited in p. 251 n.

truth of (a) would not entail the existence of anything red and triangular.* Even if, as will become clear, this account of the meaning of (a) won't do as it stands, the logical point that (a) has the form, S is in a state of kind φ, i.e., φ (S), rather than, (S) R (y), remains true when it has been corrected.

What, then, is a visual impression (e.g., of a red triangle), if it is not simply that state of a perceiver which is normally brought about by the influence of a red and triangular physical object on the eye? The answer is implicit in the above characterization of the framework of sense impressions as a "theory," certain sentences of which have been enriched by a reporting role. For even where a theoretical state of affairs can be given a definite description (in Russell's sense) in terms of the phenomena it is introduced to explain, this definite description cannot exhaust the sense of the relevant theoretical expression. If it did, the theory would be no theory at all, but at most the claim that a theory can be found. Clearly what gives sense to the primitive expressions of a formalized theory are the postulates which connect theoretical states of affairs with one another and with the phenomena to be explained. Thus, to grasp the sense of the phrase "impression of a red triangle," we must see how this phrase functions in the "postulates" of the framework of sense impressions.

Here we run up against the obvious fact that the framework of sense impressions is *not* a formalized theory. Its "postulates" are formulated in terms of analogies, the force and limitations of which must be tickled out piecemeal by exploring the logic of sample uses of the framework. Such an exploration, which, if it were not for the danger of termino-

---

* Though, as was also pointed out, if the location "a red and triangular sense content exists" were introduced as the equivalent of "Someone has a sensation of a red triangle" then we could say that the truth of (a) entails the existence of something red and triangular. But what he would be saying would be exciting only if misunderstood.

logical confusion, might be called the phenomenology of sense impressions, is an arduous and time consuming task which lies beyond the scope of this paper. In any case, my concern is with broad issues of philosophical strategy, and even a large scale map of the jungle of perceptual epistemology can bring decisive clarification. I shall therefore limit myself to a summary statement of what I take to be the outcome of such an exploration.

One item stands out above all others. Analysis reveals a *second* way in which the sense of "impression of a red triangle" is related to the sense of "red and triangular physical object." The first has already been characterized by relating "S has an impression of a red triangle" to "S is in that state . . . etc." The second consists in the fact that visual impressions of red triangles are conceived as items which are analogous *in certain respects* to physical objects which are red and triangular on the facing side. (That only one side is relevant to the analogy accounts for the fact that the red triangle of an impression of a red triangle has no back side.) Here it is essential to note that the analogy is between sense impressions and physical objects and not between sense impressions and *perceptions of* physical objects. Failure to appreciate this fact reinforces the temptation to construe impressions as *cognitive* and *conceptual* which arises from the misassimilation of the "of-ness" of sensation to the "of-ness" of thought.* It is also essential to note that the analogy is a trans-category analogy, for it is an analogy between a state and a physical thing. Failure to appreciate this fact reinforces

---

* The correct interpretation of the "of-ness" of thought does resemble in an important respect the "of-ness" of sense impressions as analyzed above. To oversimplify, a thought *of* p turns out to have the form a thought *of the* .p. kind, where the latter consists of episodes which play a conceptual role analogous to the linguistic role played in English by "p." This similarity, however, highlights rather than obscures the essential difference between the intentionality of thought and the pseudo-intentionality of sense impressions.

the temptation to construe "S has an impression of a red triangle," as having the form "xRy," where y is a strange kind of particular analogous in certain respects to the facing side of a red and triangular physical object.

With these warnings out of the way, we can turn our attention to the positive analogy. It has two parts:

(a) Impressions of red, blue, yellow, etc. triangles are implied to resemble-and-differ in a way which is formally analogous to that in which physical objects which are triangular and (red or blue or yellow, etc.) on the facing side resemble-and-differ; and similarly *mutatis mutandis* in the case of other shapes.

(b) Impressions of red triangles, circles, squares, etc. are implied to resemble-and-differ in a way which is formally analogous to that in which physical objects which are red and (triangular or circular or square, etc.) on the facing side resemble-and-differ; and similarly *mutatis mutandis* in the case of other colors.

In effect, these analogies have the force of postulates implicitly defining two families of predicates, "φ_1" .... "φ_n" and "ψ_1" ... "ψ_n," applicable to sense impressions, one of which has a logical space analogous to that of colors, the other a logical space analogous to that of the spatial properties of physical things.

In addition to these analogies, the framework of sense impressions involves a causal hypothesis, the general character of which can be indicated by saying that the fact that blue objects appear in certain circumstances to be green, and that in certain circumstances there appear to be red and triangular objects in front of people when there is no object there at all, are explained by postulating that in these circumstances impressions are brought about of the kinds which are normally brought about by blue objects (in the first case) and by red and triangular objects (in the second).

It has sometimes been suggested that the basic mode of existence of colors is "adverbial," i.e., that the basic mode of existence of blue is expressed by the context "S senses bluely." This suggestion is typically developed into the idea that physical blue is the power to cause normal perceivers to sense bluely. From our standpoint this suggestion, although it contains an important insight, puts the cart before the horse and misconstrues as basic a "color" concept which is derived by analogy from color concepts pertaining to physical objects. The violence done by this construction is reflected both by its paradoxical ring, and the reluctance of its sponsors to extend the same interpretation to the way in which shapes are involved in the impressions of sense.

7. *Beyond Direct Realism: A Kantian Critique*

The argument to date has been an attempt to spell out the relations which exist between the framework of sense impressions and the framework of physical objects, and by so doing to show exactly why neither classical phenomenalism nor hypothetico-deductive phenomenalism (let alone hypothetico-deductive realism) is a tenable position. But though the primary aim of the argument has been negative, it is clear that the argument up to this point can be more positively construed as a defense of direct realism, and therefore of a position which is phenomenalistic in that broad sense which amounts to the idea that things are, in standard circumstances, what they seem to be. It must now be pointed out, however, that if the argument to date is sound, it has a momentum which must sweep away even this broad sense of phenomenalism. If it were halted at this point, it would be inconsistent with its presuppositions.

A review of the later stages of the argument discloses that on two occasions essential use was made of premises concerning the status of theoretical frameworks. On the first occasion, the point was made that the correspondence rules of a theory correlate "theorems" in the language of the theory with inductive generalizations in the framework of the phenomena the theory is designed to explain. Since the point to be made was simply that if there are no inductive generalizations in sense content terms, then the framework of physical objects cannot be construed as a theory analogous to the theories of micro-physics, a closer scrutiny of what it is that micro-physical theories accomplish by correlating theorems with inductions and just what this correlation amounts to was not called for. On the second occasion, however, an additional theme was introduced; namely, the idea that to have a good reason for espousing a theory which postulates the existence of unobservable entities is to have good reason for saying that these entities really exist. And this idea, as we have noted, runs up against the objection that the entities postulated by theories of this type are and can be nothing but "computational devices" for deriving observation framework conclusions from observation framework premises, and that even this role is "in principle" dispensable. For, it is argued, every success achieved by the theory has the form $T \rightarrow (O_i \rightarrow O_j)$ where "$O_i \rightarrow O_j$" is a generalization which relates two kinds of situations definable in the observation framework, and which, though derivable from the theory (including its correspondence rules), must in principle be capable of *independent* inductive confirmation or disconfirmation. Now in my opinion, it must be admitted that *if* the observation framework permits the formulation of inductive generalizations—statistical or nonstatistical—which hold within limits which can be accounted for in terms of such concepts as accuracy of measurement and experimental error, i.e., the variance of which is purely "epistemic," then the "positivistic" interpretation of theoretical entities is inescapable. But must we grant the antecedent of this hypothetical? Of course, if we knew that the conceptual framework of

perceptible physical objects in space and time had an absolute authenticity, i.e., that the physical objects of the perceptible macro-world as conceived by the direct realist really
existed, we would know that any testable consequences to
which a theory could call attention would be lawlike uniformities, statistical or otherwise, in the behavior of physical
objects. *But do we know that the physical objects of the
perceptible world really exist? Is the behavior of macro-
objects even statistically lawful in a way which leaves to
theories only the job of deriving these laws from its postulates
and correspondence rules?* I have argued elsewhere[5] that the
answer to both these questions is no, and that the negative
answer to the *second,* together with the fact that *theories
explain why physical objects come as close as they do to
conforming to statistical laws which have a purely "epistemic" variance,* is what justifies the negative answer to the
first.

On the view I propose, the assertion that the micro-entities
of physical theory really exist goes hand in hand with the
assertion that *the macro-entities of the perceptible world do
not really exist.* This position can be ruled out of court only
by showing that the framework of perceptible physical objects in space and time has an authenticity which guarantees a
parasitical status for the subtle and sophisticated framework
of physical theory. I have argued elsewhere that the very
conception of such absolute authenticity is a mistake.[6] If this
contention is correct, the premise to the effect that theoretical
entities really exist, which was used in explaining the status
of sense impressions, requires us to go one step further once
its presuppositions are made explicit, and argue that the
physical objects, the perception of which they causally (but
not epistemically) mediate, are unreal. It commits us, in

[5] Most recently in "Scientific Realism or Irenic Instrumentalism," cited
in p. 248 n.
[6] Chapter 5 of *Science, Perception and Reality.*

short, to the view that the perceptual world is phenomenal in something like the Kantian sense, the key difference being that the real "noumenal" world which supports the "world of appearance" is not a *metaphysical* world of unknowable things in themselves, but simply the world as construed by scientific theory.

To say that there are no such things as the physical objects of the perceptible world is, of course, to make a point *about* the framework of physical objects, not *in* it. In this respect it differs from the assertion that there are no centaurs. As long as we are *in* the framework of physical objects, of course, we evaluate statements about particular physical objects and the perception of them in terms of the criteria provided by the framework. "Direct" realism gives an excellent reconstruction of the ways in which physical things, perceivers, sense impressions, perceptions *of* physical objects, perceptions *that* they are thus and so, privileged access to one's own thoughts, feelings and sense impressions, etc., fit together to make one framework of entities and knowledge about these entities. To say that the framework is phenomenal in a quasi-Kantian sense, as I am doing, is to say that science is making available a more adequate framework of entities which *in principle,* at least, could serve all the functions, and, in particular, the perceptual functions of the framework we actually employ in everyday life. It is not, of course, to say that there is good reason to put it to this use. Indeed, there are sound methodological reasons for not teaching ourselves to respond to perceptual situations in terms of constructs in the language of theoretical physics. For while this could, in principle, be done, the scientific quest is not yet over, and even granting that the main outlines are blocked in, the framework of physical objects in space and time, shaped over millennia of social evolution, provides, when accompanied by correct philosophical commentary, a firm base of operations with which to correlate the developing structure of scientific theory, refusing to embrace any stage without reserve as our very way of perceiving the world, *not* because it wouldn't be a *better* way, but because the better is the enemy of the best.

8. *Beyond Sense Impressions*

Let me bring this already overloaded essay to a close by discussing a topic which will bring all of its main themes into one focus. Suppose someone were to raise the following objection,

> I can understand the temptation to say that there really are such things as clouds of electrons, etc., but why conclude from this that the physical objects of ordinary perceptual experience don't really exist? Why not simply say that we must revise our conception of them and recognize that while *as perceptible physical objects* they have the qualities of sense, *as systems of imperceptible particles* they have the properties ascribed to them by scientific theory?

I reply that this won't do at all. The attempt to melt together Eddington's two tables does violence to both and justice to neither. It requires one to say that one and the same thing is both the *single* logical subject of which an *undefined* descriptive predicate (e.g., "red") is true* and a *set of logical* subjects none of which is truly characterized by this predicate, thus raising all the logical puzzles of "emergence." And if, as is often done, "red" as predicable of physical objects is tacitly shifted from the category of *primitive* descriptive predicates (where it properly belongs) to the category of *defined* descriptive predicates by being given the sense of "power to cause normal observers to have impressions of red," then the very stuffing has been knocked out of the framework of physical objects, leaving not enough to permit

---

* That the form of predication is complex ("O is now red at place p") does not impugn the undefined or primitive character of "red."

the formulation of the very laws which are implied by the existence of these powers, and are presupposed by the micro-theory which might be invoked to explain them.

The point I have in mind is essentially the same as that on which our critique of classical phenomenalism was based. For to suppose that the qualities of physical things are *powers* is to overlook the fact that the *occurrent* properties of physical objects are presupposed by the laws which authorize *both* the ascription to "circumstances"* of powers to manifest them-selves in the sense contents of percipients (stressed by power phenomenalism) *and* the assertion of subjunctive condi-tionals about the sense contents which would eventuate for a perceiver were such and such (phenomenal) conditions to be satisfied (stressed by classical phenomenalism).** As a matter of fact, the subjunctive conditionals of classical phenomenal-ism can be reformulated in the language of "powers" as the "passive" counterparts of the "active" powers of "circum-stances" to manifest themselves in the immediate experience of perceivers, i.e., as the powers of perceivers to be appeared to by the "circumstances."†

But, if the alternative to saying that physical objects are

* The concept of the "circumstances of perception" is eviscerated by power phenomenalism. "Circumstances" serve merely as the logical subjects of powers and have no other actuality.

** Indeed, we say, the "uniformities" which do obtain presuppose not only the general principles which relate impressions of sense to the impact of the physical environment on the sense organs, but also *particular* matters of fact concerning the physical environment and sensory equipment of the perceiver in question.

† Needless to say, only a realistic interpretation of this manifesting is entitled to the ordinary connotation of the terms "active" and "pas-sive" as expressing ways of looking at causal transactions. In power phenomenalism they are to be interpreted in terms of the difference between the active and passive voices of the verb "C manifests itself to S in (sense content) x," i.e., "C manifests itself to S in x," and "S is manifested to by C in x." Since, as was pointed out above, the circumstance, C, is merely the logical subject of the "active" powers, power phenomenalism is in immediate danger of collapsing into solipsism.

both single logical subjects for primitive predicates like "red" and sets of logical subjects for micro-theoretical predicates is the position, defined in the preceding section, that physical objects with their occurrent qualities don't really exist, where do their qualities, e.g., color, really exist? What really exists and has them, if physical objects don't? This question requires an answer in three stages.

The *first* stage consists in the statement that *nothing* really has them. The logic of the color predicates of the framework of physical objects is such that only a physical object *could* have color in this sense of the term, and *ex hypothesi,* there are none. (The existence of public flashes of red light complicates this point, but changes nothing of principle.)

The *second* stage consists in pointing out that our argument has led us to the idea that while visual sense impressions are not, of course, colored in the sense in which physical objects are colored, they do have intrinsic properties which have a logical space formally similar to the logical space of the colors of physical things. And this suggests that in the scientific picture of the world the counterparts of the colors of the physical object framework will turn out to be aspects, in some sense, of the percipient organism.

The *third* stage begins with the reminder that when we abandon the framework of physical objects, our conception of a *person* cannot remain inviolate. In the pretheoretical framework of physical objects, living things and persons, the situation is much as presented in classical philosophy at its best. A person is a single logical subject, not a set of logical subjects. The Aristotelian includes the physical aspects of persons in this single logical subject by attributing only a "virtual" existence to the physical parts of the body construed as logical subjects. This requires that statements about what the legs, hands, etc. of a person are doing be construed expressible in terms which mention no logical subject other than the person as a whole. For the Aristotelian, the term "leg" as referring to a part of a person, and the term "leg" as referring to an amputated limb would have radically different *logical* grammars. The Platonist, for a number of reasons into which we need not enter, prefers a framework in which a person consists of a person proper and a body, thus permitting the latter to be an actual plurality of logical subjects.* The Platonist hesitates as to whether sense impressions belong to the body or to the *psyche*. On the whole, he takes the latter course, though constantly tempted to divide the *psyche* into a team consisting of a rational, a sentient and (perhaps) a vital *psyche*. The former course would require an Aristotelian approach to the sentient body.

The purpose of the above quasi-historical remarks is to remind the reader that in the common-sense framework of persons and physical objects as we have described it, thoughts and sense impressions are adjectival to single logical subjects (as contrasted with sets of logical subjects). What are we to make of these single logical subjects in the light of scientific theory? And, in particular, is there any reason to suppose that in a new synthesis there will be logical subjects for yet other analogies of the color predicates (and geometrical predicates) of the framework of physical objects? If so, these counterparts twice removed would not be *adverbial* (as are the predicates of sense impressions) and we could say with good conscience that it is these logical subjects which "really have the colors and shapes which physical objects seem to have." But what a difference there would be between what we would mean by saying this, and the sense it has as usually advanced.

---

* A consistent development of this position requires that all the primitives of the conceptual framework to which the body belongs be such as to apply to the ultimate logical subjects of the frame. A set of logical subjects can have a property (e.g., juxtaposed) which the elements do not and cannot have, but the attribution of the property to the set must be explicable, in principle, in terms of predicates applicable to the members of the set. In other words, predicates applicable to the set cannot be primitive.

The basic roadblock is the unity of the person as the subject of conceptual activities. To do justice to this unity we must, it would seem, take it to be ultimate and irreducible, and, in effect, commit ourselves to either a Platonic or an Aristotelian ontology of the "I." That this is not so is the fruit of a line of thought initiated by Kant (in his treatment of the "I think" in the *Transcendental Deduction of the Categories* and in the *Paralogisms*). As in the case of status of the framework of physical objects, he sketched the *form* of a solution, giving it, however, a metaphysical content which must be replaced by scientific considerations. The heart of the matter is the fact that the irreducibility of the "I" within the framework of first person discourse (and, indeed, of "you" and "he" as well) is compatible with the thesis that persons can (in principle) be exhaustively described in terms which involve no reference to such an irreducible logical subject. For the description will *mention* rather than *use* the framework to which this logical subject belongs. Kant saw that the transcendental unity of apperception is a form of experience rather than a disclosure of ultimate reality. If a person is "really" multiplicities of logical subjects, then, unless these multiplicities used the conceptual framework of persons, there would be no persons. But the idea that persons "really are" such multiplicities doesn't require that our concept of a person be *analyzable into* concepts pertinent to sets of logical subjects. Persons may "really be" bundles, but the concept of a person is not the concept of a bundle.

Suppose, then, we take a neo-Hobbesian line with respect to the conceptual activities of persons, and construe these activities on the model of the computational activities of an electronic robot; one, however, which is capable of responding to its own computational activities in the language of persons.[8] What would be the implications of this line for the

---

[8] The philosophical problems involved in reconciling such a neo-Hobbesian line with the meaningfulness of human speech, with the Cartesian

status of sense impressions? The immediate consequence is obvious. By "identifying" a person in the above manner with a plurality of logical subjects, i.e., the constituent parts of the "computer," we have undermined the logic of sense impressions. For whether these parts be construed as material particles or as nerve cells, the fact that they are a plurality precludes them from serving either jointly or separately as the subjects of the verb "to sense red-triangle-wise." We must therefore either introduce another logical subject (an immaterial substance) to do this work, or turn each sensing into a logical subject in its own right, i.e., introduce a new category of entity ("phantasms" or "sensa" we might call them) with predicates the logical space of which is modeled on that of visual impressions, as the latter was modeled on that of colored and shaped physical objects. To one who is confronted by these alternatives, the familiar facts about the dependence of sense impressions on brain processes are bound to point in the second direction, which is, in effect, that of the epiphenomenalism of Hobbes.

Epiphenomenalism is a far more radical dualism than the Cartesian dualism of matter and mind. For the latter is, at least in intention, a dualism of interacting substances. Phantasms, being the counterparts of the having of sense impressions, are fleeting particulars with none of the attributes of thinghood. They neither act nor are acted on, but simply

---

argument that thinking cannot be a physical process because we can clearly and distinctly understand what we mean by a thought without thinking of thoughts as physical processes, and with the fact that thinking involves the recognition of standards or norms, are far too complex to be more than mentioned in this paper. I have, however, discussed them at length in Chapters 1, 2, 5, and 11 of *Science, Perception and Reality*. See also the correspondence with Roderick Chisholm, published as an appendix to Herbert Feigl, Michael Scriven, and Grover Maxwell (eds.), *Minnesota Studies in the Philosophy of Science*, Vol. II (Minneapolis: Univ. of Minnesota Press, 1958), pp. 521–539.

occur. Their impotence is logical, rather than a puzzling empirical fact. They are the prototype of the "events" into which modern philosophers have been prone to analyze things and the interactions of things. And if these analyses reflect a misunderstanding of the place of events in the framework of things, they have far more merit if they are viewed as attempts to construct a framework alternative to the framework of interacting things; alternative, yet in the last analysis, equivalent; a different, but philosophically illuminating mode of representation.[9] In such a framework, changing things become genidentical patterns of "events," and those irreducible metrical *Undinge,* space and time, become abstract forms of order.

These considerations suggest that epiphenomenalism, with its disparate categories of *things* (whether the material particles of Hobbes or the nerve cells of modern neurophysiology) and "phantasms," is a halfway house; that a unified picture requires a translation of the physiological context in which epiphenomena occur into the framework of "events." With this in mind, let us strain our feeling for conceptual possibilities to the limit by raising the question which more than any other must fascinate the philosopher who takes science seriously and has not succumbed to any of the reductive fallacies exposed in earlier sections of this paper. How are we to conceive the relationship between the sequence of micro-physical "events" which constitute a brain's being in the physical state appropriate to the occurrence of a red and triangular sensum, and the sequence of "events" which is the sensum? Or, to put it somewhat differently, what would be the relation between terms for sensa and the primitive vocab-

[9] For a detailed comparison of the framework of things and the framework of "events" see my "Time and the World Order," Herbert Feigl and Grover Maxwell (eds.), *Minnesota Studies in the Philosophy of Science,* Vol. III (Minneapolis: Univ. of Minnesota Press, 1962), pp. 527–616.

ulary of a micro-physics capable of dealing with inorganic phenomena? To ask this question is to realize that it is a disguised demand for the general lines of a completed scientific theory of sentient organisms. The philosopher's task can only be that of clearing the way by exposing mistaken presuppositions and metaphysical assumptions. I shall bring this essay to a close by examining some relevant dogmas.

In the first place, there is the dogma that sensa cannot be in physical space. This conviction seems to be a misinterpretation of the logical truths that *impressions* are not in physical space (which is clear) and that the pseudo-objects "of" which we "have" impressions are not in physical space. But if sensa are in physical space—not, of course, the space of physical objects, but of their micro-theoretical counterparts—*where* are they? They are, we have seen counterparts of impressions, those states of perceivers which are postulated to explain certain familiar facts of perception and misperception. The obvious, but crude, answer, then, is that they are "in the brain." A better answer is that they are where the relevant brain *events* are, for the phrase "in the brain" has the logical grammar of "thing inside thing," e.g., lump of sugar in a sugar bowl. If it is retorted that sensa don't *seem* to be where these brain events are, the answer is twofold: (a) Brain events are not perceived, so that nothing could *seem* to stand in *any* relation to them; (b) If there is a sense in which sensa can be said to "seem" to be on the surfaces of physical things, it is a highly derived and metaphorical sense which must not be confused with that in which red objects can seem to be black, or there can seem to be a book behind the mirror. Strictly speaking, sensa don't *seem*. They belong to a highly sophisticated account of the world, and simply do not belong to the framework of perceptual consciousness. It is, indeed, true, from the standpoint of this sophisticated framework that when a person sees that a physical object is red and triangular on the facing side, part of what is "really" going on is that a red and triangular sensum exists where certain cortical processes are going on; but it would be a mixing of frameworks to say, with some philosophers, that people "mistake sensa for physical objects," or "take sensa to be *out there.*" For these latter ways of putting it suggest that sensa belong to the conceptual framework in terms of which people experience the world.

Another familiar line of thought which requires close scrutiny is the move from the premise that where there is metrical *form* there must be *content,* to the conclusion that the "qualities of sense" are the content of physical things. The premise is true. The conclusion is true of the physical world of common experience, though awkwardly formulated. But the argument is obviously invalid unless a premise is added to the effect that the "qualities of sense" are the *only* contents available to embody metrical form. Certainly they are the only contents which play this role in the framework of perceptible things. But what of the framework of physical theory? Granted that the metrical properties of the framework of perceptible things are anchored in the qualities of touch and sight (a fact which Berkeley saw, but put to bad use), then must the metrical forms of micro-physical process be similarly embodied in colors and other qualities of sense? Are nuclear events "patterns of color which obey the laws of micro-physics" as physical objects are color solids which obey the laws of micro-physics? Must the color predicates of the framework of perceptible things be tacitly present (though with modified grammar) as primitive predicates of the micro-theory of inorganic things? (We have granted that they will be present in the micro-theory of sentient organisms.) To ask these questions is to answer them in the negative. A primitive predicate in a theory is meaningful if it does its theoretical job; and to do this job, as we have seen, it does not have to stand for a perceptible feature of the world.

The phrase "partial interpretation," often used in explaining the status of micro-theories, plays into the hands of "structuralism" by suggesting that a theory falls short of complete meaningfulness to the extent that the correspondence rules fall short of enabling a complete translation of the theory into the observation framework with which it is correlated. The picture is that of a skeleton which has some flesh on its bones. A philosopher who subscribes to the realistic interpretation of theories, but is taken in by this picture, will be tempted to cover the bones which science leaves uncovered with the qualities of sense, supplementing the "partial interpretation" of theoretical terms given by science with a *metaphysical* interpretation. But all such moves rest on a failure to distinguish between correspondence rules, which do *not* stipulate identities of sense, and definitions, which do. Only if correspondence rules were (partial) definitions, would the meaning of theoretical terms be incomplete. It is perhaps not too misleading to say that the meaning of a theoretical term is its use, and that if there is a sense in which there are degrees of meaningfulness for theoretical terms, it is a matter of the extent to which the theory satisfies the criteria of a good theory, rather than of degrees of translatability into the observation language.

If these contentions are sound, then there is no *a priori* reason to suppose that the content for the metrical forms of micro-physical process must be the sensa of sophisticated perception theory. And to say that this content must be *like* sensa is *false* if it means that they must be colors which nobody has seen, and *trivial* if it simply means that they are like colors in being dimensions of qualitative content.

The third and final point I wish to make is that while it would be a category mistake to suppose that sensa can be construed as a dimension of neural process as long as one is working within a framework of thing-like particulars, whether nerve cells, organic compounds, or micro-physical particles, the same considerations do not rule out the possibility that when an ideally completed neurophysiology interprets the physical concepts it employs in terms of the spatiotemporally punctiform particulars of an ideally completed micro-physics, sensa might fall into place as one qualitative dimension among others, one, however, which exists only in neuro-physiological contexts.[10] Needless to say, the idea that colors might in this sense be a dimension of neural process must not be confused with the idea that nerves are colored inside like chocolate candies.

To sum up this final section, the scientist, in his attempt to understand perception, must oscillate between the "Aristotelian" framework in which his problems are initially posed, and in which one logical subject, the person, has sense impressions, and a working "Hobbesian" framework in which, the unity of the person having been broken down into a plurality of logical subjects, the impressions become logical subjects in their own right, though of an attenuated and epiphenomenal kind. A unified picture of the perceiver can be found only at the beginning and at the end of the scientific quest. It has been my purpose to show that we are not without some glimpse of the end.

10 For an elaboration of this and related themes see "The Concept of Emergence," by Paul Meehl and Wilfrid Sellars in Herbert Feigl and Michael Scriven (eds.) *Minnesota Studies in the Philosophy of Science,* Vol. I (Minneapolis: Univ. of Minnesota Press, 1956), pp. 239–252.

COMMENTS

University of Massachusetts

THOUGH I AGREE with Professor Sellars on most philosophical issues, having cut my academic teeth on his tough but nourishing papers, I find that I have growing misgivings about his views on sense impressions. These misgivings may of course spring from misunderstanding, since the issues involved are maddeningly complex. But they are honest misgivings, and intricate enough, I think, to deserve a little airing—even though in airing them I take the risk of biting the hand that fed me.

According to him, the phrase "an impression of a red triangle" is related to the phrase "a red, triangular physical object" in two fundamental ways. The first of these is roughly that an impression of a red triangle may be characterized as that state of a perceiver normally brought about by the influence of red, triangular objects on the eye. The second is that an impression of this kind is conceived as analogous in certain respects to objects that are red and triangular on their facing side. Though this latter analogy is, in Sellars' view, a limited one, with the added peculiarity of being trans-categorial—that is, of holding between a thing and a state of a thing—it strikes me, on the contrary, as having somewhat the character of a metaphysical conceit, involving "heterogeneous ideas, yoked by violence together."

The difficulty I find with the analogy can be reduced to this. In emphasizing that impressions are to be understood as states, rather than as peculiar inner particulars, Sellars was led to assert that "*a* has an impression" has the form of "Φa," rather than "$aR\Phi$." This, however, seems clearly to commit him to a rejection of the traditional distinction between an impression and the having of an impression. Yet if the state in point, that is, the state conceived as analogous to the facing surface of a physical object, is more accurately, less misleadingly, described as "(the state of) having an impression," than the force of the analogy is exceedingly difficult to appreciate: I, for one, simply cannot imagine how *having an impression*, which is an entirely nonextended sensory state, could possibly be analogous to a facing surface. Indeed, if anything were to be conceived as analogous to a facing surface, it would presumably be the kind of thing that philosophers have called a "sense datum" or "sense content," something which is, plainly enough, a peculiar kind of particular, not a state of having something.

If my discomfort with trans-categorical analogies of this sort is not freakish—if others, too, must strain their imagination to the shattering point in attempting to perceive a likeness between physical surfaces and nonextended sensory states—then an analogy between surfaces and impressions can apparently be drawn *only if* one is prepared to regard an impression as a peculiar inner particular. For most philosophers today, who find all talk of inner particulars hilarious or grotesquely absurd, the cost of accepting this analogy will be, of course, far too great to pay. But something positive can be said in its favor, nevertheless. For one thing, if we are not quasi-behaviorists and yet admit that words do not gain meaning by private ostension but by some kind of interpersonal activity, which seems to require that the basic terms of our conceptual scheme must refer to things that we and our teachers can see and handle, then we should be strongly attracted to the idea that impressions, which are *not* publicly observable, are most easily conceived by analogy with what *is* publicly observable. Conceiving the unobservable in terms of the observable is, after all, an inveterate tendency of the human mind; for not only did we begin to think of such things as molecules on the model of observable elastic bodies, but even the ghosts, gods, and happy hunting grounds of our fathers were conceived by analogy with elements in the prosaic world around them.

Now if, keeping this analogizing tendency in mind, we then turn to impressions, it is not difficult to imagine how they may originally have been conceived in the mythy minds of our ancestors. For when the primeval hunter shouts at a bear that is clearly not there, it would be entirely natural for his fellows to think that a bearlike thing is somehow within him, promoting the cry: a tiny replica of a bear, similar, perhaps, to the tiny, colored, bearish shape that might be glimpsed in the eye of a bear-seeing man. Granting the truth of this possibly dubious conjecture does not of course commit one to hold that the ordinary man of today *must* think of his "visual sensations" in this primitive way. But the idea that impressions are things which, like daggers of the mind or little green men, can be privately apprehended *may* reflect a basic belief of the popular consciousness, and so infect the linguistic habits of ordinary speakers. The point is, when unobservables are conceived at all, they are generally conceived by analogy; and since impressions are *not* publicly observable, it is a good bet that they are conceived analogically as well. If so, the model for such things would very naturally be physical things, or their surfaces, which are intersubjectively available; and daggers of the mind would, accordingly, have the status of peculiar "mental" particulars.

If we approach the speech of ordinary men, and attempt to analyze it *without philosophical preconceptions,* we find, I think, that first person discourse often *does* reflect a belief in peculiar inner particulars. Considering, at any rate, the words a man is likely to use in describing his after-images, hallucinations, and the like—the kind of thing falling under the technical concept of a sense impression—it appears that they are generally described *as if* they were particulars, *as if* they were privately discernible objects. Thus, in the course for instance of a mescaline experiment one might describe various covert "somethings" as colored, bulgy, faded, or dim. If given a straightforward, aseptic analysis, such descriptions seem radically different from the description of a state, or of the having of something. In such cases one presumably describes something had, not the having of it; and to the extent that one's conception of a sense impression is to be justified by reference to the words normally used in describing one's experiences, to that extent the interpretation of sense impressions as states, rather that particulars, seems highly implausible. (But more of this later.)

Assuming, then, that something can actually be said in favor of an analogy between sense impressions, conceived as inner pictures, and facing surfaces of physical objects, just what can be said against it? Well, quite a lot—though in my opinion the considerations here are of a quasi-scientific, rather than a purely linguistic, nature; that is, they are based less on an unbiased analysis of what an ordinary person would ordinarily say than on a scientifically influenced picture of man and nature. I shall elaborate on this theme in a moment; but in order to prepare the way, I want to comment on the other element of the analogy, namely that of the facing surfaces of physical objects. If I am right, even if we could swallow the idea of inner surfaces, of sense impressions conceived as peculiar inner particulars, I think most of us would have trouble with the kind of outer surfaces that seem required by the analogy.

Consider, for instance, the case of a large red triangle. If the triangle is indeed red, then, as I believe Sellars has shown, it has this color even when it looks black to every available perceiver. But does this mean that the sensuous quality that comes to mind when one thinks of the color red, or when one imagines a red flag flapping in the sun, literally covers the surface of the triangle even when it is lodged in the deepest, darkest cave—that the sensuous quality is always *there*, if we could only detect it? (The sensuous quality in point here is the "redness" that traditionally is simple, indefinable, and knowable only ostensively.) Few of us, I think, would be happy to say yes; yet the analogy in point seems to demand an affirmative answer.

If what I have been saying is at all plausible, then, if there is to be an analogy between color impressions and colored physical surfaces, it appears that both impressions and surfaces must be interpreted in a way that, to me at least, is extremely unsatisfactory. But if, as I suspect, the analogy here is ultimately unacceptable, just how are we to interpret such remarks as, "I am now seeing something flat, red, and dim, though I am quite aware that it is not a physical, or publicly visible thing"? Well, a natural approach to this question might begin with an endorsement of part of Sellars' view (a part, by the way, with which I entirely agree), namely that one utters such words because one is in the same sensory state as one is normally in when viewing a red, flat object under a faint light. But this is only an approach to the question, not an answer to it; for it does nothing to settle the matter of what an impression actually is, of what the logical subject of the report happens to be.* It may well be true that anyone in this state will make this kind of report; but we cannot conclude that the report is *therefore* a description or identification of this state. Indeed, as I mentioned, when viewed

* This is really the heart of the matter. For if one were to ask a non-philosopher who, in the context, say, of a psychological experiment, is ostensibly describing his peculiar visual imagery, and says, "It is red and flower - shaped," whether he is talking about himself or something else, I am sure that he would say something to this effect: "Of course I am talking about something else; I am not just parroting noises, and I am surely not saying that I myself am red and flower-shaped!"

from a logico-grammatical point of view one seems in these cases to be describing a strange kind of particular.

Faced with the difficulty of this apparent reference to peculiar inner surfaces, philosophers have tried all sorts of escapes; for instance, to construe such puzzling statements as, "It is red," said apparently of a sense impression, as actually having the force of "I sense redly," which is ostensibly a statement about me, a fairly unproblematic sort of thing. But not only are these construals excessively contrived, they tacitly involve the abandonment of ordinary discourse, into which they are generally introduced for clarification. This is easily seen if one considers such a specimen as "It is pale and dagger-shaped." The "clarified" counterpart here would be "I sense palely and daggerly"; yet this form of words is not only never used in normal conversation, but it resists being classified as standard English.

Now, there is of course nothing sacrosanct about ordinary discourse, and hard reflection may make one want to revise certain parts of it, at least for theoretical purposes. But revisions ought not to be advanced as analyses. We can't just expect that the truth is *always* there in ordinary language, waiting to be brought to light by an inspired construal. Indeed, it seems reasonable to expect that hard philosophical thinking will occasionally reveal traces of the language's earthy origin,* two instances of which *might* be the ideas that sense impressions are inner pictures and that the sensuous quality that comes to mind when one imagines a blazing red

---

* The suggestion that ordinary habits of speech may occasionally be out of line with the news that science brings should not be excessively startling; in fact even J. L. Austin, who wrestled with ordinary speech in such an astonishingly able way, was prepared to say: "Determinism, whatever it may be, may yet be the case, but at least it appears not consistent with what we ordinarily say and presumably think." See "Ifs and Cans," in his *Philosophical Papers* (Oxford: Clarendon Press, 1961), p. 179, and also 166, fn. 1, where he remarks that "a modern belief in science" seems "not in line with the traditional beliefs enshrined in the word *can*. . . ."

sunset is always there in the dark, covering the surfaces of red but presently indiscernible objects.

If, however, one is anxious to free one's idiom of all traces of ancient beliefs, then, instead of remaining under the illusion, shared, I believe, by many philosophers today, that one is doing nothing other than *construing* that idiom, and hence not really changing it at all, one might just as well admit that it deserves a little revision (for theoretical purposes), and that this revision is best advanced on the basis of the best available picture of man and nature—which is, no doubt, the scientific picture. And if one proceeds in this way, it might be best to think of an impression as a something, unspecified as to precise logical type, which has certain phenomenal properties, that is, certain peculiar properties which we try to describe by using such words as "red," "bulgy," or "dim." This something may then turn out to be a set of cortical events.[1] True, these events will then have peculiar phenomenal properties, not presently mentioned in handbooks of neurophysiology. But these events, i.e., impressions so described, will at least be different from the having of an impression: when we speak of the having, we would then be speaking of a man's relation to what is had, his readiness to act, speak, think, or move as a result of what he has. In other words, the impression, as opposed to the having of it, will be characterized both physically, in terms for instance of the pattern of neuron firings in a certain area of a man's brain, and phenomenally, by the use of words as "red" and "bulgy" —words which, as Sellars shows, apply strictly or primarily to physical things. So characterized, the having of an impression will differ radically from the impression had; for the having of it will not be described as bulgy or dim (even when these

[1] This suggestion is amplified and defended at length in my paper, "Feigl on the Mind-Body Problem," in P. Feyerabend and G. Maxwell, eds., *Mind, Matter, and Method* (University of Minnesota Press, Minneapolis, 1966), pp. 17–39.

terms are not to be understood in the usual, physical sense);
it will rather be described in terms of the behavior, verbal or
otherwise, that is appropriate to the kind of impression had:
if, for instance, the impression is of a red triangle, then the
appropriate behavior will be similar, generally, to the behavior expected of a man in the presence of an actual (physical) red triangle under optimum conditions of illumination.
(Here it is obvious that I have no misgivings with Sellars'
analysis of the notion of *having* an impression; we diverge
only because I want to defend a distinction he apparently
refuses to make, namely that between the having of an
impression and the impression had.)

These fragmentary remarks on ordinary discourse, and on
the philosopher's inveterate tendency to purge it of ancient
conceptions and to hammer it into a happier instrument for
the expression of his considered views on man and nature,
have, I believe, an important bearing on Sellars' conception
of the relation between science and common sense, and I
want to round out my comment with a word on this subject.
For various reasons I am now, unlike Sellars, quite willing to
melt together both of Eddington's tables. I am quite willing,
that is, to regard the thing that I call a desk as a collection of
molecules, arranged in a certain way. True, I cannot see the
individual molecules that make it up; but I can see others,
such as diamonds and polymers; and I can even discern the
gross structure of smaller ones in photographs taken through
an electron microscope.

Sellars, however, has a number of arguments against this
position, two of which are short enough to consider briefly
here. The first concerns the fact that color words like
"brown" are, as he says, undefined predicates, true of single
logical subjects such as desks; while Eddington's so-called
desk is a whole aggregate of logical subjects, none of which is
truly characterized by this undefined predicate. In fact, as
Sellars insists, the framework of micro-physics has no place

for the common sense notion of color at all: when we begin to conceive reality along scientific lines, we see that outer, colored surfaces are just as peculiar as inner, colored surfaces; indeed, such outer surfaces do not really exist.

My reply to this argument, which shows perhaps that my conception of physical color is not truly commonsensical, is as follows: Though micro-particles are not strictly colored, aggregates of them generally are; they are the single logical subjects of which color words are true. Saying this does not commit me, I believe, to convert such words as "brown" into *defined* predicates, by giving them, say, a dispositional or power analysis. On the contrary, I would insist that, even according it a "primitive" character, one can still apply it to aggregates, and do so by looking at them: one trains one's eye on what is, in fact, an aggregate and, as a result, makes the appropriate identification. That this identification is correct is established not by the looking (which is not a premise), but by the standards of one's linguistic community: Would standard observers agree? Is one a standard observer oneself, so that whatever one says about the colors of objects in one's immediate vicinity has a strong prima facie claim to truth? And so on.

Another argument, which Sellars has worked out in another connection, *might,* however, be advanced against me here, *viz.*[2] the so-called grain argument. The point of the argument is this: color has a homogeneity, a continuity, which is essentially different from the gappiness of a molecular aggregate, from the gappiness of the surface of Eddington's so-called table. Since gappiness of this kind is incompatible with the continuity demanded by the usual conception of physical color, it therefore appears that molecules and colors *cannot* be melted together into a unitary picture of the

---

[2] In his "Philosophy and the Scientific Image of Man," in R. G. Colodny, (ed.), *Frontiers of Science and Philosophy* (Pittsburgh: Univ. of Pittsburgh Press, 1963), pp. 37–78.

desk we see. If we are strictly describing a desk, a bulky, smooth, colored thing, we are working within the conceptual scheme of everyday life; but when we attempt to describe what is before us in purely physical terms, in terms of the conceptual scheme of micro-physics, we conceive the object in a way that *forbids* the applicability of ordinary color concepts to it.

Again clinging to what is perhaps a nonordinary conception of physical color, a conception which does not imply that "redness," the sensuous quality, is always there, lurking in the dark, I reply as follows: Since color is, by definition, a visible property, the continuity it has is strictly a visual continuity, which means that if an object is, say, solid red, without dots and patches, then every visually distinguishable region of its surface must be red, also without dots and patches. But micro-regions of its surface need not have this color, since they are not visually discriminable. Hence the gappiness of molecular aggregates is not, it seems to me, incompatible with their having a solid, appropriately continuous color.

Now, Sellars did not actually use this grain argument in connection with physical color, at least in his paper on phenomenalism; he used it rather in connection with what might be called "phenomenal color" and the relation of such a quality to sets of neurons. I brought in the argument here only because it seems connected with his remark that color, commonsensically conceived, is *undefined,* which suggests that color words have an ostensive component, not captured by the usual verbal explanations, and grasped only by association with a colored surface. This sensuous "something" grasped ostensively may thus be continuous in a way that makes it difficult to conceive of molecular aggregates as really having color.

But while "common sense" may indeed conceive of physical color in this way, I, for one, do not: the idea that red objects placed in a dark room literally have something sensuous spread across their surfaces, or permeating their entire volume (as in the case of a pink, semi-transparent ice cube), strikes me as obviously absurd; and if common sense conceives of color in this way, then, in my view, Sellars is obviously correct in saying that, everything considered, colored objects, as conceived by common sense, simply do not exist. This might be put by saying that if Sellars is right about common sense, then common sense is scarcely the sort of thing that philosophers ought to take seriously. On the other hand, however, it is extremely doubtful whether educated men, living after the Renaissance, have thought of color in this common sense way.

In admitting that I am perhaps not a follower of common sense, I am evidently in danger of being grouped with those who do not love and find intellectual salvation in ordinary language. This may be so; but then I wonder whether the official, philosopher's program of analyzing ordinary language or common sense discourse is not slightly misconceived, anyway—at least in practice, if not in aim. For if one analyzes ordinary language in the now fashionable way, by attending to what "one would ordinarily say," rather than to the way the language is actually used by quite ordinary people (as determined, say, by the questionnaire method, or by an analysis of recorded speech), then one cannot expect that the very process of philosophizing will not alter "what one would say" when asked interesting philosophical questions. This process has, at any rate, altered my habits; for it is because I have been philosophizing, as well as studying science, that I am now extremely hesitant to speak of two things which *are,* for all I know, really championed by the ordinary or commonsensical man: namely, peculiar inner surfaces and peculiar outer surfaces.

REJOINDER
Wilfrid Sellars

I AM GRATEFUL to Professor Aune for the friendly care he has devoted to diagnosing the philosophical discomfort caused by my treatment of sense impressions. I could not ask for a better opportunity to correct misunderstandings and define substantive disagreements than is provided by the questions he raises and his own counterproposals.

At the heart of Aune's comments is a distinction, to which he believes I fail to do justice, between an impression and the *having of* the impression. Thus he writes:

> In emphasizing that impressions are to be understood as states, rather than as peculiar inner particulars, Sellars was led to assert that *"a* has an impression" has the form of *"Φa"* rather than *"aRΦ."* This, however, seems clearly to commit him to a rejection of the traditional distinction between an impression and the having of an impression.

To this the reply is "In a sense, yes, and in a sense, no." Postponing for the present the question of how the phrase "of a red triangle" in "Jones has an impression of a red triangle," is to be analyzed, the point I was trying to make is that "Jones has an impression" has the form "øJones" *rather than* "Jones R x" in the sense in which "Jones wore a smile" has the form "ø Jones" *rather than* "Jones R x." In other words, granted that there is a perfectly good sense in which both these statements have a relational form, this form is derivative form and dependent on that of the non-relational statements "Jones is impressed thusly," and "Jones smiled."

Another way of putting this is to draw a distinction between *real* relations, such as "to the left of," and *nominal* relations, such as "has" or "wore" in the above statements.[1] The "nominal" character of the latter would be bound up with their eliminability in accordance with the schema "x is R_n to a $N_V \leftrightarrow x\ V$" where "R_n" stands for the nominal relation, and "N_V" or the verbal noun corresponding to the verb "V." This terminology could be extended in such a way that impressions, smiles and, in general, N_Vs could be said to be nominal objects. This terminology, however, would be misleading, to say the least, and it is undoubtedly better to speak of smiles, feelings, impressions, sensations etc. as simply one variety of derivative objects. We would, of course, have to distinguish purely nominal relations, which carry no other burden than that of making possible the transposition of subject-verb statements into relational form, e.g., "has" in the above sense, from derivative empirical relations. Thus in "Jones' dance was *faster than* Smith's" *faster than* is derivative from the modifier in "Jones danced faster than Smith."

There is, then, a perfectly good sense in which I am as anxious as Aune to retain the distinction between an impression and the having of it. Yet I would deny that this distinction is a "real distinction" any more than is the distinction between a waltz and the waltzing of it. And I suspect that what Aune refers to as "the *traditional* distinction between an impression and the having of it" (italics mine) confuses *having* as a nominal relation with a real, if derivative, relation between a person and an impression (e.g., responding to

---

[1] Compare P. F. Strawson's distinction between "relations" and "ties," in particular the "attributive tie," in *Individuals* (London: Methuen & Co. Ltd., 1959), pp. 167 ff.

it) which might also be *called* "having." Indeed, when Aune comes to develop his own views on impressions and the having of them, it becomes clear that he has an empirical relation in mind.

2

Aune is troubled by my conception of visual impressions as states of a perceiver which have a certain analogy to the facing surfaces of physical objects. He notes that I speak of the analogy as "trans-categorial." This he regards as a "metaphysical conceit." As he sees it, only *particulars* are capable of possessing the requisite analogy to these facing surfaces. His fundamental strategy, thus, is to get me to admit that sense impressions as I conceive them must be "inner particulars." He hopes then to persuade me that the motion of inner particulars, although found, perhaps, among primitive peoples, has no place in the philosophical clarification of the conceptual framework of scientifically sophisticated people, and hence that the analogical interpretation of sense impressions, which I have developed in a number of papers, should be abandoned for a less devious analysis. As might be expected, everything hinges on what is to be understood by "particular." Granted that physical objects are particulars, then what of their facing surfaces? Aune seems to think that these also can be characterized as particulars. But if so, then might not only persons, but also their smiles, waltzing and sensations be particulars? If we adopt a reductive usage which excludes derivative objects from the category of particulars, then persons who smile, but not their smiles, would be particulars. In the context of persons and their states, Aune, without explicitly raising the issue, does seem to adopt a fairly tough usage. Thus, when he writes:

> Indeed, if anything were conceived as analogous to a facing surface, it would presumably be the kind of thing that philosophers had called a "sense datum" or "sense content," something which is, plainly enough, a

peculiar kind of particular, not a state of having something,

he seems to be ruling out the idea that impressions in my
sense, which are the counterparts of smiles and dances, are
"plainly enough" particulars. But once this terminological
tangle is cleared away, does any ground remain for Aune's
mistrust of "trans-categorial analogies"? Is it absurd to speak
of analogies between a dance and a statue? I agree with Aune
that the subjective terms of the analogy I have in mind must
be the impressions themselves and not the having of them.
My reason for this, however, is not that these havings are
states of the perceiver, but rather that these havings as such
are, so to speak, colorless, all empirical content falling in the
had. For visual impressions, as I can see them, are themselves
states of the perceiver, and I *do* think that as such they can be
analogous to facing surfaces. Aune's objection, on the other
hand, seems to be to the very notion that a *state* of a perceiver
could be analogous to a facing surface.* He seems to think
that if impressions are analogous to facing surfaces, they must
be "inner particulars" and *not* states of the perceiver. But
before bearing down on this point, a review of Aune's positive views on the subject will be helpful. Aune tells us that

> . . . an impression [is] a something, unspecified as to
> precise, logical type, which has certain phenomenal
> properties, that is, certain peculiar properties which we
> try to describe by using such words as "red," "bulgy,"
> or "dim."

---

* It must be born in mind, however, that Aune's objections rest not on a
clear and distinct thesis with respect to the analogy capacities of
states, but on a confusion of this topic with the question whether
(states of) having impressions *in his sense of "have"*— which he fails
to distinguish from the sense in which it stands for what I have called
a nominal relation—can be analogous, in the respects I mentioned, to
the facing surfaces of physical objects. A criticism of my position based
on a negative answer to the latter question would be a glaring
ignoratio.

What does Aune mean by "try to describe"? And *what* do we try to describe? In the above passage it is the *properties* which we try to describe. This suggests that the "peculiar" properties which impressions have are not the properties which the words "red" etc., stand for when applied to physical things. He further writes

> . . . the impression, as opposed to the having of it, will be characterized . . . by the use of words as "red" and "bulgy"—*words which, as Professor Sellars shows, apply strictly or primarily to physical things.* (italics mine)

In both passages there seems to be lurking a view according to which the "peculiar," "phenomenal" properties which visual impressions have are properties which we try to express *by an extended use of the perceptual vocabulary we apply to physical things.* Yet in spite of the obviously close relationship between the view he is sketching and the view he is criticizing, he refuses to speak of analogies between visual impressions and the facing surfaces of physical things.

In a somewhat more speculative frame of mind Aune tells us that the "somethings"—"unspecified as to logical type" may ". . . turn out to be a set of cortical events . . . these events will then have peculiar phenomenal properties, not presently mentioned in handbooks of neurophysiology." My feeling about this is that something like it may be true, but that the task of *analyzing* the *existing* conceptual framework of sense impressions is being confused with the task of envisaging an as yet nonexistent neurophysiological theory certain constructs in which might be "identified" with visual sense impressions. What a Pandora's box of philosophical woes is concealed in Aune's blithe "may turn out to be." And surely the source of Aune's feeling that impressions should be characterized as "unspecified as to precise logical type" is *not* that the sense impressions of the existing conceptual framework do not have a determinate logical grammar—for they do—but rather the fact that he uses the term "sense impression" to cover both the sense impressions of the existing conceptual framework and their counterparts in someday science. The latter are, indeed, "unspecified as to precise logical type."

On Aune's view, the "having" of an impression is not the metaphysical tie between a smiler and his smile, or a waltzer and his dancing, but a real relation between perceivers and their impressions. He acknowledges, parenthetically,

> Here it is obvious that I have no misgivings with Professor Sellars' analysis of the notion of *having* an impression: we diverge only because I want to defend a distinction he apparently refuses to make, namely that between the having of an impression and the impression had.

I hope it is clear from the preceding discussion that while I may have offered an analysis of the *notion* Aune refers to by the words "the having of an impression" I have not *used these words* to express the notion in question. I hope it is also clear that if I *had* used these words in Aune's sense, I would likewise have emphasized that impressions are not to be confused with the "having" of them.

3

The analogy, as I see it, between visual impressions and the facing surfaces of physical objects is to be understood in terms of an analogy between their characteristics. It should be borne in mind, as Aune recognizes, that central to the account of impressions developed in my "Empiricism and the Philosophy of Mind," and polished in subsequent papers, is the drawing of a meta-analogy between the formation of analogical concepts pertaining to inner episodes and the formation of analogical concepts in those scientific theories which postulate a domain of unobservables to redress the balance of the macro-world. The various interlocking frameworks of "inner episodes" were compared to the explanatory frameworks of physical theory.

The analogy between the properties of visual impressions and the properties of facing surfaces of physical objects was discussed in Section 6 of my essay. For our present purposes, the important thing to note is that if the analysis I have offered is correct, the families of predicates: "sφ_1" . . . "sφ_n"; "sψ_1" . . . "sψ_n," which are the analogues of physical object predicates "φ_1" . . . "φ_n"; "ψ_1" . . . "ψ_n" and generate statements of the form "x has I · sφ_i (I)," or, in less barbaric guise, "x has an impression which is sφ_i," designed to reconstruct statements of the form, "x has an impression *of* φ_i," must rest *in some sense* on a more basic level which would find its expression in the contrived sentence "x is impressed sφ_i-ly," in the way in which "Jones had a wan smile," rests on "Jones smiled wanly." This consideration brings us to the heart of the issue concerning trans-categorial analogy. Aune calls attention to the fact that

Faced with the difficulty of this apparent reference to peculiar inner surfaces, philosophers have tried all sorts of escapes; for instance, to construe such puzzling statements as "It is red," said apparently of a sense impression, as actually having the force of "I sense redly," which is ostensibly a statement about me, an eminently unproblematic, substantial sort of thing. But not only are these construals excessively contrived, they tacitly involve the abandonment of ordinary discourse into which they are generally introduced for clarification. This is easily seen if one considers such a specimen as "It is pale and dagger-shaped." The "clarified" counterpart here would be "I sensed palely and daggerly"; yet this form of words is not only never used in normal conversation, but it resists being classified as standard English.

To evaluate this we must step back a moment and consider first the case of the adjectival characterization of impressions. Consider the statement pairs:

(A-1) x had a red and triangular impression.
(A-2) x had a warm feeling.

(B-1) x had an impression of a red and triangular surface.
(B-2) x had a feeling of warmth.

In the first pair, "red and triangular" and "warm" are adjectives in a hard-nosed sense, i.e., they not only modify the nouns "impression" and "feeling" but do so in a grammatically perspicuous way. On the other hand, these adjectives clearly do not have the same sense as their homonyms which apply to physical objects. Thus, construing these predicates as analogical extensions of these homonyms and reconstructing these statements as

(A'-1) x had a red$_s$ and triangular$_s$ impression.
(A'-2) x had a warm$_s$ feeling.

would affront only a very ordinary ordinary-language philosopher. What of the "grammar" of the second pair, B-1 and B-2? It is easy to see that the expression "of a red and triangular surface" and "of warmth" serve to modify "impression" and "feeling" respectively. *In this sense* they are adjectives. But though they serve the adjectival function, they are not *in the ordinary sense* adjectives. They could, however, without discomfort, be called adjective-expressions. And clearly only the most hidebound ordinary language philosopher could object *in principle* to the claim that it is clarifying to view "of a red triangle" as a predicate, applicable to impressions, formed by joining a perceptual predicate applicable to physical objects to the preposition "of." (That ordinary language contains sensitive and subtle devices for expanding and relating conceptual structures should cause no surprise in this post-Milesian period.) It is not, therefore, flying in the face of ordinary language to suggest that "of red," "of yellow," "of a triangle," "of a circle" . . . can be compared to the families of predicate "sφ"; "sψ" introduced above. But does this make "x senses redly" or "x senses pale-dagger-shaped-ly" any more palatable? Aune argues that these contrived expressions cannot *clarify* the structure of ordinary language; that to introduce them is to *revise*. He concludes by inviting the philosophers who make these desperate moves to join with him in a frank revision of common sense. I disagree on both counts. I find these adverbial structures clarifying and I reject the view that the task of philosophy is to revise.

Let us continue with the examples we have been using, adapted to the verbal noun "sensation" which is the terminus of a different route of conceptual expansion than is "impression." Granted that

(C-1)   x senses red-triangle-ly.
(C-2)   x feels warmly,

are not standard English, does it make sense to say that they can be used to clarify *rather than* revise ordinary usage? I take it as obvious that the adverb "red-triangle-ly" and "warmly" are not explications of the predicates "red," "triangular" or "warm" as these are applied to physical objects. If they explicate anything, it must be concepts in ordinary usage which are offshoots of the latter. But, Aune urges, there simply are no adverbial expressions in ordinary usage to be clarified by such constructions. Is this true? Might it not be argued that once "of a triangle" has been recognized as an adjectival expression modifying the verbal noun "sensation" (or "impression") and as a suitable candidate for perspicuous representation by "triangular$_s$," we are committed to the view that the "grammatical space" of standard English contains the adverbial expression "(of-a-triangle)ly" as a modifier of the verb "senses" (or "is impressed"). Cannot language be said, by virtue of containing certain expressions in daily use, to be committed to the availability for use of certain *other* expressions which are themselves in point of fact never used? Let me defend this point by an example from another area. Suppose that the abstract term "Socrateskind" were introduced as a parallel to "mankind" so that one said, "Jones is a member of Socrateskind," just as he might say, "Jones is a member of mankind." Suppose, also, that the criterion for being a member of Socrateskind was to be excitingly like Socrates in intellectual make up. Suppose, however, that whereas one often said, "Jones is a man," and recognized it as a reduced equivalent of "Jones is a member of mankind," one never said, "Jones is a Socrates." Is there not a sense in which the existence of "Socrateskind" as a parallel to "mankind" involves the existence in the language of a common noun expression which has the sense of "a Socrates" as we actually use this expression, in, for example, "Wittgenstein was a veritable Socrates"?

To take a somewhat different example, suppose that, as is indeed the case, among the adjectival expressions in actual use there is one to which there corresponds no abstract singular term as "triangularity" corresponds to "triangular." Let it be "hysterical." There is, then, no such abstract singular term as "hystericalness" or "hystericality." Cannot our language, nevertheless, be said to contain an abstract singular term *expression* corresponding to the adjective? "But, of course!" someone might say. "Surely that is exactly the purpose served by the rubric 'being . . . ,' as in '(the quality of being triangular." In a perfectly valid sense, the language would contain the abstract singular term *expression* "(the quality of) being hysterical." Well, but doesn't language contain a suffix "-ly" exactly to form adverbs? Suppose the following premises are granted: (1) "sensation" is a verbal noun which stands for a category of states of persons;

(2) "of a red triangular circle" is an adjectival phrase which delineates a determinate kind of state falling under this category; does it not follow that our language contains (1) a verb which, if it doesn't exist *in actu,* exists *in posse* by virtue of a mode of self-extension intrinsic to the language, and which is the counterpart of the verbal noun in question—say "senses"; (2) an adverb which combines with this categorial verb to form a specific verb pertaining to sensing? If it be further granted that in the context "red and triangular sensation," "red and triangular" has the force of "of a red and triangular surface" and that "-ly" is available for the fomation of adverbs, then, assuming the relevant categorial verb to be "senses," are we not committed to the expression "x senses red-and-triangular$_s$-ly," where, as before, the subscript reminds us that the geometrical and color words in question are here being used in a way which is derived by analogy from their primary use?*

4

In the concluding section of this reply, I shall comment briefly on other aspects of Aune's remarks. He attacks my conception of both terms of the trans-categorial analogy between visual sense impressions and the facing surfaces of physical objects. I have already commented on his criticism of my conception of the first term. As for the second term, he interprets me as committed to the view

> that the sensuous quality that comes to mind when one thinks of the color red, or when one imagines a red flag flapping in the sun, literally covers the surface of the triangle even when it is lodged in the deepest, darkest

* I need scarcely emphasize that priority in the order of concept formation must not be confused with ontological priority. This is a point related to, but more searching than, Aristotle's point that priority in the order of knowing need not coincide with priority in the order of being. It will be remembered that on the view defended in "Phenomenalism" there are *really* no such things as the colored and shaped physical objects of the perceptual world.

cave?—that the sensuous quality is always *there*, if we could only detect it.

His mild comment following the passage quoted is: "few of us would be happy to say yes." Elsewhere, however, he expostulates

> . . . the idea that red objects placed in a dark room literally have something sensuous spread across their surfaces, or permeating their entire volume (as in the case of a pink, semi-transparent ice cube), strikes me as obviously absurd.

and goes on to say, as a gesture in my direction, that

> . . . if common sense conceives of color in this way, then, in my view, Professor Sellars is obviously correct in saying that, everything considered, colored objects, as conceived by common sense, simply do not exist.

To which he adds that "if Professor Sellars is right about common sense, then common sense is scarcely the sort of thing philosophers ought to take seriously." Aune, however, finds it "extremely doubtful whether educated men, living since the Renaissance, have thought of color in this . . . way." Well, I think it to be a *categorial* feature of the framework of percepible physical objects that they are colored throughout, even in deepest caves. They are not *believed* to be colored any more than persons are *believed* to be capable of forming intentions and carrying them out in action. Aune's use of the blanket phrase "educated men" blurs the distinction between the conceptual framework in terms of which a man responds to the world when he is outside his study, and the higher-order framework of philosophical reflection in terms of which, in the study, he reflects on the validity of the framework of perceptual experience. Aune seems to suppose that because educated people in their study are disposed to say "what really exists" are colorless atoms in the void, they must therefore *perceive* the world in terms of the conceptual framework of colorless atoms in the void. This is surely false. The conceptual framework of perception is the language of colored, shaped objects, flashes, etc., learned at mother's knee. And it must not be thought that theoretical science gradually revises *this* conceptual framework in the way a body of beliefs is revised, indeed that it revises it at all.

Aune thinks it absurd that physical objects are colored even in the deepest cave, because he *knows* that "the sensuous quality that comes to mind when [he] thinks of the color red" has no *real* existence in the object perceived, but exists rather as "peculiar, phenomenal properties" of cortical events. My objection is not that something *like* this isn't so, but that a fundamental issue in the theory of theories is being approached with a crowbar instead of a scalpel.

In elaborating his conception of the relation between science and common sense, Aune expresses his willingness "to melt together both of Eddington's tables." He considers two arguments against this. The first of these I develop in the concluding section of "Phenomenalism." It is, and I use Aune's formulation, to the effect that color predicates which apply to common sense physical objects are "undefined predicates, true of single logical subjects such as tables; while Ellington's so-called table is a whole aggregate of logical subjects, none of which is truly characterized by this undefined predicate." To this Aune counters

> My reply to this argument, which shows perhaps that my conception of physical color is not truly common-sensical, is as follows: Though micro-particles are not strictly colored, aggregates of them generally are; they are the single logical subjects of which color words are true.

He argues that this does not commit him to interpret such words as "brown" as defined predicates, by giving them, say, a dispositional or power analysis. He defends this claim by insisting that

> . . . even according it a "primitive" character, one can still apply it to aggregates, and do so by looking at them: one trains one's eye on what is, in fact, an aggregate and, as a result, makes the appropriate identification.

But what does it mean to say that "[aggregates] . . . are the single logical subjects of which color words are true"? I can readily understand the claim that a class is a single logical subject. Thus in "the class, K, is empty," *the class K* is the single logical subject of which the property of being empty is asserted. But surely "brown" is not predicated of classes? I agree, of course, that there is a sense in which a table *is* an aggregate of particles, but it is just this sense which is in dispute. As far as I can see, Aune has in mind an identity which obtains between the table and a class, not in the sense that $T = \{x,y,z\}$ but rather in a sense which might be initially represented by the schema, $T =_{df} (x_1,x_2,x_3)$ which implies that "$\varphi (T)$" stands to "$\varphi (x_1,x_2,x_3)$" as "brother (a)" stands to "male sibling (a) ." Or, more realistically, since the individual members of the aggregates to which we refer are rarely named, we can mobilize the schema $T =_{df} ('x, 'y, 'z) \lambda (x,y,z)$ so that given the truth of' (T) it would follow that there were unique objects, say x_1,x_2,x_3, such that $\varphi (x_1,x_2,x_3)$. But if something like this is in the wind, the statement "Brown (T)" would be defined counterpart of Brown $('x, 'y \ldots 'w)$ $\psi (x,y \ldots w)$ to which, if true, would correspond, in principle, the unquantified statement "Brown $(x_1 \ldots x_n)$" where "x_1," x_2," etc., are names. Now *ex hypothesi*, "brown" is a primitive predicate. But a primitive predicate, atomic statements involving which have the above form, must stand for an n-adic relation, which it obviously does not.

As for Aune's point that "brown" can be a primitive one-place predicate and still be "applied" to aggregates, the term "apply" conceals a fatal ambiguity. "Applying 'brown' to an

aggregate" may mean making a statement of the form "Brown
(. . .) " where an expression for an aggregate fills the blank,
"expression for an aggregate" being used in a strict sense to
mean "expression belonging to the conceptual space of a
set of elements, and having the appropriate logical form for
referring to an aggregate of these elements". On the other
hand, it may mean "what is, in fact, an aggregate." The
latter sense is completely uninteresting, for according to it,
Aune learned to "apply" the predicate "brown" to aggregates
of subatomic particles at his mother's knee. The problem of
in what sense tables are "in fact" aggregates is left completely
unilluminated.

WANTS, ACTIONS, AND CAUSAL EXPLANATION

William P. Alston

University of Michigan

1

THE TRADITIONAL problem of free will arises from an apparent conflict between the supposition that sometimes human beings act freely and can be held responsible for what they do, and the supposition that all human actions, along with all other happenings, are causally determined. In the immense literature which has grown up on this subject a great deal of attention has been given to the question of what it is to act freely and to be responsible, and the question of what causal determinism in general amounts to has been given a pretty thorough airing. But relatively little has been done to spell out what it would be for a human action in particular to be causally determined—what causal factors might possibly be involved and how they would have to be related to the action if they are to determine it. A few unspecific and unguarded references to "motives," "desires," "impulses," etc., are all that we usually get. Of late, however, philosophers have concentrated more heavily on this aspect of the problem, and the general tenor of the discussion has been that the idea that human actions are causally determined is fundamentally confused, and that we can see this when we look carefully at what a human action is and what causal determination is. For example:

> . . . if we are in fact confronted with a case of a genuine action (i.e., an act of doing something as opposed to

suffering something), then causal explanations are *ipso facto* inappropriate.[1]

Where we are concerned with causal explanations, with events of which the happenings in question are effects in accordance with some law of causality, to that extent we are not concerned with human actions at all but, at best, with bodily movements or happenings; and where we are concerned with explanations of human action, there causal factors and causal laws in the sense in which, for example, these terms are employed in the biological sciences are wholly irrelevant to the understanding we seek.[2]

I want to take issue with these views and, in the process of doing so, to explore some of the issues which arise when we try to imagine what causal determination of a human action might be.

I would suppose that here, as in other areas, causal determination of an event would require the truth of certain general "lawlike" statements which would represent events of that sort as determinate functions of certain sorts of prior factors, so that by knowing the values of those factors in a given case one could predict just what form that kind of event would take.* Wherever there are such principles which permit such predictions, we may speak of the class of events in question as being causally determined. It seems obvious, at first glance, that one could not *show* that this is impossible with respect to actions; surely the idea that there are such true

---

* There are well known difficulties involved in constructing a general criterion for "lawlike" statements, in contrast with other general statements. And there are further problems as to how simple the lawlike statements must be if they are to justify us in regarding events of a certain sort as causally determined. Since these problems are not special to causal determination of actions, I shall not even review them and shall pretend that we can either solve them or can somehow continue to speak of lawlike statements and causal determination in the absence of a definitive solution.

principles which have actions as the dependent variables represents an intelligible possibility. Yet this is what seems to be denied in the above quotations. I suggest that we look into the arguments which are given for this position. They can be usefully divided into those which do, and those which do not, proceed by a consideration of some particular sort of putative causal factor. We shall consider the latter first since, as we shall see, it very quickly collapses into the former.

2

Insofar as these authors give any reason for the *general* claim that no causal explanation of any sort can be given for actions, it amounts to saying that any attempted causal explanation of an action will turn out to be only an explanation of a bodily movement, and that actions are not just bodily movements.

> To give a causal *explanation* of an event involves at least showing that, other conditions being presumed unchanged, a change in one variable is a sufficient condition for a change in another. . . . Now the trouble about giving this sort of explanation of human actions is that we can never specify an action exhaustively in terms of movements of the body or within the body.[3]

It must be admitted that actions are not identical with bodily movements or other physiological occurrences, not even the simplest actions. To say that I raised my arm is not just to say that my arm rose or that certain muscles were innervated. At the very least the former differs from the latter by virtue of implying that the movement was under my control, that I could have inhibited it if I had decided to do so. When we get beyond this simplest level, much more is involved. To say that I played the violin this afternoon is to imply, *inter alia,* that a violin was in a certain sort of contact with my body. To say that I was fishing this afternoon is to imply, *inter alia,* that I was dangling bait in water for the *purpose* of catching fish. To say that I asked someone for a match is to imply, *inter alia,* that I recognized my utterance to be governed by certain linguistic rules. To say that I completed a forward pass is to imply, *inter alia,* that I was engaging with others in a game which the participants recognize to be governed by certain rules and that certain of my movements had a result which was to be termed a success in terms of the conventions of that game. And so on.

But what reason is there to suppose that an attempted causal explanation of actions could never get beyond explaining bodily movements? These philosophers have not arrived at their general thesis via a survey of all conceivable ways of attempting such explanations (vain aspiration!). I believe that a careful examination will reveal an implicit assumption that causal explanations (in any sense in which we have causal explanations in the natural sciences) always conform to a mechanistic pattern. This would mean explaining actions as the mechanical products either of inner physiological occurrences like neural impulses and muscular contractions (the project criticized by Peters), or of volitions, desires, intentions and the like, construed as immaterial mental "pushes," "forces," or "impulses" (the project criticized by Melden). To dissipate this assumption, and with it the general claim that causal explanations can bear on movements, but not actions, it is sufficient to point out the logical possibility of causal explanations of other, nonmechanistic, sorts. And to defend that logical possibility is the chief task of this paper. But first we should scrutinize briefly the claim that actions cannot be explained in terms of such mechanistic models. Let us concentrate on the physiological model, since that is more of a live issue today than the "mental mechanism" model derived from the British empiricist tradition.

Why should we suppose that causal explanations of actions in physiological terms is impossible? Peters bases this thesis on the claim that actions, unlike bodily movements, contain a logical complexity not to be found in physiological states and processes.

> There cannot therefore be a sufficient explanation of actions in causal terms because, as Popper has put it, there is a logical gulf between nature and convention. Statements implying norms and standards cannot be deduced from statements about mere movements which have no such normative implications.[4]

If what I have said about actions is true, then there are many action terms which do carry implications about "norms and standards," and so it is impossible to *deduce* statements about actions from statements about "mere movements" or to translate the one type of statement into the other. Indeed we do not need to bring in norms and standards to make this point. All the conditions of application for action terms mentioned above, in addition to conditions specifying certain bodily movements, furnish reasons for this same conclusion. But in itself this does not show that actions cannot be causally explained in terms of physiological occurrences. To suppose it did would be to regress to a conception of causality on which the cause-effect relationship is a deducibility relationship or some other logical connection; or perhaps it would involve invoking the medieval principle that the cause must contain at least as much reality as the effect.

But it is true that, if actions involve conditions of all the sorts mentioned above, it would be wildly implausible to suppose that they can receive a complete causal explanation in physiological terms. For to suppose that typing a letter could be so explained would be to suppose that a certain brain state, e.g., is not only a sufficient causal condition of certain bodily movements, but also a sufficient causal condition of the presence of a typewriter with paper in it, and of the existence of a custom of sending letters in the society to which the man in question belongs. I am not sure whether such a causal connection is logically impossible. A reason for supposing that it is would be this: It does seem obvious that any specifiable brain state could be artificially produced by electrical stimulation if our technology were sufficiently advanced. Suppose we carry this out in a completely bare room on a member of a culture in which letter writing is unknown. Could it be an empirical question as to whether this brain stimulation would cause a typewriter to materialize in the room and would suddenly introduce the institution of letter writing in the culture (or, alternatively, transport this chap, culturally, into another milieu). It is just barely conceivable, I suppose, that there is in fact a constant conjunction between a certain kind of brain state and the satisfaction of *all* the conditions that have to be satisfied for one to be writing a letter. But the above consideration casts considerable doubt on the supposition that such a regularity could have the counterfactual implications which it must have to be a causal connection. (If this brain state were produced in the conditions described, all the conditions necessary for writing a letter would be satisfied.) But even if not logically impossible the suggestion is too wildly implausible to be taken seriously.

Nevertheless, it might be a sensible project to combine physiological factors with other sorts in causally explaining actions. Let's divide the conditions which have to obtain if a given action is to be performed into those which are facts about the agent and those which are not. For typing a letter, the former group would include making bodily movements which fall within a certain range, knowing a language, intending to produce a set of written sentence tokens of the language for the purpose of communicating with someone. The latter group would include the existence of a typewriter and paper in a certain connection with the agent's hands, the normal operation of this typewriter, and the existence of an institution of letter writing in the society. I would suppose that the highest aspiration a physiological theory could sensibly have would be the explanation of the former group of conditions. It could then form one segment of a total explanatory scheme which would have to bring in the determinants of the "external" conditions. If we look at the writings of people who want to approach psychology physiologically, e.g., D. O. Hebb, they do not seem to have grasped this point. Their aspirations, when they are speaking programmatically, are pitched much higher.

3

However interesting these possibilities, it is not with physiological schemes that I wish to concern myself. As noted earlier, one can rebut the claim that any attempted causal explanation of actions will turn out to be at best explanations of bodily movements by showing that one can envisage causal explanations of actions which are of a nonmechanistic sort. It would be of particular relevance to show that there are no logical bars to giving a causal explanation of actions in terms of such "intentional" factors as wants, beliefs, and perceptions. For such factors contain the same rich logical complexity as action terms. (Wanting to congratulate Jones on his appointment is, as Melden points out in detail, at least as complex logically as congratulating Jones on his appointment.) Even Peters' gratuitous worry about a "logical gap" would be relieved. I wish to devote the rest of the paper to considering various reasons for supposing that such schemes are, in principle, impossible. Such a consideration will be of interest not only for the free will problem, where the thesis of causal determination of actions has often been put forward in such terms, but also for the strategy of theory construction in psychology, where schemes of this sort are among the alternative bases for theoretical thinking and experimentation.

In order to get before us an actual example of this sort of causal theory (or rather an actual example of an outline of

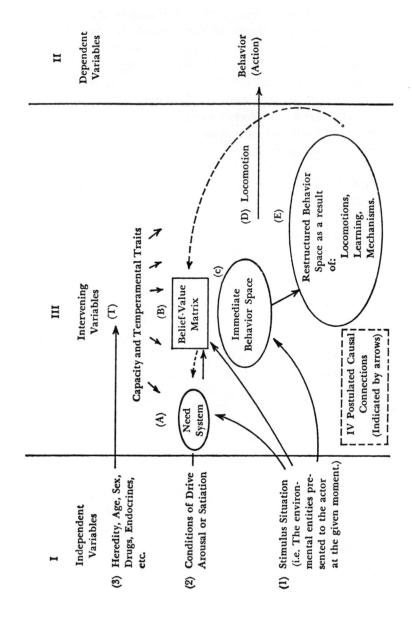

such a causal theory, the most one can find at the present juncture) consider the scheme put forward by E. C. Tolman in his essay "A Psychological Model."[5] Roughly, the "need system" consists of dispositions to find satisfaction in certain kinds of objects or situations; the "belief-value matrix" contains beliefs about and valuations of objects with which the person has come into contact; and the "immediate behavior space" is a complex of perceptions, including memories and inferences from perception, concerning objects and their interrelations, including the person himself.

As Tolman makes abundantly clear, what he gives us is not a theory, but a model along the lines of which a theory might be constructed. Before we could actually develop such a theory a number of preliminary steps would have to be taken. First, we would have to decide on suitable units. What is to count as a single belief or a single perception? Is the belief that a military outpost will hold out for the next twenty-four hours made up of a number of constituent beliefs corresponding to sub-periods of that twenty-four hour period? When I look out the window, how many perceptions shall we count? One for each distinguishable object in my visual field? (And how do we count those?) One for each distinguishable aspect of each object? Or something more global? After deciding on units, there is the problem of finding a workable way of representing the variety of such units. If explicit causal principles are to be constructed along these lines we could not simply import into the principles all the unsorted conceptual variety to be found in our ordinary ways of talking about beliefs, etc. Presumably we would have to emulate the physical sciences in representing this diversity as variations in relatively basic magnitudes. That is, for each of the "variables," independent, intervening, and dependent, we would have to find a manageable number of dimensions, which are such that each belief, action, etc., could be represented as a constellation of positions on these dimensions. Appropriate techniques of measurement would have to be developed. Except for sense perceptions, narrowly conceived, virtually nothing has been done to construct such dimensions.

And of course, we would have to make sure that our categorization of "variables" is such as to include everything that is likely to be relevant and such as to make conceptual cuts in the most useful places. On the first point, it would seem, e.g., that Tolman would have to enlarge his scheme to include emotional upsets of various kinds. On the second point, there is the question as to whether the distinctions between likings, interests, (internalized) standards, and attitudes can be ignored in the way that would be involved in lumping them all under the heading of "valuations."

Moreover, actually to apply the scheme in the prediction of behavior we would need something close to a complete inventory of the beliefs, valuations, etc. of a given individual, as well as a detailed account of the way in which he "sees" the situation in which he finds himself at the moment. This is an enormously more complicated job than simply getting at one or two or three particular factors (e.g., anxiety level and need for dominance) as one tries to do in the usual searches for correlations between a very small number of factors. To develop techniques for doing it we would have to answer many so-far unanswered questions. For example, when are we to say that a person does or does not have a certain concept?

It is interesting that a science which advertises itself as the science of behavior has done so little toward developing theories which can be used to predict action. Psychologists can tell us much more about the determinants of skills, levels of excellence of performance, emotional states, likes, attitudes, habits, perceptions, and beliefs than about what controls exactly *what* a person will do at a given time. No doubt this is primarily because of the greater complexity of the latter task. Most of the matters considered by psychologists will have an important bearing on what a person does at a given time, so that this is, in a sense, the culminating problem of psychology. But whatever the reason, the fact is undeniable. However it seems to me that Tolman's model gives us an indication of the sort of thing such a theory might be, an indication which is sufficient to provide a basis for discussing its logical possibility.

We can extend our understanding of the program by considering some of the attempts to use fragments of this kind of scheme in the actual prediction of behavior. Consider J. W. Atkinson's paper, "Motivational Determinants of Risk-Taking Behavior."[6] Atkinson works there with the "achievement motive," conceived as a disposition to strive for a certain kind of satisfaction, viz., that which comes from success in a performance as evaluated against some standard of excellence; or alternatively conceived as a capacity for taking satisfaction in such success. A great deal of work has been done in developing ways of measuring relative strengths of the achievement motive in different people, primarily by thematic apperception tests. In relating a motive to behavior, Atkinson works with the following "principle of motivation."

> The strength of motivation to perform some act (sc. insofar as only one motive is involved) is assumed to be a multiplicative function of the strength of the motive, the expectancy (subjective probability) that the act will have as a consequence the attainment of an incentive, and the value of the incentive: Motivation f (Motive x Expectancy x Incentive).[7]

He then makes certain assumptions as to how the subjective probability of the attainment of a goal and the incentive value of that goal for the individual can be measured. He then derives relative strengths of the motivation to perform tasks of varying levels of difficulty, when the motive to achieve is greater than the motive to avoid failure, when the latter is greater than the former, and when they are equal in strength.

(We are assuming an ideal case in which other motives, e.g., to win approval or to hurt oneself, are involved only negligibly.) He does not attempt to use this scheme to predict individual actions, but he does derive from it broad statistical predictions which are borne out by previous experimental studies, e.g., that people who are generally more fearful of failure than hopeful of success tend to set either extremely high or extremely low goals. There are no doubt many other factors which influence a person's choice of actions, even in this idealized situation, e.g., his current emotional state. But this shows how we might at least begin to make use of schemes like Tolman's in the actual prediction of behavior.

Now in bringing forward Tolman's model as an example, I am supposing that if this sort of theory were developed it would count as a causal theory, and that explanations of actions derived from it would count as causal explanations. And it might be thought that, quite apart from the deep difficulties to be considered shortly, such a theory would obviously not be a causal one, that it does not even *look like* a causal theory. (Tolman himself uses the term "causal connection," but I should not wish to attach much significance to that fact.) Such a reaction would most likely stem from the common practice of making a sharp distinction between the reasons for an action and the causes of an action. With such a distinction in the background one might then suppose that any explanation derived from Tolman's kind of theory, since it proceeded in terms of the wants, beliefs, and perceptions of the agent, would give us the agent's reasons for what he did and hence could not be construed as specifying causes of his action.

To neutralize this reaction, I should like to distinguish between the claim that wants and beliefs, as they figure in everyday discourse about actions, would ordinarily be called causes of actions, and the claim that causal explanations of actions might be constructed in terms of such factors. It is only the latter thesis I am concerned to defend. Indeed, it does seem to me that we do ordinarily distinguish between causes and reasons of actions in such a way that wants and beliefs cannot be regarded as causes. "I wanted to get some yard work done," or "I intended to finish that paper today," would be strange answers to "What caused you to get out of bed?" I am not sure as to the exact boundaries of the use of "cause" in connection with actions. It seems clear that "He had a sudden spasm of pain in his arm and that caused him to turn the car suddenly" and "The workers on the street started up a terrific din, and that caused him to get up" are all right. But what about "The alarm went off and that caused me to get up" or "He got such a terrible headache that it caused him to leave the meeting early"? In fact, it is difficult to find really clear cases of the use of "cause" in connection with full-blooded actions, as opposed to starts, twitches, recoils, and grimaces. However, it does seem clear that we do not ordinarily speak of causes of actions unless we are dealing with sudden intrusions of factors which work on the person more or less automatically. And it seems that we do not use "cause" where we are speaking either of cognitive factors like beliefs and realizations, or of factors like wants or feelings of obligation which, if they are not themselves cognitive, work only in connection with cognitive factors.

But the fact that we put these special restrictions on "cause" in ordinary discourse about human behavior does nothing to show that one could not construct systematic theories relating factors of these sorts to actions in a way that would justify us in calling these theories causal theories, and the explanations which they yield causal explanations. "Cause" and its derivatives are, of course, used in various ways in various contexts, and there is disagreement over when a theory or an explanation should be called causal. But I would suppose that a theory of action would have at least a prima facie claim to

be called a causal theory if it satisfied the following requirements:

(1) The theory exhibits an action as a determinate function of a certain constellation of variables such that,
given the values of all these variables, one can determine what action(s), if any, an agent performs at a
certain time (as well, perhaps, as determine various
other facts about the action not covered by a specification of *what* action it is, e.g., how long he goes on
performing it).

(2) These determining variables are such that one can
determine the values of all of them in a given instance without already knowing what action(s) the
agent in question performs at the time in question.

(3) The values of the variables in question are values
those variables have at a time prior to the performance of the action in question. That is, reading the
action off from these values is, or could be, *predict-
ing* the action.

We might strengthen these requirements in various ways,
e.g., by stipulating some minimum degree of spatio-temporal
contiguity between independent and dependent variables,
and we might weaken them in various ways, e.g., by requiring
only that the theory exhibit a certain probability of a certain
action as a function of the variables in question. But I think
it is clear that any theory which satisfies the requirements as
stated would be what is often called a causal theory, and so,
too, for any explanation derived from such a theory. More
particularly, it would seem that, insofar as such a theory were
established, we would thereby have reason to regard actions as
causally determined in the sense that is of interest in the free
will problem. For, once we get beyond animistic notions of
causal necessity and causal constraint, what makes causal de-

termination seem antithetical to free will is the possibility (in principle) of complete predictability.

Now it certainly seems that any theory of the sort envisaged by Tolman would satisfy those three conditions, and would give us the kind of predictability which engenders the free will problem. The fact that in our ordinary talk about actions we distinguish between those factors like wants and beliefs which involve intentionality, and those like external stimuli and bodily sensations which do not, by using the word "cause" in the latter case and not in the former, does nothing in itself to show that such a theory is impossible or that it would not deserve to be called a causal theory.* Indeed, I would distinguish my thesis not only from a claim that wants and beliefs are "causes" of actions, ordinarily so called, but even from a claim that the explanations of actions we give in everyday discourse in terms of wants and beliefs, are causal in character. It would be in line with the general outlook of this paper to maintain that the commonsense explanation of someone's getting up early by reference to his wanting to get a paper finished is essentially an incomplete causal explanation, that it is related to a complete specification of causal conditions in terms of a Tolman-like theory in the same way that explaining a fire in terms of someone's dropping a lighted match is related to a complete statement of the causal conditions in terms of some physical theory. This seems to me to be a plausible view, but to examine all the issues involved in criticizing and defending it and its alternatives is an arduous task for which I have no time in this paper. The point is that one could reject this interpretation of *everyday* explanations of actions in terms of wants and beliefs, and still accept the thesis of this paper that a systematic causal theory of action

---

* Of course, one may hold that there are differences between the relations of these two different sorts of factors to actions which justify these restrictions on "cause" in ordinary discourse. This claim would presumably be based on the arguments discussed below.

could be framed in such terms, and that from it causal explanations of actions in such terms could be derived. In that case, there would be a gulf between the two sorts of explanations, one of the many gulfs which open between scientific and everyday thought.

4

The main bar to supposing that a causal theory of this sort is possible is the appearance of a logical connection between such factors as wants and the actions which they are invoked to explain. It seems reasonable, at least it has seemed reasonable since Hume, to suppose that if A and B are logically connected they cannot be causally connected. And quite apart from facts about the use of the term "cause," it would seem that if wants and actions are logically connected, it would not be an *empirical* job to determine the way in which actions are a function of wants.

There are several different ways in which a logical connection seems to be involved. For one thing, it is claimed that when we "explain" an action by citing a want or intention, we are in fact simply giving a fuller description of the action; and that since the want or intention enters into the (full) description of the action, it cannot be causally related to it.

> For instance, we might ask "Why did Jones walk across the room? Was it in order to put coal on the fire or out of politeness?" But this would not be a causal question. It would be a way of eliciting what sort of action it was.[8]

> . . . on this supposition, the motive for the action is the cause of the action. This, however, is self-contradictory. As the alleged cause of the action, it cannot serve further to characterize the action. As motive it must—for it tells us what in fact the person was doing.[9]

> Since a motive, in explaining an action, makes it clear what the action in question is, any description or account of the motive must of necessity involve a reference to an action being performed, and specifically to the kind of action that is thereby specified by the explanation given.[10]

These arguments do not seem impressive to me for two reasons. First, it is only in certain types of cases that we can be secure in going from an explanation in terms of want, etc., to an account of what the agent is doing. These are the cases in which the want or intention involved is a want or intention to do something which the agent is doing contemporaneously with the action being explained. Melden's chief example is of this sort: explaining the driver's raising his arm in terms of his intention to signal a turn. Signalling a turn is going on simultaneously with raising the arm, and, furthermore, in this situation raising the arm *is* signalling the turn. Other such cases would be: explaining my writing a letter to Jones by saying that I wanted to invite him to visit us; explaining my leaving the room by saying that I wanted to avoid Smith; and explaining my laying down a certain card by saying that I did it in order to trump the trick. But there are many other cases in which we explain doing A in terms of a want or intention to do B, or a feeling that one has to do B, where B is not simultaneous with A but is a further action, which A is thought to lead to. Thus I may explain getting up early by saying that I had to meet Jones at the airport, explain my getting out my tools by saying that I want to fix a door knob, or explain my walking down the hall by saying that I intend to have it out with my boss. In these cases the explanation does not "further characterize the action" or "make it clear *what* the action in question is," or even give us materials for such characterization. To say that I am getting up early because I want to meet Jones at the airport is not to imply that I *am* meeting Jones at the airport; nor does saying that I am getting out my tools because I want to fix a door knob imply that I *am* fixing a door knob.

The second and more fundamental difficulty with this argument goes deeper and extends to all sorts of cases. Even where, in explaining an action in terms of a want, etc., we are providing, or at least providing materials for, a further description of what the agent is doing, this does not mean that

explanans and explanandum are *logically* related in a way
that would make a causal relationship impossible. When, in
answer to the question, "Why are you leaving the party?" I
reply, "I want to avoid Smith," I am, it is true, providing you
with a further account of what I am doing at the moment,
but that does not keep my wish to avoid Smith from being
among the causal conditions of my leaving the party. What
we must see is that in giving this explanation I am setting out
to explain *the fact that I am leaving the party;* I am not setting out to explain *what I am doing at the moment,* taken in
some all-inclusive sense, nor am I setting out to explain various other facts which also have to do with what I am doing
at the moment, such as the fact that I am avoiding Smith, the
fact that I am walking toward the front door, etc. We must
not let the fact that *in this situation* leaving the party *is* avoiding Smith, or the fact that what I am doing at the moment
can be correctly characterized both as leaving the party and
as avoiding Smith, make us suppose that the task of explaining my leaving the party is the same as the task of explaining
my avoiding Smith. And we should resist just as strongly the
temptation to suppose that the job of explaining my leaving
the party is a job of explaining what I am doing at the time
(taken without further specification) or of explaining what is
going on there and then. To give way to these tendencies
would be to commit the elementary blunder of supposing
that what we set out to explain is a slice of reality, a chunk
of space-time in all its concreteness. If that were so, the way
we characterize a chunk when we ask for an explanation of it
would have no implications for *what* we are trying to explain.
And, in the above situation, the questions "Why are you
leaving the party?" and "Why are you avoiding Smith?"
would turn out to be the *same* question. What we set out to
explain is always *the fact that so-and-so,* an abstract aspect of
a slice of reality, and so the aspect of the slice we pick out in
order to specify our explanandum has a great bearing on

what question we are trying to answer. If I set out to explain the fact that a person is given to compulsive hand-washing, there will be many other things that he is doing in compulsively washing his hands, which will not be adequately explained by my explanation of his compulsion, no matter how adequately that explanation does the job for which it was intended. Thus in washing his hands, the person may be destroying germs, seriously depleting the water supply, and affording amusement to his siblings. But my explanation will not be an adequate explanation of the fact that he is doing all these things, although it would be if I were setting out simply to explain "what he is doing" on these occasions.

Once we see this point, we can see that even though what I am doing at the moment can be correctly characterized both as leaving the party and as avoiding Smith, it by no means follows that the fact that I want to avoid Smith is logically related to the fact that I am leaving the party, in such a way as to make it impossible that the first figures among the causal conditions of the second.

5

There is a kind of putative logical involvement which does not disappear so quickly under scrutiny. If one begins to try to imagine what sorts of principles would be involved in a Tolman-like theory, it may seem that the connections between psychological states and actions specified by such principles would not be empirical principles at all (and so would not specify *causal* connections). Could it be an empirical discovery that wanting very much to do something would increase the likelihood of doing it; or that believing that doing something would lead to great injury to oneself, would engender a strong tendency not to do it? Could we deny these principles without overturning our concepts of want, belief, etc.? But we must be careful not to pose the problem in terms which are too simple to make contact with the real issues.

Melden speaks of "the logical incoherence, and no mere violation of empirical fact, involved in the supposition that a person might never do what he wants to do or always do what he does not want to do."[11] Of course it is obvious that it is not logically, or even factually, necessary that a person always does what he wants to do, or even that he always tries to do what he wants to do. And it is certainly not logically true, although it might be true as a matter of fact, that people usually do what they want to do. But it does seem that there is something logically odd in the supposition that people never do what they want to do. And this would seem to make "If a person wants to do x, there is a considerable probability that he will do x" suspect as a candidate for a principle in an empirical theory relating psychological factors to actions. However this particular logical involvement, assuming it does exist, does not seem particularly germane to our problem. For one thing, insofar as we are interested in causal determination from the standpoint of the free will problem, we are interested in deterministic, not probabilistic, principles. For another thing, any scheme which would be of interest to psychologists would include among the determinants of doing x, not wanting to do x, but rather wanting to do or have or be something else. The psychologist wants to get farther back in the causal chain than he would if he just traced doing x to wanting to do x. He will be more interested in seeing doing x as a function of a number of relatively generalized wants—for achievement, attention, approval, emotional stimulation, novelty, etc., plus various beliefs which relate these to specific types of actions and perceptions which relate them to the immediate situation, as in Tolman's scheme.

But analogous difficulties can be raised with respect to this more complicated sort of explanation. Suppose we think of explaining Smith's driving to town in terms, not of his wanting to drive to town, but in terms of his wanting to go to a concert (or if we want something more general, of the sort actually considered by psychologists, his wanting the kind of emotional stimulation one receives from symphonic music) plus a belief that driving to town now is a necessary condition of his getting such stimulation (or, perhaps, a belief that driving to town would put him in the best possible position for getting such stimulation). It might be supposed that any general principle which would lie behind explaining the action in those terms would be logically true.

(1) Whenever any one wants to do x and believes that doing y will put him in the best possible position for doing x, he will do y.

However this will not stand up as such. It is not self-contradictory, or even logically odd, to suppose that Jones wants to go to the concert, believes that he can only go to the concert by driving to town, and yet does not drive to town. He might want more to stay home and read a book. Or he might have some work which he has to get done that evening. Or he might not have a car available. Or he might not be able to drive. Or he might have religious scruples against driving on Friday evening. Or the whole thing might have slipped his mind until it is too late. Or he may be too emotionally upset to go to the concert.

Of course, each time we think of something which would prevent the action actually being performed we can introduce something into the formula which excludes that interference. Presumably something like this is done when schemes such as Tolman's are excogitated. Thus we can construct the more complex principle:

(2) Whenever A wants to do x, doesn't want to do anything incompatible with doing x more than he wants to do x, believes that doing y will put him in the best position for doing x, has both the capacity and opportunity for doing y, doesn't feel obliged to do anything incompatible with doing x or y, has no

scruples against doing x or y, hasn't forgotten about doing x, is not too emotionally upset to do x, then he will do y.

It may well be that even this is not complex enough, but it is difficult to tell. What factors might prevent this complex antecedent from issuing in the consequent? Well, Smith's wife might strongly oppose his driving to town on the grounds that the roads were slippery, and in the face of this opposition Smith might abandon his project. But one could say that in this case he does have a stronger incompatible want—to avoid subjecting his wife to a great deal of worry. Perhaps his pride in some way interferes with his doing y. Is this to be counted as an incompatible want, or as a contrary scruple? Or is some separate category needed here? Although it is difficult to be sure at any point that we have a statement which is universally true and which would afford firm ground for prediction, it might well seem that the closer we get to such a statement the closer we get to a statement which is *logically* true. For it may seem that in filling out the statement we are simply reflecting on our use of the terms involved rather than appealing to empirical evidence. It would seem that I don't have to perform experiments to tell that having strong scruples against doing y might well prevent y from being performed, even though the other conditions are satisfied.

Before I go into the question of the logical status of (2) let me consider the following doubt as to the pertinence of this question to the philosophy of psychology. It may be thought that even if such principles as the above are logically true, or even analytic, this has no bearing on the status of the principles in a systematic psychological theory. For psychologists like Tolman are not employing the ordinary concepts of want, scruple, etc., but are constructing technical concepts which are only misleadingly expressed in these everyday terms. But this is not really a way out. The psychological theorist simply does not have the resources to get along without depending on the vague but rich content of these everyday concepts. He can attempt to refine them in various ways, introduce intersubjectively reliable indications and measures, and pare away this or that feature, but the state of the art is not such that he can straight out *define*, e.g., "motive" in terms of some measure like the thematic apperception test. If he tries to do so, he will be left high and dry with a methodologically pure concept which fails to connect interestingly with very many of the things with which he is seeking liaisons. And there is another reason why such isolation is unrealistic even as a goal. It is surely the case that in some way we do get real understanding of a person's action if we see that he did it because he wanted so and so. One would hope that psychology would, among other things, help us to understand better what kind of understanding this is and provide us with ways of acquiring more precise and more thoroughgoing understanding of this sort, rather than turning its back and talking about something else instead. (Indeed, as we shall see in a moment, Tolman himself, when elucidating his crucial concepts, explicitly indicates their close connection with commonsense concepts.)

To return to the question of the logical status of (2), if anyone thinks that any such principle is logically true, his grounds may simply be that its denial sounds "logically odd" or "deviant." But such a claim, however currently fashionable, provides at best a sandy foundation. Like its ill-fated predecessor, "I can't imagine (conceive, envisage) its not being so," it is notoriously difficult to distinguish at sight between different sources of the inability to conceive or of the odd sound. The fact that I can't form a conception of the agent not doing y when all the above conditions hold, *may* be due to logical features of the proposition, but it may also be due to deficiencies in my powers of conception or lack of imagination on my part. Similarly, if it sounds very odd to me to say that all those conditions hold but nevertheless the chap doesn't do y, this may be because there is something logically defective about it, or it may be that (2) seems so obviously true and is borne out so pervasively by experience, that a suggestion that it might not hold falls strangely on the ears. (It certainly does sound odd to suggest that a bush might be in flames without being consumed.) And is it not rash to suppose that one can distinguish between these various sources of strangeness just by attending to the "quality" of the sound?

It is such deficiencies in the appeal to the immediate, whether of the older or the newer variety, that have led people to take a more discursive approach to the justification of claims to logical truth or falsity, and to attempt to justify such claims by appeal to formulations of the meanings of the terms involved. Thus Jonathan Cohen claims that the following proposition is analytic:

(3) If an agent believes that y is contingent upon x, desires y, has no conflicting desires, and x is in his power, then he will probably do x.[12]

(Note that we have made the antecedent much simpler, without making the claim of analyticity wholly implausible, by having only the probability of doing x in the consequent.) Cohen's conviction that this statement is analytic is based on his conviction that "It is merely part of what is ordinarily meant by 'desire' "[13] and ". . . a desire of x entails a tendency to effect x under certain conditions."[14] Presumably this means that "A desires x" is to be analyzed in dispositional terms in such a way as to make a desire a disposition to perform certain actions under certain conditions. And such definitions, or sketches of such definitions, have been proposed from time to time. But just how is such a definition to go, and just how is it to ground the logical truth of (2)?

The heroic course would be to simply dump all the other

components of the antecedent of (2) into a dispositional definition of "want."

> D1 A wants to do x = df. If A doesn't want to do anything incompatible with doing x more than he wants to do x, believes that doing y will put him in the best position for doing x, has both the capacity and the opportunity for doing y, doesn't feel obliged to do anything incompatible with doing x or y, has no scruples against doing x or y, hasn't forgotten about doing x, and is not too emotionally upset to do x, then he will do y.

Of course, the first thing that leaps to the eye is the vicious circularity involved in including in the definiens not only "want," but also a specification of the particular want specified in the definiendum. But perhaps this could be remedied by first defining "A wants to do x at t more than he wants to do anything else at t," and then finding some way of defining the more general notion on the basis of that. Even so, there are many difficulties. It does seem incredible that we should have to drag in all the factors which might conceivably prevent a want from issuing into action into a specification of the meaning of the word "want." This would be a coherence theory of meaning with a vengeance. That would mean that we have to make our basic decisions about the shape of a theory of human action, e.g., decisions as to what major categories to use in sorting out the factors that can influence what a person does, before we could say what is meant by the terms for any one of these factors. Our disinclination to go along with this may be reinforced by the following considerations. Such a dispositional definition of "want" was brought in to dispel doubts about the logical truth of (2), but this particular definition could not be effective for that purpose because, since it exactly reproduces the content of (2), any doubts about the logical truth of (2) will automatically transfer to the claim that D1 is an adequate definition. Moreover, the fact that with respect to (2) one can quite reasonably wonder not only whether it is logically true but also whether it is true without exception for any reason whatever, leaves D1 hardly an adequate statement of what we *mean* by "want." If it were, there could be no question as to whether cases might turn up in which all the conditions of (2) were satisfied but the agent did not do y. And it seems that such questions can sensibly be raised for any formula like (2) which can be constructed.

This may lead us to construct a much simpler dispositional definition of "want," one which is not enmeshed in the details of (2) in fatal ways. We might try the following:

D2 A wants to do x = df. A has some tendency to do x.

Unfortunately it is possible for A to want very much to do x but to have no tendency at all to do x, at least in any ordinary sense of "tendency." This would be true, e.g., if doing x went against such firmly held principles that there was no real possibility of A's doing it. What we need to express is the notion that the want substantially raises the probability of his doing x, that even though some contrary tendency may make it all but certain that he will not do x, still wanting to do x introduces a possible source of doubt which would not have been present otherwise. But we cannot, on pain of circularity, make our definiens read "The probability of A doing x is greater than it would be if he did not want to do x." However we can get substantially the same idea into the definition by introducing the notion of belief, as follows:

D3 A wants to do x = df. If A believes that doing y will put him in position to do x, he will be more likely to do y than he would have been without this belief.

One reason this cannot be taken seriously as a definition of "want" is that it fails to distinguish wanting to do x from, e.g., feeling obligated to do x or being under considerable pressure to do x. If the definiens is adequate for anything, it is rather for some more general notion like "being motivated to do x," of which "wanting to do x" is one species. However, this need not bother us, for even if this is true, it could still be the case that the above definiens gives part of the meaning of "A wants to do x," in such a way that this partial meaning would be entailed by "A wants to do x," and that might be enough to yield the conclusion that (2) is logically true.*

But of course D3, even if it is a completely adequate definition, cannot yield that conclusion by itself. We can't have it both ways. We cut most of the detailed content of (2) out of the definition because otherwise it would have been too close to (2) to do us much good. But having suitably purged it, (2) cannot be simply analytic of "want." We shall have to bring in definitions of the other terms as well. And we are going to have to have different sorts of patterns for the definition of at least some of them. If we were to define each of the terms in (1) by a dispositional pattern involving some selection of the other factors, as, e.g.:

D4 A is able to do y = df. If A wants to do x and believes that doing y will put him in the best position for doing x, he will probably do y.

D5 A has the opportunity of doing y = df. If A wants to do y and is able to do y, he will probably do y.

we should find ourselves rotating in a very small circle.

* It is worth noting that, insofar as Tolman explicates his fundamental concepts, the explication takes a dispositional form. He says that a "need" is "to be defined in the last analysis as a readiness to get to and to manipulate in a consummatory fashion (or to get from) certain other types of objects." (*Op. cit.*, p. 288) And he defines a belief, or a readiness or potentiality for expectation, as "a connection that makes a readiness to perceive and to behave in a certain way relative to one type of object (as end) give rise to a readiness to perceive and to behave in a certain way relative to certain other types of objects (as means)." (*Ibid.*, p. 293) Thus, insofar as Tolman really means these as definitions, he is involved in any logical connections of needs and beliefs with actions that follow from this sort of definition in terms of behavioral dispositions.

Of course other sorts of definitions might be found for some of the terms, which would then be used as a basis for dispositional definitions of the others. For example, belief might conceivably be defined in terms of perceptual thresholds. But until something like that is done, we could not begin to use a dispositional definition of "want" to ground a claim for logical truth for a formula like (2). (This is in addition to the difficulty of deriving a deterministic principle from dispositional definitions in a probability form.) And it is worth noting that, quite apart from the aim to show that (2) is logically true, one could not use D3 for anything, without having some idea of what the other factors are that influence action and how they are to be identified. For how am I to tell that a certain belief has or has not affected the probability of a certain action being performed? If I am to make use of anything other than observation of the relative frequency of the action in cases where the belief is and is not present (and unless both populations are both large and varied this result is not likely to be of much interest), I shall have to work against the background of some theory (at least a rough one) as to what factors influence action and how they interact in doing so. Otherwise, I would have no reason to think in a particular instance that it is the acquisition of a certain belief that tips the balance.

6

Over and above these difficulties, there are more basic objections to this project of framing a set of plausible and usable dispositional definitions which will ground claims of analyticity for (2). It seems to me to be a great mistake to *define* these terms, as used either in psychological theory or in everyday thought, in such dispositional patterns. In both spheres we take various sorts of things as indications of a person wanting something or other and of how much he wants it. Whether we are dealing with a quite specific want, like wanting to go to a certain concert, or something much more general like a desire for power or recognition, we make use of the following sorts of indications (sticking to the more specific case for purposes of illustration):

I-1. The way a certain belief will affect his actions, or, on a more sophisticated level, the probability of his actions. (Does coming to believe that tickets for the concert can only be purchased at a certain place lead him to go to that place?)

I-2. His readiness to "avow" the desire. (Given that he has no intention to deceive, does he tell us that he wants to go to the concert when the occasion to do so arises?)

I-3. Patterns of his thought and discourse. (In free conversation does he keep recurring to this concert and concert-related themes?) Note that this is the common sense technique which is elaborated into projective testing and psychoanalytic free association techniques.

We can think of each of these techniques as based on a hypothetical, relating wants to publicly observable behavior, albeit indirectly, via such factors as beliefs, trains of thought, and occasions. To define a want in terms of one of these hypotheticals is to give that one a certain kind of privileged position. It is to regard that connection as analytic of the meaning of "want" and the others as connections which happen to hold good of "want" as so defined. If I-1 is chosen, as in D-3, we are committed to taking beliefs affecting the probability of actions in a certain way as a logically necessary and sufficient condition for the existence of a want. This would imply that it is inconceivable that one should want to do x without a belief that doing y was necessary for doing x affecting the probability of one's doing y, and vice versa. However, it would merely be contingently the case that a want affects in certain ways one's trains of thoughts, one's fantasies and dreams, and one's readiness to give an affirmative answer to "Do you want . . . ?" We might give up our confidence in any or all of these connections without changing the meaning of the term; and in individual cases there would be nothing logically odd about the supposition that indications of these sorts might be lacking for a want.

It seems clear to me that things are not this simple. If we look closely at the way we ordinarily employ the term "want" and its close relatives, we will find reason for denying that any such indication, or any combination of such indications, is a logically necessary and sufficient condition for the application of the term, in any straightforward and unqualified sense of "logically necessary and sufficient."

Nevertheless, there are grounds for according this status to I-1, certainly more so than in the case of I-2 or I-3. If we can see that what a person is doing over a stretch of time is varying with variations in beliefs as to what he has to do in order to get into a position to attend a certain concert or get a job, we would ordinarily take that as decisively showing that he wants to attend that concert or to get that job even if indications of the other sorts are lacking.* And conversely, if variations in beliefs as to what is necessary in order to get the job do not affect the probabilities of doing what is believed to be necessary, e.g., if having come to believe that he must get to know Smith if he is to get the job, he shows, so far as we can tell, *no* inclination to get to know Smith, then we would, I believe, deny that he *really wanted* to get that job.**

It is dubious that anything analogous can be said with respect to I-2 and I-3. I-2 is certainly not a necessary condition.

---

* To make another application of a point mentioned above, this and other statements concerning sufficient reasons will not even stand a chance of being true unless we understand "want" in a very wide sense in which it includes feeling an obligation as a special case, a sense roughly equivalent to "being motivated."
** Both this and the preceding sentence are subject to various qualifications which are made explicit as the discussion proceeds.

I could quite intelligibly say that Robinson really wants a certain job, but doesn't realize that he wants it (and so, even if he has no intention to deceive, would not be prepared to avow the desire). And I sometimes say of myself in retrospect that I had wanted to do something, e.g., quit my job, without knowing it (perhaps—but not necessarily—without letting myself realize it). I-2 may be a sufficient condition; it may be impossible to think of a case in which one could intelligibly say "Smith said in all honesty that he wanted to do x but he really didn't," and where it is not clear that "want" is being used in two different senses. There is the case where, after telling myself and everyone else for years that I wanted to go to Europe, I go and find it disappointing and say, "I guess that wasn't really what I wanted to do after all." But here it is clear that the last statement means something like "That did not in fact give me the kind of satisfaction I was looking for"; and this statement is perfectly compatible with my really having wanted to go to Europe in the sense of "want" I employed when I kept telling everyone I wanted to go to Europe. With respect to I-2 it is worth noting further that even if it were a logically necessary and sufficient condition, it could not be used by itself as the basis of a definition of "want." The fact that a person is prepared in the appropriate circumstances to say, "I want to go to Europe," is a basis for saying that he wants to go to Europe only on the assumption that he is using "want" in the relevant sense; and of course the specification of that sense is just what the definition was supposed to provide.

The exact status of I-3 is less clear but at least one can be sure that it is not a logically sufficient condition. Something might keep running through my head, not because I wanted it, but for various other reasons. It might be because I dreaded it, or I may have had to think about it so much that now I can't get it off my mind. The latter might be the reason why going on a vacation keeps coming up in the thoughts of a travel agent. Or I may have obsessive thoughts of strangling someone, but honestly say, "That is the last thing in the world I want to do." We may accept the psycho-analytic explanation of such cases, according to which the person *does* want to do the action, or, alternatively, the action for which the obsessive thought is a disguised substitute. But the psychoanalytic theory is not *logically* true, and it seems clear that "unconscious desires always underlie obsessive thoughts" is not built into our ordinary use of words like "want." Moreover, it seems clear that I-3 is not a logically necessary condition. People may want something very much even though they rarely if ever think of it. In such cases we say that they *keep* themselves from thinking of it, and this suggests that these counterexamples might be avoided by changing the "indication" into a *tendency* to dwell on the action in thought. This would locate this "indication" at about the same distance from conscious thought as the first and second are from overt behavior. (Or, alternatively, one could save the universality of the connection by postulating unconscious thoughts in these cases.) But even so, it is not clear that our inclination to think that there must be such a tendency whenever anyone wants something is based on some feature of the meaning of "want" rather than on a plausible theory, the truth status of which cannot be settled by refer-ence to the meanings of terms.

Although I-1 is a more plausible candidate for a logically necessary and sufficient condition than the others, there are reasons for refusing to regard it as such. For one thing, in cases where we have I-1, but not I-2 or I-3 or both, while we do not refuse to use "want," we do so with less confidence, with more hesitation, with a feeling that this is not quite the same thing that we have in more full-blooded cases. This can lead us to label these cases as "unconscious wants" or even to maintain that "want" is being used in a different sense here. I think that the latter temptation should be resisted, but the fact that it is not wholly implausible is sufficient to show that I-1 is not clearly a logically sufficient condition for wanting something in the way in which being a male sibling is clearly a logically sufficient condition for being a brother. However, it is difficult to distinguish semantically based hesitations and lacks of confidence from other sorts, and equally difficult to say just what degree of hesitation would justify us in denying that a certain condition is logically sufficient. Hence I should not wish to place much weight on this consideration.

A more conclusive point is this: Try to imagine a state of affairs in which there would be no significant correlation between indications of these three sorts. Avowing wants would be only randomly correlated with behavioral dispositions, and so on. In such a universe, when would we say that someone wants something? It would seem that the only answer to this question is, "We wouldn't know what to say. We wouldn't know when to say that people want something." In our universe we can, in special cases, say that someone wants something when only the first indication is forthcoming, and perhaps when we have only the second. But it seems that this is only possible in *special* cases. If the high degree of intercorrelation of these indications were to disappear, we would no longer have the background against which our talk about wants goes on. The basic point of this talk lies in the way in which it ties the agent's behavior in with his reports and with various aspects of his thought and feeling. Ordinarily we take any one of the indications (at least the first two) as a sufficient indication of a want without checking the others; and sometimes we even take one sort of indication as sufficient when we have reason to think that the others are absent. But this is possible only because we can assume that generally they all go together. If this weren't the case, the concept of want would have lost its place in our talk about human behavior and experience, and it would no longer be clear what would count as a want and what would not. Of course, in such a state of affairs we could decide to take one or another of the now uncorrelated indications as a logically necessary and sufficient condition; and I would suppose that I-1 would be the most plausible candidate. But the point is that this would be a decision. The actual use of the term does not clearly mark out that choice.

In fact, we do not have to imagine anything so outré to find a case in which we would not know what to say. I have suggested that where we have I-1, but not I-2 and/or I-3, it is clear that we would apply the term (provided this does not happen too often), though with some lack of confidence. And where we have I-3 while the others are lacking, it is clear that the term does not apply. But that leaves the cases in which we lack I-1, but have I-2 with or without I-3. If a case occurred in which Smith, with no intent to deceive, said that he wanted very much to go to a certain concert, but, while believing that buying a ticket is a necessary condition of this, displayed absolutely no tendency to buy a ticket, we would not know what to say. (Of course it may be impossible ever to be sure that we have such a case.) It would seem that the presence of I-1 whenever we have I-2 (though not necessarily vice versa) is an assumption so deeply imbedded in our use of "want" that no provision is made in that use for the possibility that a person might be *mistaken* in thinking that he wants to do something (where "wants" is defined, for the moment, in terms of I-1). In *that* case it would be clear neither that the person wants to go to the concert nor that he does not want to go to the concert.

These considerations indicate that the term "want" is subject to an assumption, which is itself clearly synthetic, that there is a high degree of intercorrelation between indications of these three sorts. Subject to that assumption, indications of any of these sorts will normally be regarded as adequate, though some may be regarded as more crucial than others. Where we have this sort of situation, where an assumption of the general coincidence of logically independent criteria is built into the meaning of a word, none of these criteria or any combination thereof can be logically necessary and sufficient conditions in an unqualified way. When the assumption breaks down sufficiently, there will be no guidelines for the correct application of the term. We will not know what to say. It may well be that the combination of all the indications will be logically sufficient, assuming that a complete list can be drawn up. And in *exceptional* cases one or another indication may be taken as sufficient. But with certain kinds of breakdown of the assumption, we would not get the clear-cut decision on applicability which we would get if a logically necessary and sufficient condition, in a strict sense, could be formulated. And, if this is the case, we cannot define "want" by specifying such a condition, as in D3.

This treatment of "want" is reminiscent of Waismann's discussion of "open texture."[15] There Waismann points out that a term like "gold" is used, to put it my way, subject to an assumption that various criteria are going to go together, e.g., atomic weight, valence, type of radiation, and electrical conductivity. (Presumably here, in contrast with psychological terms like "want" an invariable coincidence is assumed.) If we tried to imagine a case in which some of the tests for gold were satisfied but not others, we would not know whether to call the sample gold or not. A new decision about the use of the term would be called for. Another case is that of a cat which suddenly grew to a fantastic size, or a cat which inexplicably appears and disappears. We wouldn't know whether to call it a cat or not.[16]

The logical status of the relatives of the everyday term "want" in psychological theory ("needs," "motives," etc.) is quite similar, but with some important differences. With them, too, indications of all three sorts are freely employed, except that I-3 is much more highly developed, in the free association technique of psychoanalytic investigation and in projective tests. Further, if we were to attempt to single out any sort of indication as definitive, as showing us what a need or motive *is*, we would not be faithful to the way the psychologist is employing the term. The operationalist temptation to do so (to say, "The achievement motive is what is measured by this test.") is now generally resisted on the grounds that it is essential to the function of such terms in psychological theory that they not be definitionally tied to any one kind of test. It is important to retain an unexplicated background of significance which can be drawn on for the construction of further tests and for suggestions as to the way a need might be related with various other factors. Again it seems that we can best represent the situation by saying that the psychologist uses a term like "need" or "motive" subject to a (logically contingent) assumption that indications of these various sorts are going to be highly correlated with each other. And if this should turn out to be false, he would not know when to say that a certain motive was present. He would have to re-examine the whole problem.

But there are some differences. For one thing, it is not so clear that the assumption in question is not one of invariable rather than general coincidence. The self-conscious theorist is in a much better position to explain away apparent counterexamples in terms of interferences which prevent the indication in question from issuing in overt behavior. Remember that, in order to get anything which is even plausible as a component in a definition of "want," we have had to state the various "indications," not as the actual occurrence of one or another kind of overt behavior in given circumstances, but rather as an increased probability of such behavior, or as a "readiness" to produce it, or as a train of thought which might or might not be expressed. This location of the "indications" at a considerable remove from the publicly observable makes it difficult ever to be sure that one of them is not present. Even if a person makes no move that would count toward getting to the concert, it does not follow that I-1 is not present, i.e., it does not follow that if he believes that doing y will put him in position to go to the concert, that belief will not raise the probability of his doing y. The absence of any attempt to go to the concert could be explained in other ways. He may not believe that anything which he could do would be likely to put him in a position to go to the concert, in which case the antecedent of the hypothetical would be empty. Or it may be that, for anything which he believed would put him in a position to go to the concert, the antecedent probability of his doing that was so low that even after the belief in question raised that probability it was still far below the threshold of action. And so on. Needless to say, this makes it difficult to be sure, even in everyday thought, that we are willing to apply the term when we know that one of the indications is missing; for it is difficult to imagine a case in which we could be sure we know that. And this casts some doubt on the judgment that a given sort of indication is or is not a necessary condition. The possibility of alternative explanations of the absence of typical overt manifestations of these "indications" is still greater in psychological theorizing, where one can postulate all sorts of interfering and repressing factors (subject, one would hope, to future test). Thus if a person in all honesty says he does not want to be president of the company, where the other indications are clearly present, one can explore the possibility that he would have realized it except for repressive mechanisms which are protecting him from a knowledge which, for some reason, would be distasteful to him. And if he never thinks of something which, on other grounds, we have good reason to think he wants, one can explore the possibility that thought about it is occurring all the same, but unconsciously. Allowing for these explanations, there is reason to hold that some psychologists use terms like "want" on the assumption that indications of our three sorts always go together. But even so, their conjunction could not be taken to be a logically necessary and sufficient condition. This is shown by the fact already mentioned that if the psychologist became convinced that the indications did not agree, he would be at a loss as to when to say that people wanted something; whereas if the conjunction really were functioning as a necessary and sufficient condition, it would be quite clear what one should say in such a situation, viz., that no one wants anything.

A more important difference comes from the fact that many theoretical concepts in psychology are still in the making; there is a self-conscious attempt to mold concepts in a way which will yield the most useful explanatory scheme. As a result, from time to time new devices for spotting "motives" are developed, and the balance of power among the various indications is constantly in danger of being upset. A psychologist may start out thinking of a motive as "a readiness to get to and to manipulate in a consummatory fashion (or to get from) certain other types of objects" (to use Tolman's terms). But he may discover that identifying and measuring motives in terms of this "definition," i.e., by actually observing what the individual does under certain conditions, is impossible, at least when we are dealing with human beings and with wants of some considerable complexity and/or abstractness.[17] He may then, shifting the emphasis to I-3, devise perceptual and fantasy tests, like the Thematic Apperception Test, for the presence and strength of motives. It may be that whatever it is that is measured by one of these devices, or a combination thereof, turns out to have very interesting and important connections with various things other than those used in the test, such as choices between alternatives, level of performance, and learning experiences, connections which are roughly in accord, for the most part, with what one might well expect for motives. The point is that the relative weight of different sorts of indications will shift with developments in theory and test construction. For that matter, new elements can be added to the list of indications. I would suppose that attention to the way a person perceives things as a measure of strengths of motives is *almost* an innovation of theoretical psychology; in everyday thought we do not have the resources for making the necessary distinctions between aspects of perception. And, of course, all this is over and above the variation that comes from differences in weight of emphasis between schools of psychology.

It is hardly necessary to point out that the above is only the barest beginning of an examination of the logical status of terms like "want" in either everyday discourse or psychological theory. But perhaps enough has been said to cast doubt on the possibility of giving straightforward dispositional definitions of such terms.

7

Even if (2) and/or similar principles should be analytic, and even if such psychological terms as "motive" are very similar to the ordinary terms contained in such principles, it still would not follow that the principles of a Tolman-type theory would themselves be analytic. For one thing, such principles would be in a quantitative form. They would represent values of certain dimensions along which actions would vary as functions of the values of dimensions along which wants, beliefs, perceptions, etc., vary. Even if it were a fact that a principle like (2), which is stated in rough, nonquantitative terms, is analytic, it does not follow that we could frame analogous analytic principles which would relate magnitudes of action to strengths of psychological factors. Not only would it not follow that such analytic principles could be constructed; it seems wildly implausible to suppose that they could. Even if we ignore the problem of representing the content of beliefs, wants, etc., in terms of positions on dimensions, it seems incredible that combinations of the strengths of these factors should be analytically related to the performance of certain actions. The only principles which even look as if they might be analytic are those, like (2), which represent a certain action as contingent on a number of factors which are present in *sufficient*(!) strength. How, by sheer logical analysis, could we determine how strong a want to go to the concert, in conjunction with how firm a belief in the contingency of that on driving to town, etc., would be required to produce the action of driving to town? Of course, if we *defined* strength of belief and want in terms of their bearing on what action would be performed, such analytic principles might be produced. But such definitions would seem to be even less plausible than similar definitions of the nonquantitative terms.

This problem of determining the exact form of the principles in a Tolman-like theory involves the problem of determining whether any concatenation of factors uniquely determines a certain action (with certain magnitudes, etc.), or whether the most we could possibly get in the consequent of such principles would be a certain probability of a certain action. (This facet of the problem is of crucial importance for the free will problem from which this essay took its start.) And here, too, we seem to be faced with alternatives which cannot be settled by logical analysis. It would strain credibility to suggest that by analysis of the concepts involved we could find out whether actions are uniquely determined by such factors or only rendered more or less probable by them (and if the latter, to what degree). If anything is clear, it is that the question of determinism cannot be settled by analysis of these concepts. But if so, no Tolman-like principle of a deterministic form could possibly be logically true.

8

The upshot of the whole discussion is that none of the arguments currently in vogue does anything to show that it is impossible that human actions should be causally determined. More specifically, an examination of the logical status of hypothetical statements relating "intentional" factors such as wants and beliefs to actions, both in everyday thought and in psychological theory, does nothing to show that such statements are logically true in such a way as to prevent them from being causal laws, in any relevant sense of that term, or prevent them from figuring in an empirically testable causal theory which could be used for prediction. Hence the free will problem cannot be dissolved in *this* way. Whether or not a causal theory of this sort, or any other sort of causal theory dealing with human action, can be established is a question which can be resolved only by the future development of psychology.

COMMENTS

Keith Lehrer

University of Rochester

PROFESSOR ALSTON'S PAPER is a combination of philosophy and speculation about the "strategy of theory construction in psychology." The principal philosophical contention of his paper is that it is logically possible to give *causal* explanations of human actions in terms of such psychological factors as, wants, beliefs, and perceptions. Other philosophers, for example, A. I. Melden, have apparently denied this. Melden does not wish to deny that it is possible to *explain* human actions in terms of psychological factors; he only wishes to deny that such explanations could possibly be *causal*.[1] Moreover, Melden is careful to point out that he is using the terms "cause" and "causal" in a restricted sense.[2] Since Alston is also using these terms in a restricted sense, it is essential that we investigate how each of them is using the terms "cause" and "causal" before attempting to judge the issue in dispute.

Let us first consider Alston's views concerning *causal* explanation. He says that the word "cause" in ordinary discourse about human behavior is not used when we are speaking of wants, beliefs, and perceptions. This seems to me to be quite doubtful. Sometimes we do. If someone asks, "What caused him to kill Smith?"—which would be a perfectly intelligible question—one might correctly reply, "He wanted revenge," "He believed that Smith was going to blackmail him," or, "He saw Jones poison his coffee."

Be that as it may, the thesis that Alston is most concerned

to defend is that in some normal sense of the word "causal" "a theory of action would have at least a prima facie claim to be called a causal theory if it satisfied the following requirements:

(1) The theory exhibits an action as a determinate function of a certain constellation of variables such that given the values of all these variables one can determine what action(s), if any, an agent performs at a certain time. . . .

(2) These determining variables are such that one can determine the values of all of them in a given instance without already knowing what action(s) the agent in question performs at the time in question.

(3) The values of the variables in question are values those variables have at a time prior to the performance of the action in question.

He then goes on to say

. . . I think it is clear that any theory which satisfies the requirements as stated would be what is often called a causal theory, and so, too, for any explanation derived from such a theory.

I believe that these remarks constitute the most fundamental thesis of Alston's paper, because the remainder of the paper is primarily an attempt to show that it is possible to construct theories that satisfy these requirements which explain human actions in terms of wants, beliefs, and perceptions. Unless such theories and explanations are causal, Alston's arguments will fail to establish his principal contention, namely, that it is possible to give *causal* explanations of human actions in terms of wants, beliefs, and perceptions.

I now want to argue that, as these requirements are stated, there is no reason to think that a theory that satisfies them has even a prima facie claim to be called causal. Suppose that a girl named "Artcele" kills her mother on the day she reaches twenty-one. Moreover, suppose that Artcele has unique fingerprints at birth, which we shall call "A-prints." In this case, we can formulate a theory, not so elaborate as Tolman's, that satisfies all of Alston's requirements. It is contained in the following statement: (T) Whenever a person is born with A-prints, he will kill his mother at noon on the day he reaches twenty-one.

That theory (T) satisfies Alston's requirements, can easily be shown. The theory exhibits an action, killing one's mother, as a determinate function of a constellation of variables, being born with A-prints, such that given the values of all variables we can determine what action an agent performs at a certain time, at noon on the day that one reaches twenty-one. Moreover, one can determine that a person is born with A-prints without already knowing that the person will kill his mother at noon of the day he reaches twenty-one. Finally, being born with A-prints is something that happens prior to the time at which one reaches the age of twenty-one.

Thus, theory (T) clearly satisfies Alston's three requirements. But, this theory does not even have a prima facie claim to be called *causal*. We have not supposed that there is any causal connection between Artcele's action and her fingerprints, and we may reasonably conclude that there is not. Ordinarily, there is no causal connection between a person's actions and his fingerprints. Therefore, no causal explanation of Artcele's action, or, for that matter, anyone else's action, can be derived from the theory.

There is an obvious objection that might be raised against my claim that theory (T) is a counterexample to Alston's thesis, namely, that the one statement of the theory is not a law. This is true. However, Professor Alston does not state as one of his requirements that the statements of the theory must be laws. Nevertheless, this may well be implict in his requirements. Earlier in his paper he does say he supposes that the causal determination of human actions would require the truth of certain "lawlike" statements.

Thus he might wish to qualify his requirements by adding the restriction that the statements of the theory must all be laws, i.e, true lawlike statements. With this qualification Alston's thesis would not be subject to the counterexample that I have raised. However, with this qualification, his thesis would then be vacuous and his requirements redundant. To see that this is so, we need only ask what sort of *law* Alston has in mind when he speaks of the truth of lawlike statements. Obviously, the answer is—*causal laws*. Consequently, with the proposed qualification, Alston's thesis would be the thesis that a theory of action, the statements of which are causal laws, would have at least a prima facie claim to be called a causal theory if it satisfies the three requirements. Of course, the three requirements would be entirely redundant. Any theory the statements of which are causal laws not only has a prima facie claim to be called a causal theory, it *is* a causal theory.

Moreover, even with the qualification that would make Alston's fundamental thesis concerning causality vacuously true, his difficulties would not be at an end. Some of his subsidiary theses on that subject would appear to be quite doubtful. For example, he says,

> The main bar to supposing that a causal theory of this sort is possible is the appearance of a logical connection between such factors as wants and the actions they are invoked to explain. It seems reasonable, at least it has seemed reasonable since Hume, to suppose that if A and B are logically connected they cannot be causally connected.

But is does not seem at all reasonable to me to suppose that if two factors A and B are logically connected, they cannot be related by a causal law.

Consider, for example, the following statement: (L) "All mules are barren mules." This statement is a law, but the two factors that are related by this law are logically connected. Being a barren mule entails being a mule. Of course, being a mule does not entail being barren, so the statement is contingent. If one should have any doubts about whether (L) is a law, he need only notice that (L′) "All mules are barren," is a law. Once it is seen that (L′) is a law, if follows that (L) is also a law, because (L) and (L′) are logically equivalent statements.

Moreover, even if it should be denied that (L′) is a law, it is easy to see from this example how to construct a general proof to the effect that if there are any causal laws relating two factors that are not logically connected, then there must also be causal laws relating factors that are logically connected. Suppose that A and B are not logically connected and that the statement: (S) "All A's are B's," is a causal law. Let us then define a third factor, C. By definition, something is a C if and only if it is both an A and a B. It then follows that the statement: (S′) "All A's are C's" is a causal law, because (S) and (S′) are logically equivalent.* However, factors A and C are logically connected; being C entails being A. Of course, (S′) is contingent, because being A does not entail being C.

Therefore, we may conclude that factors that are logically connected are sometimes also related by a causal law. It is less clear what logical connections *cannot* obtain between two factors that are related by a causal law. Thus, Alson says in criticizing one of Melden's arguments,

> Even where in explaining an action in terms of a want, etc., we are providing a further description of what the agent is doing, this does not mean that explanans and explanandum are logically related in way that would make a causal relationship impossible.*

* The thesis that every statement that is logically equivalent to a law is itself a law is controversial. I do think that the thesis is true, but there are difficulties that I cannot discuss adequately in the present context. For example, if *L* is a law, then *L* is logically equivalent to conjunc-

It is difficult to judge the merit of what Alston has said for two reasons. In the first place, he has not satisfactorily explained what sorts of logical relationships do rule out the possibility of causal relationships. Secondly, Melden's explanation of what he means by "causal explanation" is so unclear that it is impossible to tell what would, or would not, refute his arguments. To see that this is so, let us briefly examine Melden's own words on this subject.

In the second chapter of his book, Melden says,

> For the present I am concerned with "cause" either in the Humean sense of this term or, if this is alleged to be inadequate in certain respects, to the use of the term in scientific explanations of, say, physical or physiological events, in that sense of the term in which it is in fact employed in physics or physiology.[3]

He later adds in a footnote,

> For purposes of my argument it matters not whether or not we accept as adequate Hume's account of causation in the natural sciences—all that is important here is the recognition insisted upon by Hume that natural events (e.g., explosions, cell divisions, etc.) which are causally related are logically independent of one another.[4]

Thus, as Melden is using the term "cause," a cause and its effect must be logically independent. What he is attempting

---

tion C that contains L as one conjunct and tautologies as the other conjuncts. Such a statement surely would not *look* like a law, but I should wish to argue that it would be nonetheless. Roughly my reason is that what determines whether something is a law is its deductive role in explanation, and exactly the same things are deducible from L as from C. However, for the purposes of the present argument, I only wish to maintain that if two statements are logically equivalent *in the way that* (S) and (S′) are, then if one of the statements is a law, so is the other. Since (S) and (S′) are logically equivalent in quite a special way, this thesis does not seem to me to be nearly so controversial as the more general these. It is, of course, all that my argument requires.

to prove in his book is that when we cite motives, intentions, wants, etc., to explain human action, the explanation is not causal in this restricted sense, because motives, intentions, wants, etc., are not logically independent of what they explain. But what in the world does Melden mean by the expression "logically independent"? In a familiar sense of that expression two events are logically independent if and only if (i) it is logically possible that both should occur, (ii) it is logically possible that neither should occur, and (iii) it is logically possible that either should occur without the other. However, it is not this sense of the expression "logical independence" that Meldon has in mind. For, Melden wishes to argue that wanting to raise an arm and raising it are not logically independent,[5] while in the familiar sense they are. It is possible both to want to raise an arm and to raise it; it is possible to neither want to raise an arm nor raise it; it is possible to want to raise an arm and not to raise it; and, finally, it is possible not to want to raise an arm and to raise it, nonetheless. The proof that all these things are possible is that they all do happen.

It must be some other sense of the expression "logically independent" that Melden requires. But he nowhere tells us what that sense is. Of course, it will not do simply to say that two events are logically independent if and only if they are not logically related in any way at all, because any two events are logically related in some way. For example, the two events will always be logically related in terms of some third event which entails them both, namely, the complex event of the conjoint occurrence of both of them.

Moreover, some of Melden's arguments to show that motives and the actions they explain are not "logically independent" make matters more problematic. For example, he argues that when a person's motive for raising his arm is to inform others that he is preparing to make a turn, then the motive and the action are logically connected, because citing the motive was giving a fuller characterization of the action; it was indeed providing a better understanding of what the driver was doing. But no Humean cause could possibly do this; any alleged cause, in this sense, of the action of raising the arm . . . would merely explain how the action of raising the arm came to be.[6]

This is most puzzling. If I say of a hard egg that it is a hard-boiled egg, then surely I am *both* giving a fuller characterization of the egg, providing a better understanding of what the egg is like, *and* explaining how the egg came to be hard. Moreover, boiling an egg to make it hard would *seem* to be a paradigm case of a Humean cause; the cause and effect surely seem to be logically independent. However, if anything that further characterizes an action, like a motive, is not logically independent of the action, it would seem reasonable to conclude that anything that further characterizes an egg, like being hard-boiled, is not logically independent of it. But then what could Melden possibly mean by "logical independence"? And what does he mean by the expression "further characterization"? This argument is so puzzling, one hardly knows where to turn.

In the absence of any elucidation, it seems impossible to tell whether motives, intentions, and wants are logically independent of the actions they explain. Consequently, I do not see how Alston can be so confident that he has refuted Melden's arguments to show that the explanations that we give of human actions in terms of motives, intentions, and wants could not be causal. For, how can he possibly know what Melden means by "causal explanation" since Melden explains "causal explanation" in terms of "logical independence"? Moreover, I do not see why Alston thinks that he means the same thing by "causal explanation" that Melden does, nor, consequently, why he thinks that to show it is possible to give *causal explanations,* as he is using that expression, would show that it is possible to give *causal explanations* as Melden is using it.

Finally, even as Alston is using the expression "causal explanation," it is difficult to tell whether he has succeeded in showing that it is possible to give causal explanations of human actions in terms of such psychological factors as wants, beliefs, and perceptions. In the first place, it is not perfectly clear what *he* means by "causal explanation" either. Secondly, though he believes that certain logical relations rule out the possibility of causal explanation, he nowhere explains satisfactorily what logical relations have this effect. What he does say on this subject appears to be false.

REJOINDER
William P. Alston

FIRST I SHOULD like to say something about Professor Lehrer's purported counterexample to my set of conditions for a theory of action being (at least prima facie) a causal theory, viz., (T) "Whenever a person is born with A-prints, he will kill his mother at noon on the day he reaches twenty-one." Lehrer is correct in supposing that I would point out that the "theory" does not contain any lawlike statement.* Even if (T) were put forward by someone who believes that possession of A-prints cannot be shared, it could hardly be claimed to satisfy my conditions. For, so construed, it does not "exhibit an action as a determinate function of a certain constellation of variables." A variable is something which can vary; insofar as we believe possession of A-prints to be unique, we are not regarding it as a variable. And we are not claiming to represent a certain kind of action as a *function* of certain factors, unless we are putting forward a *general* formula for inferring a certain kind of action from those factors. Indeed (T), so construed, cannot be regarded as a *theory* of any sort. What grounds are there for calling it a theory? If I firmly believe

---

* We should not be too hasty in making that point. (T) *could* be used to make a lawlike statement. If one supposed that there could be a number of people with A-prints, he might draw counterfactual implications from (T). There is nothing in the content of the sentence which prevents it from being used to formulate a law, unlike, e.g., "All the books in this room at noon on November 12, 1963 have hard covers."

that possession of A-prints is unique, then it is only with tongue in cheek that I would say, *"Whenever* a person is born with A-prints . . ."* What is this but a jocular reformulation of the statement that in the one and only case of A-prints, the person in question killed his mother at noon on his twenty-first birthday? Hardly a theory. Thus the requirement that the theory contain lawlike statements is not, as Lehrer suggests, implicit in my conditions. It is quite explicit, provided we take seriously terms like "variable" and "function."

Lehrer further contends that if this "implicit" requirement is made explicit, the other conditions will become unnecessary. But he gives plausibility to this claim only by quickly switching from the requirement that the theory contains *lawlike statements* to the requirement that it contain *causal laws. Of course,* if the requirement is the latter, nothing else is needed to insure that the theory is a causal one. But it should have been obvious that the whole point of the other conditions was to give at least a partial account of what distinguishes causal laws from other lawlike statements. But Lehrer's switch may not be a mistake. It may reflect a conviction that in calling something a lawlike statement we are thereby calling it a causal law, that the latter adds nothing to the former. This conviction seems to be embodied in Lehrer's discussion of the thesis that two factors logically connected cannot be related by a causal law. As a counterexample to this thesis he puts forward the statement: (1) "All mules are barren mules," which he claims to be a causal law and to involve two factors which are logically connected. The claim that (L) is a causal law is supported by beginning with the claim that (L') "All mules are barren" is a causal law, and then arguing that since (L) and (L') are logically equivalent (L) is a causal law also. Since I do not wish to contest the principle that anything logically equivalent to a causal law is itself a causal law, I shall concentrate on (L') in order to avoid irrelevant distractions. It is quite clear that "All mules are barren" is, or could be, a "lawlike statement," as that term is used by contemporary philosophers of science. But unless we are simply going to rule that "causal law" is to be used as a synonym for the technical term "lawlike statement" (and why on earth should we?), it seems clear that (L′) is not a causal law. I could support this judgment by appealing to a generalization of the conditions I laid down in my paper for a theory of *action* being a causal theory. But since the adequacy of that account is a point at issue, it would be better to rest the case on more neutral considerations. It could be pointed out that in saying that all mules are barren, we are not saying of anything that it is the (or a) cause of anything else. But, as I brought out, we might have a causal explanation where we would not speak of any of the components as a cause of any of the others. Refusing to call something a causal law unless it holds that one thing is an *effect* of another or that one thing *results* in another might also be regarded as too parochial. But the least we can require without completely losing contact with the explanatory activities within which the concept develops is that the putative causal law be equivalent to a statement of the "P because of Q" form. This is certainly not a sufficient condition, even if we add the stipulation that the P and Q be general propositions. "Senators cannot be sued for libel because they have Congressional immunity" is not a causal law. But it is a very modest proposal for a necessary condition. And (L′) fails this test as well. In putting (L′) forward we are saying neither that things are mules because they are barren, nor that things are barren because they are mules. Any temptation to suppose that we are saying the latter should disappear once we realize that to say that mules are barren because they are mules would be to say that there is no further explanation to be given; mules are just that way and that is all there is to be said on the matter. ("They act that way because they are Russians.")

This unfortunate choice of examples does not seem to me to affect the substance of Lehrer's neat demonstration of the point that logical connection does not rule out causal connection. His point could be reformulated for any lawlike statement of the form (1) "P because of Q." If we can assume that (1) entails (2) "P and Q because of Q," and hence that (2) is thereby guaranteed a status as a causal law, we can reformulate Lehrer's point so that it applies to genuine causal laws. (2) asserts a causal connection between factors which are logically connected because of the fact that "P and Q" entails "Q." But his excessive generosity with the term "causal law" does vitiate the account he offers of the conditions under which it is logically possible for a statement to be a causal law.

> . . . it is logically possible that the statement, (X) "All A's are B's," is a causal law if (i) statement (X) is logically consistent, (ii) being A does not entail being B, and (iii) the factors A and B are such that taken individually it is logically possible that each of them should be a factor in some causal law.

It is clear that "All mules are barren" satisfies these requirements, and no doubt they were designed so that it should. But in the light of the above remarks it seems clear that not only that statement, but ever so many other statements of that form which satisfy those requirements, are not causal laws at all.

Lehrer professes himself puzzled as to what sort of logical relations I suppose to rule out the possibility of causal relations. To be sure, I did not give a systematic discussion of the bearing of logical relations of various kinds on causal relationships. But I should have thought the paper made it clear that it was the logical relation which holds between two factors A and B when the hypothetical, "If A, then B," is logically true, which I took to rule out the possibility of a causal connection. Why else should I have been so concerned to show that the hypothetical relating wants, beliefs, etc., to action is not analytic?

Finally I should like to do something toward correcting a distortion of perspective in Lehrer's reading of my paper. Lehrer calls my statement of conditions under which a theory of action would be a causal theory "the most fundamental thesis of Alston's paper" and "the thesis that Alston is most concerned to defend." In fact, I put little store by the adequacy of such account as I give of the terms "causal theory" and "causal explanation." The points which most interest me are these: various people are attempting to construct theories of the sort typified by Tolman's model; theories, and explanations, of this sort are often called "causal"; and some philosophers who have argued that causal explanations of human actions are impossible have put forward arguments which might seem to have force against theories and explanations of this sort. What I was fundamentally concerned to do was to examine possible logical bars to the development of such theories, particularly logical bars stemming from the nature of the concepts of want, action, etc. The bulk of the paper is devoted to a consideration of these concepts and their place in the theories I was considering. Allusions to contemporary controversies over the possibility of causal explanations of human actions were intended to serve as a jumping-off point for these discussions. If I have succeeded in allaying widely prevalent doubts about the possibility of empirical theories of the Tolman sort, I have done what I set out to do, and the question of whether such theories are properly called "causal" seems to me to be of only minor importance.

NOTES FOR ALSTON ESSAY

1. R. S. Peters, *The Concept of Motivation* (London: Routledge and Kegan Paul, 1958), p. 12.
2. A. I. Melden, Free Action (London: Routledge and Kegan Paul, 1961), p. 184.

3. Peters, *op. cit.*, p. 12.

4. Peters, *op. cit.*, p. 14.

5. In T. Parsons and E. A. Shils (eds.), *Toward a General Theory of Action* (Cambridge, Mass.: Harvard University Press, 1951), p. 286.

6. In J. W. Atkinson (ed.), *Motives in Fantasy, Action and Society* (Princeton, New Jersey: Van Nostrand, 1958), pp. 322–339.

7. Atkinson, *op. cit.*, p. 324.

8. Peters, *op. cit.*, p. 55.

9. Melden, *op. cit.*, p. 88.

10. *Ibid.*, p. 90. These arguments, as well as others I shall be citing later, are specifically directed against the claim that the explanations of actions in terms of wants, etc., that we give in everyday discourse are causal explanations. Although, as noted above, this is not the claim which I am defending, these arguments are clearly relevant to that claim. For if wants, etc., are logically related to any action they might plausibly be brought in to explain, this would create just as much difficulty for the project of constructing a systematic causal theory of action, in these terms, as it would for the attempt to interpret everyday explanations of actions in these terms as causal.

11. Melden, *op. cit.*, p. 144.

12. Jonathan Cohen, "Teleological Explanation," *Proceedings of the Aristotelian Society,* N.S. LI (1950–51), 264.

13. *Loc. cit.*

14. *Ibid.*, p. 265.

15. Friedrich Waismann, "Verifiability," in A. Flew (ed.), *Logic and Language,* First Series (Oxford: Basil Blackwell, 1952), pp. 117–144.

16. For an extended discussion of the term "religion" see William P. Alston, *Religious Belief and Philosophical Thought* (New York: Harcourt, Brace and World, 1963), pp. 1–13.

17. See D. C. McClelland, "Methods of Measuring Human Motivation," in J. W. Atkinson, *op. cit.*, pp. 7–42.

NOTES FOR LEHRER COMMENT

1. A. I. Melden, *Free Action* (London: Routledge and Kegan Paul, 1961), pp. 16–17.

2. *Loc. cit.*

3. *Op. cit.*, p. 16.

4. *Ibid.*, p. 105.

5. *Ibid.*, pp. 127–128.

6. *Ibid.*, p. 88.

THE MEN THEMSELVES; OR
THE ROLE OF CAUSATION
IN OUR CONCEPT OF SEEING

Roderick Firth

Harvard University

PHILOSOPHERS and psychologists have traditionally drawn the line between the mental and the nonmental, the psychological and the physical, in such a way that the perceptual verbs ("see," "perceive," "hear," "smell," etc.) are said to designate states or activities of the mind. To classify these verbs in this way need not prejudice any basic ontological issues in the philosophy of mind, but there is an obvious respect in which perception serves to link other, nonperceptual, mental states and activities to our physical environment, so that perceiving can be said to have an intermediate status, neither exclusively physical nor exclusively psychological. As the verb "see," for example, is most commonly used, to say that I see such and such a physical object implies that there is a certain relationship—a "psycho-physical" relationship—between me and the object. Difficult problems arise, however, when we attempt to define this relationship—or even, in some cases, to identify instances of it. Thus Descartes, in the second of his *Meditations*, feels that he should warn us that we may easily be led into error by our use of the word "see" in ordinary speech. For when we look from a window at men passing below in the street, we say that we see the men themselves; and yet, Descartes asks,

> what do I see from the window except hats and cloaks which might cover artificial machines? . . . I judge that they are men and thus I comprehend, solely from

the faculty of judgment in my mind, that which I believed I saw with my eyes.

Many philosophers have agreed with Descartes that there
is a lack of precision in our use of sentences of the form "A
sees x," and have thought that such sentences can be misleading to the unwary epistemologist. The danger is sometimes
said to lie in the fact that there is more than one sense of the
word "see" in everyday speech, some senses "stricter" and
more basic than others. Thus G. E. Moore has extended the
Cartesian line of argument to the point of declaring that we
never see any solid material object in the relatively strict and
narrow sense of "see" in which we see the front surface of
such an object.

> For it is obvious that though I should be said to be now
> seeing *the half-crown,* there is a narrower, and more
> proper, sense, in which I can be said to *see* one side of it
> —not its lower side or its inside, and not therefore the
> whole half-crown.[1]

It would be difficult to exaggerate the extent to which
arguments of this kind have determined the form of traditional theories of empirical knowledge. The philosophical
motivation for distinguishing what we see from what we
thereupon judge to exist is very similar to that which has led
to the introduction of technical terms like "direct awareness"
and "immediate perception," and the correlative terminologies of "sensible ideas," "impressions," and "sense data."
Indeed, if we agree with Descartes that ordinary language
leads us to confuse what we see with what we "comprehend
. . . from the faculty of judgment," it is very difficult to resist
the traditional conclusion that to see an "external object" is
ultimately to interpret or to make a "judgment" about something which, if we are to avoid the appearance of inconsistency, cannot be just another external object. It is clearly a
matter of some philosophical importance, therefore, to decide

whether there is any truth in Descartes' remarks about the ordinary use of "see." What are the considerations which actually lead us in everyday speech to say that we see some one particular thing rather than another?

Strangely enough, this is a question to which philosophers have given very little attention. The literature of epistemology is overflowing with discussions of what we might loosely call the "internal" or "phenomenological" aspects of perceptual experience: the role of sensing in perceiving, the respects in which hallucinations may be indistinguishable from perceptions, the sense of "judgment" in which perceiving can be said to involve judgment, the phenomenological differences between seeing what we take to be a building and seeing what we take to be merely a false facade, etc. But when Descartes decides that it is somehow more accurate to say that he sees hats and cloaks than to say that he sees men passing below, he is not trying to answer the question, "What do I seem to see?" or "What does it look to me as if I am seeing?" or any other question about the internal character of his perceptual experience. He grants that he is having a perceptual experience of the kind which would ordinarily lead him to say, "I see men passing below"; and he is chiefly concerned, therefore, not about what he seems to see, or thinks he sees, but rather, as we might say, about what he really *does* see. No doubt there is some kind of criterion for deciding, at least in most cases, whether it is correct in everyday speech to say that someone really does see such and such an external object; but very few philosophers have made any serious effort to formulate this criterion.[2]

Descartes himself, for example, makes no attempt to formulate the criterion which leads him to say that he does not see men in the street below his window. He believes, however, that the hats and cloaks which are passing below are worn by actual men; so when he decides to say that he sees the hats and cloaks, but not the men, he presumably does so because he thinks that the hats and cloaks are related to him in a way in which the men are not. The relational criterion which he employs, when stated fully enough, might also be a criterion for denying that he sees at that moment the back of his own head or objects in far distant lands, and such examples immediately suggest that his criterion might be formulated, or partly formulated, in *causal* terms. The men passing below (if we assume that no parts of their bodies are uncovered), the linings of their cloaks, and objects in far distant lands, do not have the same kind of causal influence on Descartes' visual experience that the hats and cloaks do; and it is important to ask, therefore, whether it is a supposed difference in causal influence which leads us to say in everyday speech that we see one particular external object rather than another. It will not be possible within the limits of this essay to attempt a final answer to this question, but it may be possible to raise, and perhaps to clarify, some difficult problems concerning the role of causation in our concept of seeing.

It should be observed that we can pose our question in this way without committing ourselves to the Cartesian realism which philosophers sometimes call "the causal theory of perception." Cartesian realism is appropriately called a "causal theory of perception" (or, more accurately, a "causal theory of perceptual justification") because of the heavy epistemological burden which it imposes on the causal relationship between physical objects and perceptual experience: it implies that our knowledge of the physical world can be justified only by means of a nondeductive and noninductive inference from experiential effect to physical cause—an inference which Descartes himself defends by appealing to the goodness of God. But this theory is of course just one among many philosophical interpretations of a body of common preanalytic knowledge concerning the causation of perceptual experience, and every plausible epistemology must account for this common knowledge, not deny it. Even Berkeley, whose metaphysical speculations lead him to the conclusion that God is the "active" external cause of our perceptual experience, maintains that this active cause manifests itself in the form of psycho-physical causal laws. To put the point somewhat crudely, God causes a particular kind of perceptual experience to occur only if certain particular causal conditions obtain in and near the perceiver's body; and it is just such constant manifestations of God's benevolence, according to Berkeley, that we commonly call the "causal laws" of perception. It follows, therefore, that if we seek to find a causal criterion for assertions of the form "A sees such and such an external object" we are begging none of the issues which have traditionally separated the "causal realists" from Berkeley and their other critics.

We can also phrase our question in causal terms without committing ourselves to what might be called "the causal theory of perceptual *judgment*." Philosophers and psychologists have traditionally maintained that we commonly use the perceptual verbs in such a way that to say that we perceive an external object entails that we make some judgment about the object—or, at least, that we take for granted some facts about the object. And it is possible to argue that part of what we always take for granted is that the object which we perceive *causes* our perceptual experience in a certain way. It is not implausible, for example, to hold that in smelling a skunk as we drive along a country road, we normally judge, among other things, that our olfactory experience is caused by a skunk. An analogous judgment may occur in hearing the sound of a distant bell. In the case of vision, however, which is felt to be characterized by a special "immediacy," this causal analysis of perceptual judgment is less convincing; and some philosophers have argued that in our natural unphilosophical states of visual perception we are "naive realists" in our perceptual judgments, implying by this that we fail to distinguish our perceptual experience from the perceived object in a way that would even allow us, at the moment, to judge that the latter is the cause of the former.

It would be an exaggeration to say that these phenomenological issues are entirely irrelevant to the central question raised by Descartes' argument. If it became clear that a causal judgment is literally a part of all or most perceptual experiences, including those of vision, we should then have good reason to think that the question, "Do I really see such and such a thing?" is often a way of asking ourselves for a reassessment of such a causal judgment. Thus Descartes' decision that he sees cloaks but not men could be construed as a reassessment of his spontaneous perceptual judgment that the men were having a relatively direct causal influence on his perceptual experience. If we knew, therefore, exactly what kind of causal influence we spontaneously judge an object to have when we see it, we should then be able to specify our criterion for deciding, on reflection, whether or not a past perceptual judgment was mistaken; and no doubt this would also be our criterion for deciding in general whether we see one particular thing rather than another.

It is important to recognize, however, that we can search for such a criterion of seeing without assuming that it can be discovered by analysis of our spontaneous perceptual judgments. For if there is a causal criterion of seeing, there may nevertheless be only a very weak logical connection, if any, between the truth of a spontaneous perceptual judgment and the truth of a statement that our perceptual experience is caused in a certain way. This might not be obvious if we were to formulate perceptual judgments as if they were to the effect that we *see* something. It does become obvious, however, if we adopt the convention that perceptual judgments are to be expressed only in demonstrative sentences: "This is a cloak which . . . ," "This (or that) is a thing which. . . ." For then the question whether perceptual judgments are causal judgments is simply a question concerning the manner in which these sentences should be completed. If the causal theory of perceptual judgment is correct, none of these sentences can be completed without a clause asserting a causal relationship between the indicated object (the cloak, the skunk, etc.) and the speaker's perceptual experience. But if we are "naive realists" in some of our spontaneous perceptual judgments, some of these sentences would have to be completed in a different way, perhaps by a much weaker clause which merely asserts that the indicated object exists in such and such a direction from the speaker. In that case the question whether we *see* the object could be construed as an independent question which does not call for a reassessment of our perceptual judgment. We could grant that normally when we look from our windows we perceptually judge, and judge *correctly,* that there are men as well as hats and cloaks below us. But we could also maintain, without inconsistency, that on these occasions we see only the hats and cloaks. The men, we might decide, do not satisfy our causal criterion. (There is, however, little reason to think that Descartes would want to argue in this manner. The "judgment" that he speaks of is apparently not a "perceptual judgment"—i.e., a constituent of perceptual experience—but a supervening inferential act which is *based on* perceptual experience.)

It is clear, therefore, that the search for a causal criterion of seeing does not commit us to the causal theory of perceptual judgment. It does not even commit us, indeed, to the more general doctrine that seeing involves some kind of judgment, nor, of course, to the traditional correlative doctrine that whenever we see something we have a visual sense experience. Once we have decided that perceptual experience can be analyzed into certain constituent parts (e.g., sensing and judging) we are faced with a variety of special problems concerning the causation of perceptual experience—whether, for example, sensing and judging can vary independently of one another, and whether a statement of the form "A sees such and such an external object" implies that the external object influences not only A's sense experience but also A's perceptual judgment. For the reasons we have already considered, we can properly set aside all these problems. We can simply ask what external causal conditions of someone's perceptual experience (however such experience may be analyzed) must obtain in order for us to say correctly that he is seeing a particular thing. Even when restricted in this way, the question turns out to be much more difficult than it might appear at first thought.

If we look at an egg on the breakfast table, we should ordinarily not be willing to say that we see the light which is reflected from the egg and which stimulates our eyes. And we should also not be willing to say (to take an extreme example) that we see the hen which laid the egg. Both the hen and the light are parts of the causal process which has produced our perceptual experience, but in this case they do not play a causal role of the kind which qualifies them to be called objects of our present perception. We do, however, see the egg, and we see it *because* light is transmitted from it to our eyes. This suggests that for A to see x it is necessary that light be transmitted from x to A's eyes.

If we are seeking a causal criterion for the ordinary use of "A sees x," we must be careful, of course, not to read into the word "light" any esoteric physical theory about the constitution of light. We must not, for example, interpret "light" to mean light waves; and perhaps even the word "transmit" suggests a kinetic theory of light which is not essential to the common man's conception of visual stimulation. In fact the word "light" may be ambiguous in an important way even when we carefully abstract it from scientific theories about the constitution of light. Perhaps the common man identifies light as something originating in an incandescent source (e.g., the sun or a candle) and beyond that thinks of it only as something which *helps* us to see other objects, not as something which is logically necessary for seeing them. If he thinks of the light which falls on nonincandescent objects merely as something which makes those objects easier to see—somewhat as an illuminating example makes an argument easier to understand—light so conceived would be logically distinct from light conceived as the mediating agency through which these objects actually stimulate the eyes of the perceiver; and in that case the identification of the two via the concept of reflection, would be a bit of physical theory which is not yet fully embodied in our common sense concepts. It will simplify our present task, however, if we use the word "light" as if it refers unambiguously to something which we can say is "emitted" from an incandescent source, "transmitted" to other objects, "reflected" from objects, and which, when transmitted to our eyes, may "stimulate" them and thereby influence the character of our visual experience. If this terminology misrepresents our common sense conception of light and vision, the necessary corrections can be made without affecting the general form of our conclusions. For our present purpose we need only assume that the common man believes that between the perceiver and the external object which he sees, there is *some* mediating agency which can be interrupted or otherwise affected by interposing other objects; and this assumption would, to say the least, be very difficult to refute.

Let us begin our search for a causal criterion of seeing by considering some problems that arise when we ask whether for A to see x it is necessary that light be transmitted from x (i.e., from at least one part of x) to A's eyes, thereby affecting A's visual experience. A full explanation of our use of the word "see," even after we have ruled out metaphorical expressions like "seeing in the mind's eye," must provide some account of our willingness to say that we see people at remote times and places when we watch a newsreel or look at the screen of the television receiver. Let us assume, however, that such uses are derivative, and concentrate our attention on "central" cases in which there is no mediating screen or other material thing that can be said to contain a picture of the perceived object. In speaking about such cases let us say that A and x are "directly light-connected" if light is transmitted from x to A's eyes and thereby affects A's visual experience. In these terms, then, the problems now to be considered are problems which arise when we ask whether "direct light-connection" is a *necessary* condition of A's seeing x in such cases. At a later stage we shall consider some problems which arise when we ask whether direct light-connection is a *sufficient* condition of A's seeing x.

We cannot maintain that direct light-connection is a necessary condition of A's seeing x unless we are willing to agree with Descartes' denial that he sees the men who are passing below him in the street. For if we suppose that the bodies of the men passing below are *completely* covered by their hats and cloaks, it will then be true that no light is transmitted from the men to Descartes' eyes. This will be true, to be sure, only if the word "man" is understood in such a way that a man's hat and cloak are not parts of the man; but this is surely Descartes' intention, for otherwise he would not have contrasted the hats and cloaks with what he calls "the men themselves" ("homines . . . quos etiam ipsos . . . dico me videre"). Descartes can of course concede that the word "man" is sometimes used in such a way that clothing is considered to be as much a part of a man as his hair, his fingernails, or his heart. He could even concede, indeed, that "There are clothes below" is sometimes part of what we *mean* when we assert "There are men below," so that a man's clothing is being conceived, it might be said, as part of his essence. But Descartes is clearly using the word "man" in such a way that the "men themselves" cannot be identified with their clothing either in whole or in part. It follows, therefore, that if the men themselves are completely covered by hats and cloaks, just as Descartes says that artificial machines might be covered, then we must either agree with Descartes that he does not see them, or we must deny that direct light-connection is a necessary condition of seeing.

This may be an uncomfortable dilemma, and there may be some temptation to suppose that we can escape between its horns by finding some other way to combine the men and their clothing into a single entity. We cannot say, as we have just observed, that the clothing is part of the men themselves; but we might perhaps say that light is transmitted to Descartes' eyes from *cloaked and hatted men,* or from *men wearing cloaks and hats,* and maintain that these are the "objects" that Descartes sees. Participial expressions like "cloaked and hatted men" would normally be interpreted, of course, in such a way that it is logically impossible to see cloaked and hatted men, or men wearing cloaks and hats, unless one sees men; and on this interpretation we obviously do not avoid the horns of our dilemma. But it might be argued that there is no objection to thinking of each "passer-by" as a single composite entity of which a hat and a cloak and a person are three parts. And since light is transmitted to Descartes' eyes from two of these parts—the hat and the cloak—it follows that light is transmitted to Descartes' eyes from the composite object which we are calling a cloaked and hatted man. Thus it would seem that we could deny that Descartes sees *only* hats and cloaks, since he also sees cloaked and hatted men. Yet at the same time we could retain the causal requirement of direct light-connection, namely, that for A to see x, light which affects A's visual experience must be transmitted to A from at least one part of x.

This proposal deserves further consideration as a means of preserving the causal requirement of direct light-connection, and we shall return to it shortly. It also serves as a useful warning that we must move cautiously from the premise that A does not see such and such objects (e.g., men) to the conclusion that A sees *only* such and such other objects (e.g., hats and cloaks). But this proposal is of no help at all as a device for avoiding the choice that Descartes' argument forces on us. It offers us at best a proof that Descartes can see a composite object of which a hat and a cloak and a man are three essential parts, and that he can see this object even though the hat and cloak are the only parts of the object from which light is transmitted to his eyes. But this has no direct bearing on the question originally raised by Descartes, for such a composite object is not a man as Descartes is using the word "man." We may grant that Descartes sees composite objects, each of which contains a man as one of its parts. But to see an object is not to see every part of that object. When we see a house, for example, we may see the front and the side of the house, but we do not necessarily see the back of the house. Similarly, from the fact that Descartes sees a composite object, and sees several parts of that object, it does not follow that he sees the human part of that object. Thus it is clear that the appeal to composite objects does not provide a third alternative to make our choice less difficult: we must either agree with Descartes that he does not see the men who are passing below, or we must deny that direct light-connection is a necessary condition of seeing. Which alternative shall we choose?

To many of us it will probably seem easier to accept the second alternative and maintain that Descartes sees the men passing below. It may seem perfectly obvious, indeed, that Descartes is in some respect misusing words when he asserts that he sees only the hats and the cloaks. We may feel, of course, that what he is *trying* to say is something with which we should agree quite thoroughly if it were explained to us with sufficient care. But if we are hoping to find the common man's criterion of seeing, the important question is whether Descartes' statement is true in some ordinary sense of "see," not in some extraordinary philosophical sense. It is certainly true that if we were looking through Descartes' window, and were asked casually whether we see the men passing below, we should reply without hesitation that we do; and it may seem evident, therefore, that the principle of direct light-connection must yield to a fact about ordinary usage.

If reasons of this kind lead us to choose the second alternative—i.e., to deny that direct light-connection is a necessary condition of seeing—we may still hope to find a causal criterion of seeing if we can formulate a new causal requirement which is weaker than the condition of direct light-connection. The most promising possibility is one suggested by the fact that in Descartes' example the men and their clothes are related in a variety of very intimate ways. No light is transmitted to Descartes' eyes from the men themselves, but the men do give form and movement to their hats and cloaks and thus have an influence on Descartes' visual experience that is only slightly "indirect." Perhaps it would be possible, therefore, to formulate a causal requirement that we could call a condition of "indirect light-connection" in contrast to the stronger condition of direct light-connection. For A to see x, we might say, it is necessary *either* that light be transmitted to A's eyes from x, and thereby affect A's visual experience, *or* that x have a certain causal relationship (R) to something else (y) from which light is transmitted to A's eyes and thereby affects A's visual experience. If we can characterize this causal relationship R in a satisfactory way, the requirement of indirect light-connection would allow us to say that we can sometimes see objects even when they are completely covered by other opaque objects.

There is, however, a very different way of construing the problem raised by Descartes' argument, for a philosopher who is accused of misusing words can often reply that his critics are not sufficiently sensitive to the influence of contextual factors on the meaning of words in everyday speech. In this case such a reply would have considerable plausibility.

It must not be forgotten that Descartes has just warned us that we can easily be led into error by the terms of ordinary language, and has granted that he would ordinarily say that he sees the men and not only their hats and cloaks. In this carefully prepared context, it can be argued, Descartes is quite right in denying that he sees the "men themselves," for in everyday speech it is precisely the function of the intensive pronoun, along with warnings about the ambiguity of language, to draw a distinction which might not be drawn in the course of a more casual conversation. In this case, furthermore, the distinction (between a man and a man plus his clothing) is not one of technical philosophy, but one that is thoroughly familiar to anyone who understands the old adage that clothes do not make the man. It might even be argued, indeed, that in the context provided by Descartes it would actually be a departure from the ordinary use of words to say that we *do* see the men themselves. Such a statement might suggest that the men are wearing transparent hats and cloaks, or that the speaker possesses a supernatural vision that can penetrate opaque objects.

If we decide for reasons like these that Descartes is right when he denies that he sees the men passing below, it may then be possible to maintain that even in everyday speech the requirement of direct light-connection is an essential part of our criterion of seeing. It will be necessary, of course, to explain why we seem so often to dispense with this requirement—why we should be willing, for example, in a casual conversation with Descartes, to say that we see men passing below his window. Up to a point, however, this fact can readily be explained by making a simple semantical distinction formulated in terms of what we earlier called a "composite object." We could maintain that when we speak of seeing a man the word "man" is sometimes used broadly to refer to a composite object which may include among its parts clothing and other accessories surrounding the human body, and at other times is used more narrowly to refer to the human beings themselves. But in whatever sense the word "man" is used, we could argue, it is incorrect to say that we see a man unless, in that sense of "man," light is transmitted to our eyes from some part of the man.

This explanation can be generalized for all of the most central, nonderivative, cases in which we use sentences of the form "A sees such and such an external object," and if we accept it we can retain the requirement of direct light-connection in formulating our criterion of seeing. It becomes clear on reflection, however, that to preserve the requirement of direct light-connection in this way does not really simplify our search for a criterion of seeing. For to complete our task we shall then be obliged to give an account of the conditions under which we may legitimately construe a number of objects as a single composite object of sight. What is the principle of composition, we must ask, that allows us, by lumping together a man and his clothes, to say that we see a man? It is clear that ordinary usage does not sanction a completely unrestricted principle of composition. For some unlikely purpose we might wish to give a name to the "composite object" composed of a hat, a cloak, and the Mississippi River; but we should certainly not want to say that Descartes *sees* such a composite object when he looks from his window, even though light is transmitted to his eyes from two parts of that object, namely, the hat and the cloak worn by one of the men passing below. Thus one composite object may be a possible object of sight for a perceiver at a given time and place, and another composite object may not; yet the parts that the perceiver sees of one object may be identical with the parts that he sees of the other.

It is not enough to say merely that we must analyze or clarify the concept of a "possible composite object of sight," for an analysis of this concept would not necessarily account for the fact that we use one noun rather than another to name the composite object in making a statement of the form "A sees x." The composite objects that Descartes sees below him are composed of hats and of cloaks as well as of the things Descartes calls the "men themselves"; yet these composite objects of sight, if we accept the position we are now considering, are commonly called "men" and not "hats" or "cloaks," and they are called "men," interestingly enough, even though the hats and cloaks are the only parts of the composite objects which are seen. What we must formulate, then, is the principle of composition which allows us to combine various objects in such a way that in making a statement of the form "A sees x" we can apply the same noun to the composite object x which, in a narrower sense, we should apply only to a certain *unseen* part of that object. If we call this unseen part the "core" of the composite object, we can say that the principle which we must formulate is a principle for the composition of objects of sight that are "semantically core-determined."

Some conception of the character and difficulty of this task can be gained by comparing our composite man with familiar composite objects that are not semantically core-determined. A coin or any other solid object can be thought of as a composite object—composed, for example, of a front part, a back part, and an inside part—and just as the men are completely covered by their hats and cloaks, so we might think of the inside of the coin as "completely covered" by the rest of the coin. But the analogy is perhaps even closer if we compare our composite man with a solid object like an egg which is commonly agreed to consist of three easily distinguishable parts—yolk, albumin, and shell. Referring to the yolk as the "core" of the egg, and to the man himself as the "core" of the composite man, we can say that the cases are analogous with respect to the fact that these two cores are covered by "surface parts" in such a way that no light is transmitted from the cores to the eyes of a perceiver. And we can recognize many other important respects in which these two cores are similarly related to the eggshell and the clothing, respectively. Yet the analogy breaks down in a crucial way, for we should normally be willing to say that we see men, even when the men themselves are completely covered by their clothing, but we should not normally be willing to say that we see the yolk of an unbroken egg. This difference between the two cases epitomizes the difficulty of formulating an adequate principle of composition for semantically core-determined objects of sight. What is the rule, we must ask, which allows us to say that we see a man when the man himself is completely covered by his clothing, but does not allow us to say that we see the inside of a coin or the yolk of an unbroken egg?

Since we are searching for a causal criterion of seeing, it is natural to wonder whether the distinction between the case of the man and the case of the egg may not lie in the fact that there is a special kind of causal relationship among the parts of the composite object that we are calling a "man." Although the two cores are similarly related in many ways to the corresponding surface parts, the yolk is a core that is not naturally thought of as exerting a causal influence on the eggshell, whereas the man himself is a core that is thought of as giving form and movement to his clothing and thus as having a relatively direct causal influence on the sense organs of the perceiver. Thinking in these terms, the principle of composition that we are seeking might perhaps be formulated by reference to a causal relation R′ between the core of a composite object and the surface parts of the object. A composite object x is a possible object of sight for perceiver A, we might maintain, and is also semantically core-determined, whenever there is a certain causal relation R′ between the core of the object and other ("surface") parts of the object from which light is transmitted to A's eyes. Our major problem, of course, would be to define this causal relation R′ with sufficient precision. We might perhaps suppose that the essential distinction between the case of the egg and the case of the man can be illustrated by pointing out that the clothes would collapse into a pile if the man himself were miraculously annihilated, whereas the shape of the eggshell would remain unaffected by the annihilation of the yolk. But if this is so we shall have to explain why it is usually so much more natural to say that we see the man than to say that we see the feathers inside a pillow and the wine contained in a wineskin.

When we attempt to formulate a principle of composition in causal terms, it immediately becomes evident that the causal relation R' is identical with the causal relation R which was referred to in our earlier formulation of the condition of "indirect light-connection." It turns out, in other words, that no matter which of the two alternative positions we take with respect to Descartes' argument, we are ultimately faced with exactly the same problem. If we decide that the standards of ordinary speech allow us to agree with Descartes that he does *not* see the men passing below—understanding by "men" what Descartes means by "men themselves"—a causal criterion of seeing must give some account of the relation between the core (in this case a man himself) and the surface parts (in this case a hat and a cloak) of a semantically core-determined composite object of sight. Otherwise we shall not understand the rule which allows us to say, in a more casual conversation, that we see men even when we can see no uncovered part of a human body. And if we decide, on the other hand, that it is correct to say that Descartes *does* see the men themselves passing below, then again we shall have to give some account of the same relation between the men and their clothing. For only in this way can we show that it is possible to formulate a causal condition of "indirect light-connection" to replace the stricter requirement that, for A to see x, light must be transmitted from x to A's eyes. The task of defining this relation (R or R') in causal terms is a formidable one which cannot be attempted here. But before turning to other matters it is possible to point out that some of the difficulties that must be overcome arise from what we might call the "indeterminacy" of the concept of seeing. These difficulties, at least, do not seem to be fatal.

When we attempt to define the relation R (or R') in specific terms, it soon becomes clear that our concept of seeing is so indeterminate that we cannot hope to formulate a causal criterion that is not dependent on context. We cannot even begin to define the *extent* to which one object must influence another in order to bear the relation R to that object. We should often have no hesitation in saying that we see a boat on the bank of the river, even though the boat is completely covered by a tarpaulin. This is particularly true if the tarpaulin is laced tightly to the hull so that the hull determines the shape of the tarpaulin in much the same way a man determines the shape of his clothing. If a tent were constructed over the boat, however, supported entirely by poles and battens, it is only in very special circumstances that we should still be willing to say that we see the boat.[3] And between these two extremes, of course, there is no limit to the conceivable ways in which the boat could influence the shape of the tarpaulin. Whether the extent of influence is sufficient in a given case to justify saying that someone sees the boat, depends on the context in which the statement is made. In a dispute about the color of the hull we should probably consider it incorrect to say that we see the boat unless the paint is exposed to view; but in a dispute about the location of the boat, we might possibly be willing to say that we see the boat even though she is covered by a tent that reveals very little about her shape and size, and nothing at all about her color.

The example of the boat and the tarpaulin, furthermore, is scarcely an adequate sample of the wide variety of cases in which one object must be said to bear the relation R to another object. We sometimes say that we see a snake as it wriggles through the grass, even though we know that it is only the movement of the grass that has any direct causal influence on our perceptual experience. We sometimes say that we see a jet airplane merely because we can see its lengthening vapor trail, and at night we sometimes say that we see an automobile merely because objects along the road are illuminated by its headlights. If we are to succeed in formulating a causal criterion of seeing, the relation R (or R′) must be construed broadly enough so that all of these cases are examples of indirect light-connection, or, alternatively, of direct light-connection between a perceiver and a semantically core-determined composite object of sight.

The indeterminacy of the concept of seeing, however, is not a good reason for doubting that our criterion of seeing is a causal criterion; for the most plausible explanation of this indeterminacy might lie in the very fact that the concept of seeing *is* a causal concept. When we make a statement in everyday speech about the causation of a particular event, we are usually free to select a cause, as our special interests may dictate, from a very wide range of causal conditions. If a hunter accidentally shoots himself we may say that his death was caused by loss of blood, or by a severed artery, a bullet, a rifle, a defective safety lock, and so on indefinitely, not to speak of more general environmental conditions or the hunter's acts, attitudes, character traits, etc. Consequently, if to say that A sees x is to imply that x is a cause of A's visual experience, it would not be surprising to discover that we are free to identify the object of sight as best suits the context and our interests—free to say either that we see the boat or that we see the tarpaulin which covers the boat, free to say that we see the plane or that we see the vapor trail extending behind the plane. There is, of course, no more reason to suppose that in such cases we are choosing between *contradictory* statements, than there is to say that the statement, "The death was caused by a gunshot," is logically incompatible with the statement, "The death was caused by a severed artery."

In everyday speech we sometimes recognize the indeterminacy of our concept of seeing by drawing a distinction between what we see and what we see "strictly speaking"; and this fact, too, is easily explained on the assumption that our concept of seeing is a causal concept. Such a distinction is of no help, of course, in dealing with the problem raised by Descartes, or in formulating a causal criterion of seeing. The distinction itself is always relative to context, so that what we see strictly speaking in one context is what we simply *see* in another context; and even if we were to decide that Descartes should be said to see the men but to see only their hats and cloaks strictly speaking, we should still be no closer to finding the criterion which justifies saying that he sees the men. Nevertheless, the mere fact that we sometimes make a distinction in these terms may be at least some slight reason for supposing that seeing is a causal concept; for some such linguistic device is often necessary when we want to distinguish degrees and kinds of causal influence. "The prisoner was injured by the mob," we may say, "although strictly speaking by only three or four men in the mob."

There is some temptation to say that we are distinguishing two *senses* of "see" whenever we draw a distinction between what we see and what we see strictly speaking; but it is doubtful that this is a desirable way to use the word "sense." There is no limit to the degrees and kinds of causal influence that an object of sight may have on the eyes of a perceiver, and if seeing is a causal concept there is no more reason for saying that "see" has indefinitely many senses than for saying the same of any other causal verb, including the verb "cause" itself.

A special problem is raised by Moore, however, when he speaks, in the passage we have quoted, of the "narrow sense" of "see" in which he can see only one side of the half-crown. If we assume that Moore has what we should ordinarily call an "unobstructed" view of the coin, his visual experience is affected by light which is transmitted to his eyes from one side of the coin. Since this is enough to satisfy the requirement of direct light-connection, no new problem is raised if we agree with Moore that he sees the coin. And no new problem would be raised if Moore were also to say that he sees the front side of the coin but does not see other parts of the coin; for if by "other" parts we understand nonoverlapping parts (i.e., parts which do not include any portion of the front side) then it is true that Moore is directly light-connected with the front side and not with any other part. But what Moore actually says is not just that he sees the coin, sees the front side of it, and does not see any other part of it—all of which would follow from the requirement of direct light-connection on the supposition that there is only one relevant sense of "see"; he also asserts that the sense in which he sees the front side is a "narrower and more proper" sense of "see." To account for this assertion in causal terms we should have to assume that for his narrow sense of "see" Moore has in mind a criterion which is stricter than direct light-connection, and thus that he is not merely making a distinction between two degrees or two kinds of direct or indirect light-connection.

There is no special reason to believe, however, that this stricter criterion cannot itself be formulated in causal terms. Let us suppose, for example, that Moore is thinking of the front side of the coin as a two-dimensional abstraction, and not as a three-dimensional slice which might in principle be shaved off by a plane. In that case the front side would itself have no back or inside and would therefore be distinguished from every nonoverlapping part of the coin by the fact that light is transmitted to Moore's eyes from *all* of its spatial parts (or, at least, from all of its parts that are large enough to reflect light). On the basis of this distinction a causal criterion of seeing in Moore's "narrow sense" might perhaps be formulated by including a requirement that for A to see x light must be transmitted to A's eyes from all spatial parts of x. This is a requirement which might have been of special interest to Moore in an epistemological context, for it can be argued with some plausibility that the entities which it allows us to "see" have a special epistemic status. But even if this requirement does not represent exactly the narrow sense of "see" which Moore has in mind, there is no reason to think, on the basis of what Moore actually says, that it would be harder to formulate a causal criterion for this sense of "see" than for other senses of "see."

The problems which we have so far considered are problems which arise when we ask whether direct light-connection is a *necessary* condition of seeing. But new and very different problems arise when we ask whether direct light-connection is a *sufficient* condition of seeing, and these problems must eventually be solved before we can decide whether it is possible to formulate a causal criterion of seeing that is both necessary and sufficient. We cannot attempt to deal with these problems in any detail within the limits of the present essay, but it is possible to give examples which will at least serve to provide some conception of their nature. By way of conclusion, therefore, let us consider very briefly two difficulties which seem to prevent us in some cases from saying that A sees an external object x, even though light is transmitted from x to A's eyes and thereby affects A's visual experience.

There is, first, the difficulty which is immediately suggested by the etymology of the words "transparent" and "translucent." The rules of ordinary usage allow us to say, of course, that we can see objects, although only indistinctly, through glass which is translucent but not transparent. But our eyelids are also sufficiently translucent so that if we turn our faces towards the sun, and close our eyes, our field of vision is sometimes suffused with a pinkish glow. Are we prepared to say in such a case that we see the sun? And if exactly the same visual experience can be obtained by turning our faces, with eyes shut, towards a white wall in the blazing sun, shall we then say that we see the wall? Do we see the patches of sand and kelp far below us when these produce changes in the color of the sea under our boat? Except in very special contexts, we should naturally hesitate to say that we see any of these objects, even though in each case light is transmitted from the object to our eyes and thereby affects our visual experience.

In these cases the light from the object reaches our eyes without being reflected from another object on the way, but cases of seeing by reflection raise a second difficulty which is no less serious. We do not want to say that we see a source of light—the sun, a candle, a reading lamp—whenever light from that source is reflected from the pages of the book we are reading. And if some of this light from the lamp reaches our eyes even more indirectly by reflection from the ceiling to the book, we do not want to say that we see the ceiling. This problem cannot be solved simply by stipulating that for A to see x the light from x must not subsequently be reflected by any other object before it reaches A's eyes. For in that case we could never say that we see our own faces when we look into a looking glass, a pool of water, or a piece of polished metal. And we could never say that we see anything at all when we look through a reflecting telescope, periscope, microscope, or any other optical device which uses a mirror to reflect light to the eye of the observer.

There may be some temptation to meet this second difficulty by simply conceding that in fact we never do see our faces or any other material thing in a mirror: what we see in a mirror is always a mirror image (likeness, resemblance, representation, reflection) and never a material thing. Since mirror images do not themselves emit or reflect light, this would imply that there are some things, namely mirror images, which can be seen even though light can never be transmitted from them to the eyes of the perceiver; but perhaps to concede this is not necessarily to give up hope of finding a causal criterion for the visual perception of *material* things. It might be argued that the criterion for asserting that A sees x varies with the ontological type of x, or else (which may come to the same thing) that to speak of seeing a mirror image is to use "see" in a special sense which has little relation to the criterion we are seeking. This is a familiar line of argument often available at crucial junctures in philosophical analysis, for it is just at these junctures that we are most likely to find in everyday speech a special terminology, like this terminology of mirror images, which permits us to formulate statements we can assert to be ontologically irreducible.

The obvious alternative in this case is to maintain that the function of the image terminology in everyday speech is to enable us to talk conveniently about some of the peculiar features of seeing things *by way of* mirrors. We do not fail to see an object when we see that object by way of a mirror; and therefore to assert that someone sees an image or reflection of his face in the mirror is not to imply that he does not see his face. This is an interpretation of the linguistic facts which commends itself for heuristic as well as ontological reasons. It permits us to continue our search for a criterion of seeing which is general enough to allow for the possibility of seeing material things in a looking glass and through a reflecting telescope. And if there is such a criterion we shall certainly not find it without searching.

Here are two examples, then, of further difficulties which must be met if we hope to formulate a causal criterion of seeing in terms of light: 1) We are sometimes, but not always, willing to grant that we see an object when light is transmitted from that object to our eyes through a translucent substance; and 2) We are sometimes, but not always, willing to grant that we see an object when light is transmitted from that object to our eyes by reflection from another object. It might seem that the best way to deal with these two problems is to formulate a causal criterion that specifically exempts certain cases of translucence and reflection from the general rule. As a general rule, we might say, for A to see x it is at least a sufficient condition that our visual experience be affected by light which is transmitted from x to A's eyes without being reflected on the way. But, we might add, 1) A does *not* see x if the light passes through certain kinds of translucent substance between x and A; and 2) A *does* see x if the light from x to A is reflected only by mirrors. The basic objection to this proposal emerges very clearly, however, when we ask ourselves just how we actually identify the "certain kinds of translucent substance," and exactly what we mean by "mirror." Allowing for unavoidable vagueness, it would no doubt be possible for the physicist to specify, in the technical terms of optics, one set of conditions which would correspond to the proper kind and degree of translucence and another set of conditions which would distinguish mirrors from other things with reflecting surfaces. But these would not be conditions familiar to the common man, and they would therefore be of no help in formulating a causal criterion which might actually determine the use of "see" in everyday speech. We may even begin to wonder, indeed, as we attempt to construct the special rules needed to cover instances of translucence and reflection, whether we are not attempting to avoid an unavoidable circularity. For perhaps the common man decides whether a translucent object is also somewhat transparent by experimenting to find out whether he can see through it. And perhaps he decides whether an object is a mirror by finding out whether he can see his face in it. Since there may be better ways of dealing with the problems raised by translucence and reflection, the failure of this particular method is no cause for despair. But it does help to show, in any case, that there are challenging obstacles to overcome before we shall know whether it is possible to formulate a causal criterion of seeing.

COMMENTS

Charles E. Caton
University of Illinois

I TAKE PROF. FIRTH to be wrong on several matters which appear to be of some importance to his paper. These are: the role of the intensive pronoun in cases like Descartes' example of not seeing the men themselves; the meaning of certain ordinarily rather commonplace locutions used by Firth when raising the questions he wishes to discuss; and lastly, the circumstances under which people talk.

1. *The Function of the Intensive Pronoun*

Firth says,

> . . . in everyday speech it is precisely the function of the intensive pronoun, along with warnings about the ambiguity of language, to draw a distinction which might not be drawn in the course of a more casual conversation.

This is the nearest he ever gets to discussing how the intensive pronoun is used, despite the fact that the intensive pronoun figures importantly in his reasoning at certain junctures. Although quite obviously this pronoun is used to "draw a distinction," I think Firth consciously or unconsciously thinks of the difference between the men themselves and the men *simpliciter* as on a par with the difference between the men with hats on and the men *simpliciter*. I have in mind especially a passage in his discussion of the "principle of composi-

383

tion" of objects of sight, a principle which (when adequately formulated) is to allow us to say we see a man or a boat which is completely covered by something that reveals the form underneath but which is to prevent us from saying we see the yolk of an unbroken egg or a boat under a tent:

> If we decide that the standards of ordinary speech allow us to agree with Descartes that he does *not* see the men passing below—*understanding by "men" what Descartes means by "men themselves"*—a causal criterion of seeing must give some account of the relation between the core (in this case a man himself) and the surface parts (in this case a hat and a cloak) of a semantically core-determined composite object of sight. Otherwise we shall not understand the rule which allows us to say, in a more casual conversation, that we see men even when we can see no uncovered part of a human body. And if we decide, on the other hand, that it is correct to say that *Descartes does see the men themselves* passing below, then again we shall have to give some account of the same relation between the men and their clothing. (my italics)

It looks to me as if *the men themselves* is here being thought of as on a par with *the men* or *the men in hats and cloaks*. Indeed, Firth says that "men" may be understood to mean what Descartes means by "men themselves," as if these might be synonymous. Note, too, his referring to the "core" as "*a* man himself," as one might talk about both "*the* man in the street below" and "*a* man in the street below."

Surely this is the wrong way of handling the *intensive pronoun*. Let me take a case which does not involve seeing something in order to indicate the general use of the intensive pronoun. If I pay Jones five dollars I owe him, there are different things that may be suggested by the questions whether I paid Jones himself and whether I paid him myself, and by the answers. That I paid Jones himself may mean that I paid him rather than his secretary; it may also mean that

I paid him rather than the company he represents. That I paid him myself may mean that *I*, rather than the company I represent, paid him; it might also mean that I personally handed over the money rather than sending it by mail.

Perhaps it will be said that "him himself" and "I myself" are ambiguous or multivocal; but it is clear that "him" and "him himself" and "I" and "I myself" are altogether different. In fact, I think that one cannot really say what a particular intensive pronoun means out of context. Although we might ask what Descartes meant by "the men themselves," we should not expect to be able to state the meaning of "the men themselves" in the abstract or to state necessary conditions of any correct use of it.

Secondly, I think it is characteristic of this use of intensive pronouns that, when they are used by someone in a particular context, there will be some definite contrast implied between the thing (whatever it is) and the thing itself. But, as in my earlier example, *what* the contrast is may vary from case to case. When we can't figure out what the contrast is, as in the case we are faced with, we ask, "What did he mean by 'seeing the men themselves'?" meaning, to what was seeing the men themselves then and there being opposed? Usually, of course, this will be clear and often it will even be explicitly indicated: "Did he see the men themselves or just their hats and cloaks?" But, of course, in many cases, it will be clear, without a contrast being explicitly indicated, what contrast is intended or what range of contrasts. Firth *seems* not to notice these features of the use of intensive pronouns and to assimilate them to other sorts of modifiers.

It might be thought that at least there is no misunderstanding on Descartes' part: it seems quite clear in the context*

* The only translation I can find that involves "themselves" is that of John Veitch (many editions), who makes Descartes refer to "the analogous instance of human beings passing on [sic] in the street below, as observed from a window. In this case I do not fail to say

that what is being contrasted with seeing the men themselves is seeing the men without seeing their faces.* But perhaps Descartes himself is partly at fault here: for he suggests that one should say that one sees only hats and cloaks, not the men themselves. But when would we say this? Perhaps when the men were behind a door and their hats and cloaks were in an anteroom we had passed through. However, Descartes allows us to plump for *either* the men themselves *or* hats and cloaks. We are not allowed to choose *the men's* hats and cloaks (some evidence of the presence of the men, at least) or the men *in their* hats and cloaks although their faces are hidden—which is more than evidence of their presence and which is, of course, what Descartes saw. In other words, I suggest we would normally have, in the context indicated by Descartes, a contrast suggested between seeing men without seeing their faces and seeing the men's faces as well—*not,* as under Firth's handling, between seeing men and seeing some composite object, part of which is a covered man.

The difference here is not exactly over whether one saw a man or not: according to both Firth and me, there is a sense in which one did and a sense in which one didn't; the difference is over what this legitimizes. In his view, this means that one is entitled to look for criteria of seeing some-

that I see the men themselves, just as I say that I see the wax; and yet what do I see from the window beyond hats and cloaks that might cover artificial machines, whose motions might be determined by springs? But I judge that there are human beings from these appearances, and thus I comprehend, by the faculty of judgment alone which is in the mind, what I believed I saw with my eyes." . . . *nisi jam forte respexissem ex fenestrâ homines in plateâ transeuntes, quos etiam ipsos non minus usitate quam ceram dico me bidere.*

* It is, I think, *faces* and not *any* part of their skin that is important in connection with seeing men. ("Bodies," with Firth, is clearly wrong: one can see a man's body without seeing his *bare* body.) Cf. G. J. Warnock, "Seeing," *Proceedings of the Aristotelian Society,* LV (1955), 209: "Some parts of some objects are more significant than others. One would be readier to say simply that one had seen Lloyd George, if one had seen only his face, than if one had seen only his feet." Prof. Chisholm, in the passage referred to by Firth, agrees.

thing in the one sense as against the other. But—for the reasons indicated above—I think that all that is implied is that if one says one saw something and someone asks whether one saw the thing itself, then, depending on what one *did* see and on what the other person is querying, one will be able to say that one did or didn't see the thing itself. For example, if I saw robbers escaping in their car, I may or may not have seen the robbers themselves in the sense of seeing their faces. But I might see the occupants of the car without seeing their faces, so that in this sense I *did* see the robbers themselves; but if facial identification were sought, I did *not* see the robbers themselves in *that* sense.

Honesty compels me to say that I feel that I have accommodated myself too much to Firth's type of thinking. I *did* see the robbers, but not their faces. "Did you see the men themselves?" is a peculiar, but perhaps barely possible, way of asking whether one saw their faces—and a still more peculiar, and I think *not* really possible, way of asking whether one saw *any* of their skin. If these are *not* possible, then Descartes' example should get even shorter shrift; Descartes is just wrong in saying he didn't see the men themselves (he did, even if not their faces) and Firth is just wrong in thinking that Descartes didn't see the men themselves and equally wrong in trying to figure out in what sense (according to what principle of composition, etc.) Descartes saw or didn't see the men themselves. If ". . . Descartes decides that it is somehow more accurate to say that he sees hats and cloaks than to say that he sees men passing below," then Descartes just decides badly. He should have said he didn't see their faces.

2. *Commonplace Locutions Misinvoked*

It may seem petty to complain about Firth's phrasing of the questions he is discussing, but it is occasionally so unperspicuous as to raise real questions.

I will fix on the locution "leads us to say," as in the question, what leads us to say such and such? This phrase occurs repeatedly as Prof. Firth introduces his main topic, e.g.,

> . . . it is important to ask . . . whether it is a supposed difference in causal influence which leads us to say in everyday speech that we see one particular external object rather than another.

Now perhaps this question, formulated by Firth in terms of our *being led to say* such and such, can be reformulated without using this locution. But what I would like to point out is that, if we consider what this phrase ordinarily means —and we are not told that it means anything unusual here— it is not wholly clear that there *is* such a question and, indeed, there is reason to think that there isn't. Take a case: early in March, walking home, Jones spots his first robin of the season. Striding in the door, he announces, "I just saw a robin!" The question of what *led him to say* this would seem odd in this situation. Asking what led someone to make a perfectly ordinary remark in a situation it obviously fits is generally odd, I think. This suggests that such a question only arises when someone has said something unusual, e.g., that Senator Goldwater is basically leftist or that St. Thomas Aquinas was an existentialist. The question of what led a person to say a certain thing is thus, I think, rather like questioning what the person actually meant by saying that, or what he had in mind. Note, in particular, that these questions never arise in the abstract but only with reference to what someone said on some particular occasion. This is what inclines me to think that there really isn't any such question as the one Firth asks in "whether it is a supposed difference in causal influence which leads us to say in ordinary speech that we see one particular object rather than another." Although, indeed, one might very well ask what leads Descartes to say that he sees hats and cloaks out his window when plainly what he saw were men or, if you like, men completely obscured by their hats and cloaks. So the answer to Firth's question, literally taken, would have to be a *rejection* of the question. Firth wants a *criterion* for judgment in matters of sight, but, if I am on the right lines concerning "leads to say," then no general criterion is to be expected, but, at the most, only reasons for saying what one was led to say in the particular case, and, indeed, not always this.

Of course, if he found the foregoing persuasive, Firth might want to rephrase the questions I have quoted. And no doubt this rephrasing would, in line with the rest of his discussion be in terms of how light is involved in saying correctly that one sees something. I will defer comment on this possibility, since it will be covered by implication in the following comments on his general line of reasoning.

3. *The Circumstances Under Which People Talk*

I would like to make a conjecture on what is basically wrong in Firth's approach.

It seems to me that, if one deliberately concerns oneself with ordinary language as he does, one ought to keep in mind that most of the time people talk to other people.* Though this is obvious, I do think that occasionally it eludes Firth. Occasionally, he seems to regard the meanings of quite ordinary locutions as functions of a person (who speaks a lan-

---

* Cf. Warnock, *loc. cit.,* p. 209: "The question what it is proper to say will often depend also on the conversational context. For example, where the task is to find some object, it will not mislead to say that one sees it as soon as one has located it; but where the interest is in the object's appearance, inability to give an account of this might call for qualification of the claim to have seen it. Thus, if one were trying to locate the cricket pavilion on a very dark night, one might say that one saw it (implying "Now I know where it is") on seeing only a very small though recognizable part; but if one had seen only the top left-hand corner of a painting otherwise completely covered, to say simply that one had seen it (suggesting "I know what it looks like") would be improper."

guage, of course) and of a situation—thought of as more or less physical—in which the person finds himself; whereas, in most cases, the meanings are these functions plus the state of knowledge of the speaker, his interests, the other person being addressed, together with *his* interests, what *he* knows, etc., *and* of what this other person has just said (if anything) and what the speaker has already said (if anything). The fact that what we say (can say, would say, ought to say) is a function of these various things seems to me to cut at least two ways to the detriment of what Firth *seems* to assume: first, things that he seems to regard as matters of *convenience* aren't really, but rather are matters which vary with these forgotten aspects; and, secondly, questions that he *seems* to think have definite answers, really don't, if these aspects are remembered. Take the tarpaulin-covered boat. He seems to hold that if we are so placed that we can see a tarpaulin-covered boat, then we are

> free to identify the object of sight as best suits the context and our interests—free to say either that we see the boat or that we see the tarpaulin which covers the boat . . .

But if it is remembered that one almost always is talking to someone else, then I wonder at least if this is accurately put. Coming over rough terrain, I get the tarpaulin-covered boat in sight first and call back to my companion—call back what? That I see the tarpaulin? No; this would imply that I *don't* see the boat. So I say I see the boat. If my companion goes on to ask, "Can you see the boat itself?" should I answer "No, only the tarpaulin," or worse, "No, only *a* tarpaulin"? Obviously not: what I should answer is, "No: it's covered with a tarpaulin" or, in a slightly different case," with *the* tarpaulin." Both these responses imply, of course, that I'm sure the boat is under the tarpaulin. If I'm not sure it is, then I should not have made either response, but rather something like "I can see something covered by a tarpaulin." If I'm not even *this* sure, then perhaps "I see what looks like a tarpaulin —maybe with something under it." To represent these different responses as ones we are "free" to make, depending (only?) on "the context and our interests," is to call our certainties and uncertainties about what we see either parts of "the context" or matters of "our interests"—which seems a curious description at best. Further, an obviously decisive factor in determining the right response is what the other person says—the person forgotten or slighted by Firth. With this crucial interlocutor put into the context of one's interests, what would or should be said is made to appear a matter of a speaker's response to his environment, apparently thought of as more or less *physical*. Here indeed is an egocentric predicament: with only his ability to speak and uncommunicative objects to keep him company, looking around, he has to decide what it takes to say he sees something.

4. A Final Comment on Firth's General Approach

One last worry that I have concerns the question of what use or uses of "see" Firth is discussing. He seems to be confining himself to utterances of the form "A sees x," as they ordinarily occur, including past tense versions of such sentences and being fairly liberal about longer, grammatically more complex expressions.* The general question to which his questions constitute a prolegomenon is whether in order for A to see x there must be light transmitted from x to A's eyes or from something related in some specified though per-

---

* How liberal? Gerund phrases like "the man mowing the grass" are not explicitly excluded and "see" has, when so completed, a force quite different from what it has when completed with nouns or noun phrases not involving gerunds (e.g., "the man in the white suit"), as Warnock has made clear (*loc. cit.*), and with which Chisholm appears to concur (*loc. cit.*).

haps quite general way to x. To defend the legitimacy of this question against obvious counterexamples, Firth assumes that certain uses of sentences of this form are metaphorical (seeing something in the mind's eye) and that certain other, obviously nonmetaphorical uses (seeing someone in a newsreel) are derivative from a set of central uses he is discussing.

Now the difficulty I see lurking here is, of course, that of avoiding trivialization. To make at all secure any results achieved by pursuing Firth's indicated lines of attack, one would have to be able to identify a use of "A sees x" as central, or derivative, or metaphorical. What does Firth provide? He invites us to

> . . . assume . . . that such uses [as the newsreel and television cases] are derivative, and [to] concentrate our attention on "central" cases in which there is no mediating screen or other material thing which can be said to contain a picture of the perceived object.

That is, we are to search for a causal criterion of seeing only for certain "central" cases and these "central" cases are to be distinguished from other (literal) remarks of the form "A sees x" (inflected and/or expanded, as above) by the characteristic that in the "central" cases "there is no mediating screen or other material thing which can be said to contain a picture of the perceived object." But this suggestion does not seem to fit even the two examples that he uses. That is, I don't see in what sense (except some technical one as yet unexplained) a television or motion picture screen can be said to *contain* a picture of what one sees. Admittedly, a picture is *projected* on the screen, but this feature is not present in all the cases Firth would want to count as derivative, nor is it quite the same in these two cases.

If "contain" is just a poor choice, it is open to him to try anew to mark off the derivative cases. But here one would have to deal also with trying to see figures in the clouds, looking at ink blots while taking a projective test, taking an eye examination, looking at a painting (representative or abstract), looking into a crystal ball, describing dreams and drug-induced imagery, and scrutinizing photographs and aerial maps. Of course the list is not complete but any disjunction that will handle all of these must be rather long or vague. It is open to Firth to throw out some (figures in the clouds, the crystal ball) as metaphorical—but if one calls "I see x" uttered during an eye examination "metaphorical," then it seems to me *this* term is being made technical.

Scrutinizing a group portrait of the signers of the Declaration of Independence, one might be asked, "Do you see Ben Franklin?" and reply, "Yes, I see him—there by the table": a relevant case, surely, since it is not metaphorical to say so (remember newsreels and television aren't) and since no light is transmitted from Ben Franklin to the observer's eye. Some causal relation R or R' intervenes between Ben Franklin, long gone, and something, doubtless the picture, which emits light transmitted (without reflection) to the observer's eye. This "causal" relation, surely, will be (a) tenuous—the painter of the picture may never have seen Ben Franklin, nor necessarily may any of the painters he is following in their representation of Franklin (cf. Jesus)—and (b) widely different from what could plausibly be attributed to other cases, equally literal. It seems to me doubtful Firth could reduce this variety to manageable size even if he brought in more of the context than he appears willing to deal with (whether in connection with "see" itself or in connection with the causal condition). For example, suppose he brings in what one or more of the interlocutors are up to, to aid in dealing with the cases he wishes to count as derivative: in *any* talking, it seems, one must know this in order to take rightly what is said: "My father!—methinks I see my father."—"Oh, where, my lord?"—"In my mind's eye, Horatio."

Do we, then, in the Ben Franklin case have a counterexample to one of Firth's schematized conjectures of necessary conditions of seeing? Of course not. But unless we are given some definite and clear answer to the question *why* we don't, I don't see how he can claim to be working on any clear, definite problem. And I see the danger of the set of "central" cases expanding and contracting as examples agree or disagree with the necessary condition which eventually will emerge—thus trivializing the inquiry.

Let me try to characterize the dialectic here in the abstract. There is a question raised concerning a set of things S; as often, it transpires that some things are S literally and others only metaphorically or derivatively; to deal with this complication, a criterion of genuineness C is introduced for S's. Regrettably, the criterion turns out to be either wrong (some literal S's don't satisfy it) or vague (one can't tell whether they do or do not), so that apparent counterexamples can be dealt with at leisure and at liberty by trading, consciously or unconsciously, on the vagueness of C. (I don't say that Firth has done this; I say only that this seems to be just over the horizon.) What to do? I think: *either* define S so as not to need C *or* make C clear and definite and risk taking your lumps.

REJOINDER
Roderick Firth

PROFESSOR CATON devotes the first few pages of his *Comments* to discussion of the intensive pronoun as it occurs in the expression "the men themselves," and concludes that if Descartes or someone else makes a statement involving the intensive pronoun, one can ask what *he* meant by the phrase involving the pronoun, but we should not, he warns, "expect to be able to state the meaning of 'the men themselves' in the abstract or to state necessary conditions for any correct use of it." His statement is inaccurate as it stands, for it surely seems to be possible to state *some* necessary conditions for any correct use of such phrases, including the condition that they must be used in a context which indicates the kind of distinction the speaker intends to draw by using the intensive pronoun. What Caton means is that there is not any *particular* distinction which all speakers are required to draw every time they use a particular intensive pronoun. But I do not understand why he should suppose that I or anyone else could disagree with him about this. Indeed, in the passage he quotes, I actually use the very words "what Descartes means by 'men themselves'," having previously pointed out (which is sufficient for my argument at this point) that Descartes uses this expression to refer to things that are not composed in part of hats and cloaks.

Throughout the next few pages of his *Comments* Caton maintains of Descartes' own argument that "it seems quite clear in the context that what is being contrasted with seeing the men themselves is seeing the men without seeing their faces." I think that Caton is mistaken about this, for I do not believe that Descartes would have asked the rhetorical question, "What do I see from the window except hats and cloaks?" if he thought it possible to reply, "You see ears and hair and hands protruding from under the hats and cloaks." The point which Descartes is making is not just that we are normally willing to say that we see men when we do not see their faces, but (more dramatically) that we say that we see men even when their hats and cloaks prevent us from seeing their hands, faces, hair, or any other parts of their bodies which would otherwise be uncovered. The contrast which Descartes has in mind, therefore, is the contrast between seeing the men themselves and seeing the men without seeing *any* uncovered parts of their bodies.

This issue concerning Descartes' exact intentions is itself of little philosophical importance, but Caton seems to draw the inference that some of the problems which I have discussed would disappear if only Descartes and the rest of us would speak correctly.

> Descartes is just wrong in saying that he didn't see the men themselves (he did, even if not their faces) and Firth is equally wrong . . . in trying to figure out in what sense (according to what principle of composition, etc.) Descartes saw or didn't see the men themselves.

Contrary to this I have argued at some length in my essay that we shall end up with the same philosophical problem (viz. trying to define the relation that I call "R" and "R'") whether we decide that Descartes is right *or* wrong in asserting that he does not see the men themselves; and nothing that Caton has said seems to me to provide any ground for rejecting this conclusion. Indeed, if Descartes had simply said that he sees the men but not their faces, the central problem concerning R and R' could be raised by asking Caton to formulate a criterion of seeing which would justify *this* assertion. What is the relationship between Descartes and the men in the street which makes it true to say that he sees the men, yet false to say that he sees their bones, brains, etc., and false to say that he sees their faces (*because* they are covered by hats!) yet true to say that he sees their shoulders (*although* they are covered by cloaks!)?

Since I agree with Caton's suggestion that I could if I wished find substitutes for my "commonplace" expressions, and since in my essay I do in fact (as my own illustrations show) consider other people and what they say to be part of the context of an utterance, I shall pass over his discussion of these matters to his final section. In this he criticizes me for not attempting to explain more fully what I mean when I say that I propose to limit my discussion to "central cases" (as opposed, for example, to cases in which we can say that we see a man only because we see a picture of him). I do not deny that this distinction needs to be defined more precisely. It should be observed, however, that the precise formulation of distinctions of this kind will not be a matter of primary importance until philosophers are able, sometime in the future, to formulate a criterion of seeing which is plausible enough to deserve systematic testing against possible counterexamples. The cases that I have selected for discussion (seeing the men, the egg, the coin, the boat, etc.) give rise to basic problems which we cannot avoid if we hope sometime to formulate an adequate criterion of seeing; and of course these particular cases would give rise to these particular problems (and not some further problems) even if I had selected them entirely at random.

NOTES ON FIRTH ESSAY

1. G. E. Moore, *Philosophical Studies* (London: Routledge and Kegan Paul, 1922), p. 188.

2. Among recent attempts, that of R. M. Chisholm in *Perceiving* (Ithaca, N.Y.: Cornell University Press, 1957), pp. 142–156, deserves special mention. The present essay, although its conclusions differ at most points from those reached by Chisholm, was originally stimulated by, and is indebted to, his discussion of the problem.
3. Cf. G. J. Warnock, "Seeing," *Proceedings of the Aristotelian Society,* LV (1954–55), 208–209.

INDEX

Observational framework (*see* scientific, theoretical)

Ogden, Charles K., 78

Pain
analysis of concept of, 142–43, 147–53
I know that I am in, 128–31, 166–69, 172–73
possible innate idea of, 141
privacy of, 138–42, 160, 170
signals, 191
-s, direct access to one's own, 67–68, 116–17, 127, 130, 136
-s, incorrigibility of, 127–31, 141, 166–67

Perceive
directly, 224–27, 235. *See also* seeing

Person
concept of, 59–61, 62–65, 68, 84, 153–58, 266–70
identification of a, 61, 63–64, 89–97, 101, 104–06, 110–12, 116–20
identification of a, by action, 68–70
-al identity, 71, 89–94, 103
-al identity as logically primitive, 62, 68
-s, knowledge of other, 63–74, 77, 84–87, 123–26, 131–35, 146, 149–58, 246

Peters, R. S., 302–05, 307

Phenomenalism
classical, 217–47, 260, 265
the new, 246–50

Physical objects
and classes of micro-particles, 282–84, 299–300
and colors, 217–22
and surfaces, 218–22
as theoretical entities, 247–50, 261
framework of, 247–50, 256, 261–64, 266, 297

Physicalism, 61–62, 65–67, 71, 78, 178, 186–94, 202–03

Physicalistic terms, 12

Possible, 236–38

Practical syllogism, 182

Price, H. H., 235

Pronoun, intensive, 383–87

Proposition, 128–30

Psychological, distinguished from the non-psychological, 12, 19, 36–37

Psycho-physical laws, 100–01

Public objects. *See* physical objects

Quine, W. V. O., 38, 41, 48

Rational
agent, 179–80
preference function, 179–81

Rationality, 42–43, 49
definition of, 42–43

Realism
critical direct, 253–55
direct, 216–21, 250–55, 263
hypothetico-deductive, 247–50
naive, 216–17, 361–63

Representationalism, 251

Rhees, Rush, 131–32

Richards, I. A., 79

Russell, Bertrand, 60, 257

Ryle, Gilbert, 61

Scientific
reasoning, 182
theories, analysis of, 143–45, 248–50, 255, 261–64, 273
theory as part of mental concepts, a, 143, 145–52, 158
theory of other minds, 145, 147

Seeing, 219, 222–25, 277, 357–82, 385–94, 396–97
and pure seeing, 222–23
and thinking, 222
criterion of, 359–65, 368, 370, 373, 375–76, 381–82, 389
directly, 218, 223 235
pure, 221
the men themselves, 358, 366–74

The manuscript was prepared for publication by George A. Masterton.
The book was designed by Sylvia Winter.
The type face is Baskerville designed for John Baskerville about 1750.
The book is printed on Warren's Olde Style white wove
and bound in Holliston Mills' Novelspun cloth over boards.
Manufactured in the United States of America.

The paperback edition of this book is printed on EB Neutratext Antique paper
and bound in Riegel's Carolina cover.